MEMOIRS

W. B. Yeats

MEMOIRS

Autobiography - First Draft

Journal

TRANSCRIBED AND EDITED BY

Denis Donoghue

THE MACMILLAN COMPANY

NEW YORK, NEW YORK

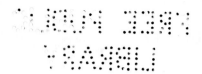

The Macmillan Company
866 Third Avenue, New York, N.Y. 10022

FIRST AMERICAN EDITION 1973

Library of Congress Catalog Card Number: 72-11279

Printed in the United States of America

Contents

List of Illustrations

Introduction

I

In this volume of Yeats's prose I have brought together his Journal, begun in December 1908, and the first draft of his Autobiography, begun in 1915. I hope they will make a lively companionship. In Yeats, the relation between the man and the poet is as vivid as it is difficult. In 'A General Introduction for My Work' he distinguished between the poet and 'the bundle of accident and incoherence that sits down to breakfast',[1] but there is no evidence that he thought the distinction complete or that he pressed it exorbitantly. He did not dispute his father's assertion that 'to be a poet it is necessary first of all to be a man', or the further assertion: 'The high vitality and vivid experience, the impulses, doings and sufferings of a Tolstoi, a Shakespeare or a Dante – all are needed.'[2] The relation between man and poet is the concern of these memoirs, the perceiving subject takes himself as object, ponders his own case. The result, both in the Autobiography and the Journal, is work of notable candour, remarkable in a poet who found it hard to be candid.

The Autobiography and the Journal differ, however, in many respects. Written twenty-five or more years after the events described, the Autobiography required not merely an act of memory on Yeats's part, but an approach to the meaning of the lives it recited, not least his own. He does not tell everything he remembers: he does not rehearse, like Rousseau, the succession of feelings that constitutes the history of his soul. Yeats is not given to the intrinsic pleasure of confession, he is concerned with the meaning of a life, not with its mere content. Besides, the reality mediated by autobiography is to Yeats as much social as personal. He does not scorn the private life, but he assumes that the available meaning of a

---

[1] *Essays and Introductions* (London, Macmillan, 1961), p. 509.
[2] *John Butler Yeats, Letters to His Son, W. B. Yeats, and Others, 1869–1922*, edited by Joseph Hone (London, Faber & Faber, 1944), p. 93.

man's life is the relation between that life and the society which, in part, it defines. In the Autobiography Yeats appears to move from one life to another according to the easy regulation of memory; but, in fact, the movement is conducted according to his more exacting sense of a time, a decade, a generation, that network of conditions and relationships in which the historical moment is revealed. We call the movement a memoir to indicate that its content is public and historical. Yeats is concerned with a particular person for the pressure he exerts upon his society, and for the pressure, perhaps equal and opposite, exerted by society in return. Such a person is presented in his symbolic moment, as if he were a character in a play, fixed in his characteristic gesture. What such a man is, beyond his nature as a *dramatis persona*, Yeats does not presume to say. He is not here a psychologist, indulging himself in what Yeats regarded as the modern vice of curiosity. A man's life is significant in its bearing upon other lives: a memoir is an approach to that significance.

But Yeats does not surrender to history; he creates for himself and his associates a new history out of the mere facts of their lives. A person may be content with mere fact, but a memoirist is not; he is not content until his persons have become personages, surrounded by an aura which is their enacted presence. Yeats's memory reconstitutes these presences, fixes them in space as they were not perhaps fixed in time. The persons so recovered achieve their identities by being placed in relation to their time. It may not be a great relation. Many of the figures described in Yeats's Autobiography are minor figures, and without his attention they might hardly have survived as more than footnotes in literary history. But a minor character achieves his identity by finding an enabling role to play. He need not be Prince Hamlet. Identity is a form of transcendence, and a person who achieves it is redeemed from the chances of daily experience. Yeats moves from one person to another, handing each a script, his part in the play. He does not merely enumerate the events of a plot: behind the several scripts, he composes a generation, many lives engaged in a play of history.

Yeats's word for the movement of a mind under these auspices is reverie. 'I have changed nothing to my knowledge; and yet it must be that I have changed many things without my knowledge; for I am writing after many years and have consulted neither friend, nor letter, nor old newspaper, and describe what comes oftenest into my memory.'[1] It may be said that this disclaimer, from the Preface to *Reveries over Childhood and Youth*, is merely Yeats's charming excuse for not bothering to get the facts right. If he is proved wrong, he has not claimed to be right. But the passage is more than charming: it is Yeats's tribute to the sinuous ways of memory. His confidence in the ostensibly lawless ways of reverie comes from his confidence in the imagination: it may be wrong in the short run, but in the long run it is right, and seen to be right. Logic is the straight road of the mind and it is good enough for straight purposes, but in the end its achievement is null. Reverie is memory under the sweet sway of intuition, it knows best and, however wayward it appears, it will arrive in good time. Yeats's style in the Autobiography is often rough, his first draft is imperfect, but for most of the way it moves with the freedom of reverie and meditation.

The tone of the Journal is different. The entries record events of the day, for the most part, and nothing can be seen across a gap of twenty-five years. Everything now depends upon chance, to begin with, and whatever the day brings of matter and impertinency. Some entries are, as Yeats said, notes to be worked up into essays; or, in richer examples, thoughts for verse. But Yeats thought it possible to make a virtue of that necessity. 'Every note must first have come as a casual thought,' he wrote in no. 5, 'then it will be my life.' By 'life' he meant, on this occasion, spontaneous energy as distinct from 'logical process'. But it was difficult to remain convinced, faced by the daily abrasions of chance, that the permanent values of that life were still in force. 'I am content to live it all again', one of the speakers says in Yeats's 'Dialogue of Self and Soul', but the diarist of 1909 found it hard to be patient with Dublin, theatre business, management of men. The diary is often an examination of conscience, with attendant scruple and perhaps morbidity. Throughout, Yeats gives an impression of living on his nerves. Many entries are tetchy, the day's events exacerbated, worked up for venom. The man who thought psychology vulgar spends many pages peering into his own

[1] *Autobiographies* (London, Macmillan, 1955), p. 3.

motives, accusing and forgiving himself by turns, knowing himself morbid. The interest of the Journal is in Yeats's response to immediate experience – the events before and after Synge's death, for instance, or the quarrel between Sir Edmund Gosse and Lady Gregory. The interest of the Autobiography is in Yeats's sense of the meaning of events, defined at a time when nothing much remained of those events but their meaning, in Yeats's version or another. And in the foreground, standing out boldly against Autobiography and Journal, there are the poems.

II

The complete draft of the Autobiography is published for the first time; some passages have appeared, inaccurately transcribed for the most part, in certain biographical and historical studies of Yeats. The complete text of the Journal is also published for the first time; certain parts of it, published as *Estrangement* and *The Death of Synge*, were included in the *Autobiography* (1938) and the standard *Autobiographies* (1955). A further selection from the Journal, transcribed by the late Curtis Bradford,[1] was published as *Reflections* (Cuala Press, 1970).

Reveries over Childhood and Youth, the first of Yeats's autobiographical volumes, was published by the Cuala Press on 20 March 1916, though the printed date is 1915. Yeats started work on the book in January 1914 and completed it on 25 December. It was a book of persons and places: the persons, notably the poet's father John Butler Yeats, George Pollexfen, John O'Leary, J. F. Taylor, Edward Dowden; the places, Sligo, London, Howth, Dublin, but mostly Sligo. On 26 December 1914 Yeats wrote to his father:

> Yesterday I finished my memoirs; I have brought them down to our return to London in 1886 or 1887. After that there would be too many living people to consider and they would have besides to be written in a different way. While I was immature I was a different person and I can

[1] Author of *Yeats at Work* (1965). Professor Bradford made a preliminary transcript of the Journal and the Autobiography some years ago. These and other manuscripts are splendidly described in *Yeats at Work*.

stand apart and judge. Later on, I should always, I feel, write of other people. I dare say I shall return to the subject but only in fragments.[1]

He returned to the subject at once. 'I am going on with the book', he told his father in a letter which Allan Wade dates '*circa* November–December 1915', 'but the rest shall be for my own eye alone.'[2]

It was a time of memoirs, celebrations, and libels. Katharine Tynan's recollections, *Twenty-Five Years*, appeared in 1913, Lady Gregory's *Our Irish Theatre* in 1914. George Moore had still to be punished for *Ave* (1911), *Salve* (1912) and especially for an insolent account of Yeats, Lady Gregory and Synge which he published in the *English Review* in January–February 1914 and again, with just enough alteration to deflect Lady Gregory's threat of law, in *Vale* (1914). Yeats wrote two 'poems of hatred' on that occasion, placing one of them, 'Notoriety', as the closing rhyme of *Responsibilities* (1914):

> till all my priceless things
> Are but a post the passing dogs defile.[3]

John Butler Yeats told his son that Moore 'was not worth powder and shot',[4] but the poet was not put off by that consideration. In the event, however, his public reply to Moore, 'more mob than man', did not come, except for 'Notoriety', until *Dramatis Personae* in 1935.

Yeats completed the first draft of the Autobiography at the end of 1916 or the beginning of 1917, but he did not propose to himself the indiscretion of publishing it. He looked at the manuscript again in March 1921 when he was preparing *Four Years*, but there is no evidence, apart from a passage on Maud Gonne, that he kept the manuscript open beside him while he composed those official reveries. The first draft brought his memoirs from 1887 to 1898, with occasional glances toward 1899 and 1900: Yeats's reference to '1896 or thereabouts' on the envelope containing the loose leaves of manuscript is inaccurate. Much of the plot of the first draft, and

---

[1] *The Letters of W. B. Yeats*, edited by Allan Wade (London, Rupert Hart-Davis, 1954), p. 589.
[2] Ibid. p. 603.
[3] *Collected Poems*, second edition (London, Macmillan, 1950), p. 143.
[4] *John Butler Yeats, Letters to His Son*, p. 174.

most of its characters, appeared in the official versions, mainly in *Four Years* and the other sections of *The Trembling of the Veil* (1922). Further characters from the first draft were recalled in *Dramatis Personae* and the 1938 *Autobiography*, but they appeared there in different forms.[1] The most haunting presences of the first draft did not emerge in Yeats's print at all, or emerged for a moment only, his 'dear shadows', more types than persons. A comparison of the first draft with *The Trembling of the Veil* and *Dramatis Personae* shows that while Yeats added much new material he excluded much for tact and privacy: intimate conversations with Maud Gonne, a memoir of his relationship with 'Diana Vernon', an account of his sexual development in youth and early manhood, meditations upon his own character. Many details of the Jubilee Riots of 1897, the Wolfe Tone Association, and the Rhymers' Club, were set aside. The justification of publishing the first draft arises mainly from the interest of these suppressed or altered matters.

As for the Journal; Yeats referred to it in a letter of March 1909 to Florence Farr:

> I have a large MS book in which I write stray notes on all kinds of things. These will make up into essays. They will amuse you very much. They are quite frank and the part that cannot be printed while I am alive is the amusing part.[2]

Four of those notes were made up into 'The Folly of Argument', an essay in the *Manchester Playgoer*, June 1911, and two went into a section of *Per Amica Silentia Lunae* dated 25 February 1917, but ample selections from the Journal were withheld until the publication of *Estrangement* (1926) and *The Death of Synge, and Other Passages from an Old Diary* (1928). Of the first 95 entries in the Journal, Yeats chose 61 for *Estrangement*, these dating from 14

---

[1] 'Four Years: 1887–1891', published simultaneously in the *London Mercury* and the *Dial*, June, July, August 1921; issued as a book by Cuala Press in December 1921. 'More Memories', published in four parts by the *London Mercury*, vol. VI, nos. 31, 32, 33, 34, May, June, July, August 1922 and by the *Dial*, May to October 1922. *The Trembling of the Veil* was published by T. Werner Laurie in October 1922. 'Dramatis Personae 1896–1902' was published in the *London Mercury*, vol. XXXIII, nos. 193, 194, 195, November and December 1935, January 1936; and in book form by Cuala Press on 9 December 1935.

[2] *Letters*, p. 526.

January to 12 March 1909. Of the next 155, he chose 50 for *The Death of Synge*, these dating from 12 March 1909 to October 1914. The Journal begins in December 1908, contains 3 entries for that month, then 197 for 1909, 30 for 1910 (though the sequence is broken at one point), 3 for 1911, 10 for 1912 (broken sequence again), 1 for 1913 (the date of another entry is doubtful), 2 for 1914. Thereafter, entries are few, but there are irregular notes between 23 November 1915 and 30 October 1930.

In preparing *Memoirs* as a practical text I have adopted the following procedures. Where a manuscript reading is doubtful, I mention the doubt. Where Yeats deleted a word and replaced it by another, in prose passages, I give the second version in the main text, and the first in a footnote only if it is clearly decipherable and interesting. Yeats's handwriting is difficult: the manuscript is designed rather to remind the author than to inform a reader. As for spelling and punctuation, Yeats never mastered those skills. In the present volume errors of spelling and punctuation have been silently corrected: readers of a practical text do not take much pleasure in the editorial *sic*. Words or dates given in square brackets mark the editor's attempt to repair a defect of sense or to establish the context of a passage. An ' × ' before a line of verse means that the entire line is cancelled in the manuscript. For instance, ' × But when Time has touched/changed that form' means that Yeats deleted 'touched', wrote 'changed' instead, and subsequently cancelled the whole line.

Denis Donoghue

Autobiography

Autobiography[1]

I BEGAN to read Ruskin's *Unto This Last*, and this, when added to my interest in psychical research and mysticism, enraged my father, who was a disciple of John Stuart Mill's. One night a quarrel over Ruskin came to such a height that in putting me out of the room he broke the glass in a picture with the back of my head. Another night when we had been in argument over Ruskin or mysticism, I cannot now remember what theme, he followed me upstairs to the room I shared with my brother.[2] He squared up at me, and wanted to box, and when I said I could not fight my own father replied, 'I don't see why you should not'. My brother, who had been in bed for some time, started up in a violent passion because we had awaked him. My father fled without speaking, and my brother turned to me with, 'Mind, not a word till he apologizes.' Though my father and I are very talkative, a couple of days passed before I spoke or he apologized.

[3]Everything had become to [me] a form of ethics, and as I walked the streets I used to believe that I could define exactly the bad passion or moral vacancy that had created, after centuries, every detail of architectural ugliness. The only buildings that gave me pleasure were Hampton Court, Westminster Abbey, and the New Law Courts; I hardly distinguished among them – I was a romantic in all – though once the size, the oppressive weight of the New Law Courts made me miserable for an afternoon. I had [thought] suddenly, while passing along Fleet Street to call upon a publisher,

---

[1] On the envelope containing the manuscript, Yeats wrote: 'Private. A first rough draft of Memoirs made in 1916–17 and containing much that is not for publication now if ever. Memoirs come down to 1896 or thereabouts. W.B.Y. March 1921.' John Butler Yeats (1839–1922) and his family moved from Dublin to London (58 Eardley Crescent, Earls Court) in the spring of 1887.

[2] Jack B. Yeats (1871–1957), painter and dramatist.

[3] 'I imagine that he feared for my sanity. Everything had become abstract to me.' deleted.

what could the most powerful soul do against weight and size? Then I called up to the mind's eye a London full of moss and grass, and a sort of preaching friar far off among fields, and I said to myself, 'the right voice could empty London again'. Perhaps, I cannot be certain after so many years, I had begun to overvalue moral zeal and exhortation, and that would account for my father's anger.

I went on Sunday evenings to the Socialist lectures at Kelmscott House,[1] and I was one of a little [group] of regular attendants who were always invited to supper in the great, little-furnished room where one wall and part of the ceiling was covered by [a] beautiful Persian carpet, and on another hung Gabriel Rossetti's 'Pomegranate'. I no longer read *The Earthly Paradise*, which had delighted me when I was seventeen, and Morris had not yet written the prose romances which were to delight me in later years. There were moments when I thought myself a Socialist and saw Morris more as a public man and social thinker. When I first met him, some trick of manner reminded me of Grandfather, and when that passed off I discovered in him something childlike and joyous that still leaves him my chief of men. There was a project among young Socialists, some sort of a mission to Paris, and a French class was started. I joined and for two or three weeks I worked hard and made great progress. I was the teacher's favourite pupil, and was confident that I would soon know French. I had, however, mentioned the class at home, and my father proposed that my sisters should join it. I made excuses, and my father grew angry, so I had to ask leave for them to come. I had not even been able to explain to myself why it would make it impossible for me to learn my lessons. I had no longer the praise, the exciting novelty of strange faces. I was but once more a figure in the comedy of domestic life, and I was soon idle and careless.

One of my sisters took work under May Morris as an embroideress.[2] She worked at Kelmscott House and her stories – she is full of humour and observation – represented Morris to us as angry, lovable, and helpless. She described his afternoon quarrels with the milkboy, who would rattle his cans on the railings as Morris was

[1] Upper Mall, Hammersmith.
[1] Susan Mary ('Lily') Yeats worked with May Morris from 1888 to 1894.

taking his sleep, and of the parrot that, when he was translating
Homer, speaking the lines aloud, would follow him up and down the
stairs imitating the murmur of the verses. 'He is always afraid', she
said once, 'that he is doing something wrong, and he generally is.'

As the months passed I became less of a Socialist, and would
explain my attendance at the debates by saying, 'I must learn to
speak. A man must know how to speak in Ireland just as a man in
old times had to carry a sword.' I disliked the working-men revolutionists, their perpetual overstatement and above all their attacks on
religion, and at last I ceased to attend the debates and lectures after
a speech as exaggerated as any of their own on the slowness of
change and the dependence of all ideas of equality of wealth on
Christianity. My first book, *The Wanderings of Oisin*, had now been
published,[1] and Morris at a chance meeting at Holborn Viaduct had
praised it to me and said, 'it is my kind of poetry', and would have
said much more had he not caught sight of one of the decorated iron
lamp-posts then recently, I believe, set up [by] the Corporation, and
turned upon it with frenzy, waving his umbrella. Had [I] been a
little more patient with his working-men revolutionists, I now might
have come to know him as poet and artist, though I was still too
obsessed with abstract ideas to measure all his worth.

II

In what year did I first meet Oscar Wilde?[2] I remember that he
seemed to think that I was alone in London, for he asked me to eat
my Christmas dinner at his house.[3] I was delighted by his pretty
wife and children, and his beautiful house designed by Godwin.[4] He
had a white dining-room, the first I had seen, chairs, walls, cushions
all white, but in the middle of the table a red cloth table-centre with
a red terracotta statue and above it a red hanging lamp. I have never
and shall never meet conversation that could match with his.
Perplexed by my own shapelessness, my lack of self-possession and
of easy courtesy, I was astonished by this scholar who as a man of

[1] *The Wanderings of Oisin, and Other Poems* (London, Kegan Paul, Trench, 1889).
[2] September 1888.
[3] 16 Tite Street.
[4] Edward William Godwin (1833–86), architect and stage-designer.

the world was so perfect. He had not yet written a successful play
and was still a poor man, and I saw nothing of the insolence that
perhaps grew upon him later. 'Ah, Yeats,' he said that Christmas
day – he had been reading to me from the proof sheets of his unpublished *Decay of Lying* – 'we Irish are too poetical to be poets; we
are a nation of brilliant failures.'

Neither then nor later did I care greatly for anything in his writings
but the wit – it was the man I admired, who was to show so much
courage and who was so loyal to the intellect. 'He is one of our
eighteenth-century duellists born in the wrong century,' I would say
of him to some young men of letters who decried him, as the fashion
was among us; 'he would be a good leader in a cavalry charge.' Or
then I would say, 'He is like Benvenuto Cellini, who, because he
found it impossible to equal Michelangelo, turned bravo out of the
pride of his art. Wilde is cowed by Swinburne and Browning.' Yet
like us all it was from Pater that he had learned, but in him the
cadence became over-elaborate and swelling, the diction a little
lacked in exactness. In that witty fantasy he had read me, he had
derived the pessimism of German philosophy from Hamlet, and
when he came to the sentence, 'The world has grown sad because a
puppet was once melancholy', I said, 'Why have you varied the
word; are not sadness and melancholy the same?' And all he could
say was that he wanted a full sound for the close of the sentence.[1]

He spoke with a deliberate slowness, in drawling speech copied
from Walter Pater's speech, somebody told me, and this had become
an artistic convention that gave him greater freedom of language.
He could be elaborate when it pleased him, without seeming
affectation. 'I do not like *King Lear*, give me *The Winter's Tale* –
"Daffodils, that come before the swallow dares". What is *King Lear*
but poor life staggering in the fog?' The next moment would come a
swift retort, some eddy of spontaneous wit. 'I never travel anywhere
without Pater's essay on the Renaissance, that is my golden book,
but the last trumpet should have sounded the moment it was
written – it is the very flower of the Decadence.' 'But', said somebody,

[1] 'Schopenhauer has analysed the pessimism that characterises modern thought, but
Hamlet invented it. The world has become sad because a puppet was once melancholy.'
'The Decay of Lying', *Intentions* (London, Methuen, 1913), pp. 32–3. First published
in 1891.

'would you not have given us time, Mr Wilde, to read it?' 'Oh no, plenty of time afterwards in either world.'

III

I was much among the Theosophists, having drifted there from the Dublin Hermetic Society.[1] Like the Socialists, they thought little of those who did not share their belief, and talked much of what they called Materialism. All good work, whether practical or in the arts, had been done, they held, with the conscious aim of improving mankind, and they were very conscious themselves of possessing that aim. I would say that so much in life had no aim but itself, and there would be an evening of argument. I began to see everything in an argumentative form and became alarmed for my poetical faculty.

I was a member of their Esoteric Section, an inner ring of the more devout students, which met weekly to study tables of oriental symbolism. Every organ of the body had its correspondence in the heavens, and the seven principles[2] which made the human soul and body corresponded to the seven colours and the planets and the notes of the musical scale. We lived in perpetual discussion. Among the symbols of one[3] of the seven principles was indigo, extracted from the plant in some particular way. I got with some trouble a bottle of this indigo and got various members to try experiments, fixing their minds upon the bottle and then [allowing them] to drift. They got impressions of mountainous country, and I began to divide up the different qualities of landscape according to the principles, that I might escape from the astral when I thought of them.

I was always longing for evidence, but ashamed to admit my longing, and having read in Sibly's *Astrology*[4] that if you burned a flower to ashes, and then put the ashes under a bellglass in the moonlight, the phantom of the flower would rise before you I persuaded members of the Section who lived more alone than I and so could

[1] Founded in 1885, the Society met at 3 Upper Ely Place, later at 13 Eustace Street.
[2] Saturn, Jupiter, Mars, Sun, Venus, Mercury, Moon.
[3] Venus.
[4] This experiment, more elaborate than Yeats's account suggests, is described in Ebenezer Sibly, *A Complete Illustration of the Celestial Science of Astrology* (London, 1788), pp. 1114-16.

experiment undisturbed to burn many flowers without cease. Presently I was called before an official of the Section and asked with great politeness to resign.[1] I was causing disturbance, causing disquiet in some way. I said, 'By teaching an abstract system without experiment or evidence you are making your pupils dogmatic and you are taking them out of life. There is scarcely one of your pupils who does not need, more than all else to enrich his soul, the common relations of life. They do not marry and nothing is so bad for them as asceticism.' He was a clever man, had taught himself much mathematics and written a great deal of bad poetry, and he admitted all I said, but added 'that Madame Blavatsky[2] had told them that no more supernatural help would come to the movement after 1897 when some cycle or other ended. At whatever sacrifice of the individual, they had to spread their philosophy through the world before that date.' I resigned, and found afterwards that he had been urged to action by a fanatical woman – women do not keep their sanity in the presence of the abstract.

Madame Blavatsky herself had as much of my admiration as William Morris, and I admired them for the same reason. They had more human nature than anybody else; they at least were unforeseen, illogical, incomprehensible.[3] Perhaps I escaped when I was near them from the restlessness of my own mind. She sat there all evening, talking to whoever came – vast and shapeless of body, and perpetually rolling cigarettes – humorous and unfanatic, and displaying always, it seemed, a mind that seemed to pass all others in her honesty. Unlike those about her, I had read with care the Psychical Research Society's charge of fraudulent miracle-working. 'She is a person of genius,' Henley[4] had said to me, 'but a person of genius must do something – Sarah Bernhardt sleeps in her coffin.' I could not accept this explanation, but finding those charges, so weightily supported, incompatible with what I saw and heard, awaited with impatience the explanation that never came. To her devout followers

[1] 1890.

[2] Helena Petrovna Blavatsky (1831–91). In 1875, with Colonel H. S. Olcott, she founded the Theosophical Society in New York; the London branch was founded in 1878. She came to London in 1884, and the Blavatsky Lodge began in 1887.

[3] 'I have no theories about her. She is simply a note of interrogation.' Yeats to John O'Leary, 7 May 1889, *Letters* (Wade), p. 125.

[4] William Ernest Henley (1849–1903), poet, and editor of the *National Observer*.

she was more than a human being – one told me how he heard often her Master's mystic ring in the middle of the night, and though the sound was faint and sweet the whole house was shaken; and another whispered to me, 'She is not a living woman at all, the body of the real Madame Blavatsky was discovered thirty years ago on the battle-field of ——.'[1] I do not remember the Russian name.

I never saw her encourage any fanatics and saw her discourage some. One night she came home from seeking change of air in a Channel island, and having sat down in her chair in front of the green baize table where she played patience perpetually, she began undoing a big brown-paper parcel. 'This is a present for my maid,' she said, and brought out a large family Bible. 'And not even annotated,' commented some woman onlooker. 'Well, my children,' was the answer, 'what is the use of giving lemons to those who want oranges?' Another night I found her in low spirits because she could not persuade this same maid to have her child baptized. She often warned me against some excess of belief or practice. One night I was sitting silent among a talking group, and noticed that there was a curious red light falling on a picture in a room I could see through folding doors. I walked towards the picture, and as I came near it vanished. I came back to my place and she said, 'What was it?' 'It was a picture,' I said. 'Tell it to go away.' 'It is already gone.' 'That is right,' she said, 'I thought it was mediumship and it is only clairvoyance.' 'What is the difference?' I said. 'If it were medium-ship, it would stay in spite of you. Beware of that – it is a kind of madness, I have been through it.'

Sometimes I thought she dreamed awake, and that when she told some adventure of the soul or the body had been asleep with open eyes. 'Once,' she said, 'my knee was very bad, and the doctor said I would be lame for life. But in the middle of the night the Master came in with a live dog split open in his hands, and he put the dog over my knee so that the entrails covered it, and in the morning I was well.' She was full of strange medieval learning, and a cure known to the medieval doctors, with their conception of transferred vitality, may have floated up in a dream – unless indeed such dreams, once

---

[1] Yeats's blank. According to legend, Helena Petrovna was killed at the battle of Mentana.

actual events, linger on in the spiritual world and are perhaps the instruments of healing. Perhaps those modern miracles of hers, where there is evidence of contrivance, were the work of dreaming hands, or of a mind that was overmastered by a vision that was like a dream. 'She would do one marvel for me.' 'Oh no,' she said when Mrs Besant[1] asked her to, 'I should remember my enemies.'

Sometimes when she was in low spirits she would speak to me of literature, or of her own youth, as though her habitual topics had grown wearisome to her. One night she said, 'I go on writing as the Wandering Jew walks. I once used to blame and pity the people who sell their souls to the Devil; I now only pity them – they do it to have somebody on their side,' and began to talk of de Musset, whom she had known and disliked, and Balzac, whom she had met but once, and George Sand, with whom she had dabbled in magic, 'and neither of us knew anything about it'. Though she would be, I was told, remorseless where her movement was concerned, taking people away from their business perhaps and sending them to the ends of the earth, she made upon me an impression of indulgence and generosity. I remember how careful she was that the young men about her should not overwork. I overheard her saying to some rude stranger who had reproved me for talking too much, 'No, no, he is very sensitive.'[2]

IV

I was introduced to the kabalist MacGregor Mathers,[3] not yet married to the sister of the philosopher Bergson, in some Fitzroy Street studio, and accepted his invitation to join an Order of Christian kabalists, 'the Hermetic Students'.[4] I am still a member and, though

[1] Annie Besant (1847–1933), Theosophist author and lecturer. 'Mrs Besant, you may not have heard, has turned Theosophist and is now staying with Madame Blavatsky. She is a very courteous and charming woman.' Yeats to Ernest Rhys, c. September 1889, *Letters* (Wade), p. 137.

[2] See Appendix A, pp. 281–2.

[3] Samuel Liddell Mathers (1854–1918). His translation of Knorr von Rosenroth's *Kabbalah Denudata* was published in 1887. The marriage to Moira Bergson took place on 16 June 1890. Mathers was dismissed from the Order of the Golden Dawn on 21 April 1900.

[4] 1887.

I attend but little, value a ritual full of the symbolism of the Middle Ages and the Renaissance, with many later additions. One passes from degree to degree, and if the wisdom one had once hoped for is still far off there [is] no exhortation to alarm one's dignity, no abstraction to deaden the nerves of the soul. 'We only give you symbols,' MacGregor Mathers had said to me, 'because we respect your liberty.' And now I made a curious discovery. After I had been moved by ritual, I formed plans for deeds of all kinds I wished to return to Ireland to find there some public work; whereas when I had returned from meetings of the Esoteric Section I had no desire but for more thought, more discussion.

Now too I learned a practice, a form of meditation that has perhaps been the intellectual chief influence on my life up to perhaps my fortieth year. MacGregor was now married and the curator of a private museum a little out of London.[1] A friend,[2] a member of the Order, returned from a visit to him with a most wonderful tale. He had made her fix her attention on a certain symbol, and by a process she could not describe a seashore and a flight of seagulls had risen before her. Then my turn came for a visit, and I was made to look at a coloured geometric form and then, closing my eyes, see it again in the mind's eye. I was then shown how to allow my reveries to drift, following the suggestion of the symbol. I saw a desert, and a gigantic Negro raising up his head and shoulders among great stones. There was nothing in the symbol, so far as I could judge, to have called up the result – if it was association of ideas, they were subtle and subconscious. As I watched the kabalist I discovered that his geometrical symbols were a series which I could classify according to the four elements and what the ancients called the fifth element, and the subdivisions of these.

I now began to experiment myself, finding that many people, after fixing their attention on the symbol, would pass not into reverie as I did but into a state of partial or complete hypnosis. Later on I discovered that it was enough to give their visions what direction I would if I myself called up the symbol to the mind's eye. My mind would influence theirs directly. I then noticed that various systems of

[1] The Horniman Museum at Forest Hill. He lost the post in 1891.
[2] Florence Farr.

evocation, of command, or of prayer were more powerful because of more prolonged attention than these detached symbols, and that I could discover occasionally among the symbols that came at my command some that I could never have heard of, though they had historical foundation and could not be the result of chance. I allowed my mind to drift from image to image, and these images began to affect my writing, making it more sensuous and more vivid. I believed that with the images would come at last more profound states of the soul, and so lived in vain hope.

V

My father had introduced me to an old friend of his, Edwin Ellis, a painter and poet.[1] The youngest member of my father's 'brotherhood',[2] those young painters who in the late sixties had found themselves between two worlds, 'one dead, one powerless to be born', he was about fifty. His painting was without interest, academic form without charm of colour or expressive line, and often a little vulgar, with big eyes and commonplace prettiness. I discovered that his mind lost its force and sincerity in the exact degree of its approach to daily circumstance, to observed objects; moving among poetical or philosophical intuitions expressed in symbolic or abstract form, it was subtle and profound and more rapid and abundant than any mind I have ever known or even heard of. He would sometimes say of himself, 'I am a mathematician with the mathematics left out.' He had also a curious psychic sensitiveness that would make him constantly aware of what one thought or felt, before one had spoken, and he often told of what seems to go beyond any mere reading of another mind – of an absolute clairvoyance.

He had a half-mad foreign wife, who was so jealous that for long periods he would not be allowed to go without her company beyond sight of the window. He would walk with me perhaps as far as the pillarbox at the corner of the street I must take on my way home and say, 'I can go no farther, my wife will be angry.' He had little money,

[1] Edwin John Ellis (1848–1916). Yeats reviewed his poems, *Fate in Arcadia* (1892) and *Seen in Three Days* (1893), in the *Bookman*, September 1892 and February 1894 respectively. *Uncollected Prose*, I, pp. 234–7, 317–20.
[2] John B. Yeats, J. T. Nettleship, George Wilson, and Ellis.

a hundred a year perhaps, and she some hundreds, and he often [spoke of] a man's duty to a wife who has had [more] riches than he, or he would sometimes explain that she had once had a very remarkable intelligence but had lost it after a brain fever. He had carried off his first wife from an American husband who after the elopement had described him as the most foolishly quixotic of men, and the second wife had nursed the first on her deathbed. He had had before his first marriage many casual sexual adventures – models and women of the town – and his conversation, which was often exceedingly witty, was wholly concerned with religion and sex; yet when he spoke of the character of women, which he did frequently, it was obvious that he judged all by his present wife. She came to seem in his eyes normal woman, and he was [so] uncomplaining that he always made one understand that he would not have had any suggestion to offer at the creation of Eve.

He had a studio at the top of the house, and though Mrs Ellis would sometimes say, 'It is such a pity that Edwin cannot colour,' he could there have some life to himself. An art student when Gilchrist, under the influence of Rossetti, had published his *Life*,[1] he was an enthusiastic scholar of William Blake. I had inherited from my father a like enthusiasm, and on turning over a copy of the poems, in his studio,[2] I found on a sheet of notepaper a series of attributes of the different districts of London to different human faculties and destinies. I recognized certain attributes of the cardinal points I had heard of among the kabalists, and Ellis and I began the four years of almost continual study that resulted in our interpretation of the mystical philosophy of the Prophetic Books.[3]

With a youthful contempt of domestic compromise and complaisance, I became the elder man's protector. He must have so much time daily for his work, he must be free to read in the British Museum, and so [on]. Sometimes I was turned out and weeks would pass and Ellis and I would have to meet at some Aerated Bread Shop near the British Museum. The longest expulsion followed a sudden conviction of his wife's that I had thrown a spell upon her – she had

[1] Alexander Gilchrist's biography of Blake appeared in 1863.
[2] Ellis's, at 40 Milson Road, Kensington.
[3] *The Works of William Blake, Poetic, Symbolic, and Critical*, edited by Edwin John Ellis and William Butler Yeats (London, Bernard Quaritch, 1893).

mistaken for the making of symbols a habit I have of beating time to some verse running in my head. And then I would be forgiven and fed with very rich cake covered with almond paste that neither pleased my palate nor suited my digestion. At her moments of sanity, that seemed to come with exhaustion, she had intelligence and a kind of anxious kindness. Once when I was poorer than usual and received an anonymous gift of two pounds, I only discovered after years that she had sent it.

Those four years were a continual discovery of mystic truths yet about us;[1] we believed that he felt supernatural assistance, and he himself passed through various curious states and exaltations. Once we were investigating Blake's doctrine of the origin of the sexes, and unable to come to any conclusion. He put down his palette and brushes and said, 'Come out into the street, I must walk up and down.' And then, when we had turned for the second or third time, 'If I had remained a moment longer, I should have been in trance. I might have stayed a long while in it. My relatives would have heard of it and our collaboration would perhaps have been stopped.' In the evening I took up the theme, and as I talked my mind became exceedingly lucid and confident. It was now nightfall, and Ellis lay upon a sofa listening. I noticed a faint flickering on the ceiling and vaguely wondered what it could be, when Mrs Ellis came in and said, 'Why are you sitting in the dark?' Ellis said, 'Why, it is dark, and I am lying down. I thought I had been sitting up in a brightly lighted room.'

I owe to my discussions with this man, who was very sane and yet I think always on the border of insanity, certain doctrines about the Divine Vision and the nature of God which have protected me for the search for living experience, and owe to him perhaps my mastery of verse. In the freedom I had won for him he wrote and published much poetry that still seems to me to have great occasional beauty and wisdom. He wrote always at great speed, and if you pointed out a fault would re-write all he had done in some entirely new way. He could not revise, and yet his technical criticism of the work of others was profound, and no detail too slight for his philosophy. I had still the intellectual habits of a provincial, and fixed my imagina-

[1] Doubtful reading.

tion on great work to the neglect of detail – my *Wanderings of Oisin* were but the first of a whole *Légende des Siècles*, and so on – but I learned for the first time that I might find perfect self-expression in the management of a cadence. He complained that 'Shy in the doorway' in one of my early poems[1] was abominable, because 'Shyin' was the name of a Chinaman, and though I did not alter the line I acquired a more delicate attention to sound.

VI

I was greatly troubled because I was making no money. I should have gone to the art schools, but with my memories of the Dublin art schools I put off the day. I wanted to do something that would bring in money at once, for my people were poor and I saw my father sometimes sitting over the fire in great gloom, and yet I had no money-making faculty. Our neighbour, York Powell,[2] at last offered to recommend me for the sub-editorship of, I think, [the] *Manchester Courier*. I took some days to think it over; it meant an immediate income, but it was a Unionist paper. At last I told my father that I could not accept and he said, 'You have taken a great weight off my mind.' My father suggested that I should write a story and, partly in London and partly in Sligo, where I stayed with my uncle George Pollexfen,[3] I wrote *Dhoya*, a fantastic tale of the heroic age. My father was dissatisfied and said he meant a story with real people, and I began *John Sherman*, putting into it my memory of Sligo and my longing for it.[4] While writing it I was going along the Strand and, passing a shop window where there was a little ball kept dancing by a jet of water, I remembered waters about Sligo and was moved to a sudden emotion that shaped itself into 'The Lake Isle of Innisfree'.

[1] 'To an Isle in the Water'.
[2] Frederick York Powell (1850–1904), Regius Professor of History at Oxford University, had a house in Bedford Park, London. The Yeats family moved to 3 Blenheim Road, Bedford Park, at the end of March 1888.
[3] Yeats's maternal uncle (1839–1910): 'a melancholy man/Who had ended where his breath began.' In 1893, in London, he became a member of the Order of the Golden Dawn.
[4] *John Sherman and Dhoya* was published by T. Fisher Unwin in November 1891. 'I have to get to work at my story – the *motif* of which is hatred of London.' Yeats to John O'Leary, 19 November 1888, *Letters* (Wade), pp. 94–5.

Then for the sake of money, and that I might while earning it study what I called 'the tradition of Ireland', I edited for a popular series the stories of Carleton[1] and a volume of Irish fairy tales[2] – getting I think seven guineas for the Carleton, I think twelve for the fairy stories. I would often walk in from Bedford Park to the British Museum, where I worked, to save the pennies for a cup of coffee in the afternoon. I probably brought my lunch in my pocket, and I can remember blacking my stockings to hide the rents in my boots. I did not, however, mind the rents or my long walks, for I had formed an ascetic ideal. No matter how rich I became, I was confident that I would always walk to my work and eat little meat and wear old clothes. I chose a deliberate poverty as a foppery of youth.

I had much more trouble with my senses, for I am not naturally chaste and I was young. Other young men that I knew lived the life Edwin Ellis told me of, but I had gathered from the Romantic poets an ideal of perfect love. Perhaps I should never marry in church, but I would love one woman all my life. I wrote many letters to Katharine Tynan,[3] a very plain woman, and one day I overheard somebody say that she was the kind of woman who might make herself very unhappy about a man. I began to wonder if she was in love with me and if it was my duty to marry her. Sometimes when she was in Ireland, I in London would think it possible that I should, but if she came to stay, or I saw her in Ireland, it became impossible again. Yet we were always very great friends and I have no reason to think she ever thought of me otherwise.

My struggle with my senses made me dread the subject of sex, and I always tried to change the subject when Ellis began any of his stories and reminiscences, and was often made uncomfortable by Mrs Ellis who, because I was very delicate, assumed that I was living a dissipated life. Once, when York Powell began to show some friends,

---

[1] *Stories from Carleton: With an Introduction by W. B. Yeats* (London, Walter Scott, 1889).

[2] *Fairy and Folk Tales of the Irish Peasantry: edited and selected by W. B. Yeats* (London, Walter Scott, 1888).

[3] Katharine Tynan (1861–1931) published reminiscences of Yeats in her *Twenty-Five Years* (1913) and *The Middle Years* (1916). In 1893 she married Henry A. Hinkson, an Irish magistrate and novelist. Nora (Tynan) O'Mahony recalled in a letter to Austin Clarke – the letter is not dated, but a probable date is 1930 – 'the night when Willie Yeats proposed to my darling Katharine' (Huntington Library MSS. H.M. 26340).

among whom I was, caricatures of the night life of Paris by some famous French artist, I left the table and walked up and down at the end of the room. Yet women filled me with curiosity and my mind seemed never long to escape from the disturbance of my senses. I was a romantic, my head full of the mysterious women of Rossetti and those hesitating faces in the art of Burne-Jones which seemed always anxious for some Alastor at the end of a long journey. And I added to the almost unendurable strain of my senses a conviction that I was without industry and without will. I saw my father painting from morning to night and day after day; I tried to work, not as long as he, but four or five hours. It is only during my recent years that, though I am working very steadily, more than two hours' original composition brings me almost at once to nervous breakdown. In almost all the members of my family there is some nervous weakness.

VII

I was always conscious of something helpless and perhaps even untrustworthy in myself; I could not hold to my opinions among people who would make light of them if I felt for those people any sympathy. I was always accusing myself of disloyalty to some absent friend. I had, it seemed, an incredible timidity. Sometimes this timidity became inexplicable, and [it is] still [in]explicable and painful to the memory. Some scholar in seventeenth-century French poetry asked me to breakfast with him one Sunday in the Temple, and there was a younger Oxford [man] who shared his rooms. After breakfast I could not make myself go, though I wanted to go and though he and his friend to give me a hint began talking of church, for which they had perhaps no liking; I was miserable and could not go. I called on some woman, an old friend of my father's, and found her engaged with what looked like a committee. I felt certain I should not stay, and yet I talked on and even tried experiments with some symbol or other, and went away in utter misery when the meeting, or whatever it was, broke up. I never ventured to call again.

Then something happened which by some caprice of the conscience is still the most painful of all my memories – even now I write in the hope of laying it at last. I find that a painful thought will sometimes affect the mind before it enters the consciousness, or without ever doing so – it affects us like moon or sun when, still below the horizon, they throw upward their light. I had introduced as a neophyte of my Order a Dublin friend, a fellow-student there once at the art schools. He was initiated, and afterwards somebody said there was an entrance fee of a couple of pounds. He said, 'Well, if one accepts a thing, I suppose one should pay for it,' and laid the money down on the little table. I knew he was poor and that no poor man was ever asked to pay anything, and yet I said nothing. I was like a man in nightmare who longs to move and cannot. I knew the woman who had asked for the money well, and that if I said one word it would be returned, and I did not speak. The thought of that moment returned again and again at night, with most bitter self-accusations. I kept picturing him in Paris, where he was going to study art, stinted in this or that because of his loss. I thought to send him the money myself, but I never had two pounds, and presently I heard he was dead.

VIII[1]

I began to make friends among[2] frequenters at the Museum, and sometimes MacGregor Mathers, whose brown velveteen jacket and marked features had interested me, even before our meeting, would join me at my coffee in the dim smoking-room of the Wheaten,[3] a restaurant long passed away; at other times it would be a young Socialist,[4] who acted as Morris's secretary and was engaged to May Morris. 'She is very beautiful,' he would say, 'Morris says so.' Or Ernest Rhys, dreamy and amiable and weak of will, who would say, 'I have been ten years in London and I have not begun even one of the books I left mining engineering to write.'[5] Lionel Johnson lived near but never, I think, entered the library – he seemed to have all

[1] Yeats numbers this section VIIa, so the numbers diverge henceforward.
[2] 'other young men of letters, who read' deleted, replaced by 'frequenters'.
[3] Doubtful reading. See Plate 1. Perhaps Wiener Café as in Pound's *Canto LXXX*.
[4] Herbert Halliday Sparling.
[5] '... a Welshman, lately a mining engineer, Ernest Rhys, a writer of Welsh translations and original poems.... Between us we founded the Rhymers' Club.' *Autobiographies*, p. 165.

the books he needed in a long, low-ceilinged room in Fitzroy Street. He had private means and so his books grew always more numerous. 'When a man is forty,' he would say, 'he should have read all the good books in the world, and after that he can be content with a half a dozen.' He had already immense erudition, and we would tell each other of the number of languages he had mastered. He was content that books should be his world.

I called on him for the first time at five one afternoon at the suggestion of some friend – Ernest Rhys perhaps – and the door was opened by a manservant. Horne,[1] afterwards the great authority on Botticelli, and Selwyn Image,[2] now Slade Professor, and an architect Mackmurdo shared the house[3] and servant. 'Is Mr Johnson in?' I said. 'Yes sir.' 'Can I see him?' 'He is not yet up, sir.' 'Is he ill?' 'Oh no, sir,' and then with an accent of slight emotion as though the feat touched him to admiration he said, 'but he is always up for dinner at seven.' The habit had begun with insomnia, but was now deliberate. Johnson slept through the distraction of daylight, when one might be tempted by the conversation of ladies or the green trees in the park, and began to work when we had all gone to our beds. Between seven and eleven or twelve he would sometimes receive us, and I used to feel that it was not fair to meet, tired with my day's work, a mind still in its morning vigour.

He became for a few years my closest friend, and what drew me to him was a certain elegance of mind that seemed to correspond to his little, beautifully formed body, the distinction, as of a Greek carving, in his regular features. He was the first disciple of Walter Pater whom I had met, and he had taken from Walter Pater certain favourite words which came to mean much for me: 'Life should be a ritual', and we should value it for 'magnificence', for all that is 'hieratic'. He had no sympathy with my speculations, though much with the disquiet that caused them, for all [had] been discussed for centuries: all that could be known was already recorded in books. 'I need ten years in the wilderness,' he would say to me, 'and you ten years in a library'; and once, finding me gloomy and misunder-

---

[1] Herbert Percy Horne (1865–1916), architect.

[2] Image (1849–1930), designer and artist in stained glass.

[3] 20 Fitzroy Street. The architect friend was Arthur Mackmurdo (1851–1942), who founded the Century Guild in 1882.

standing the reason for that, said, quoting I know not what Catholic saint, 'God asks nothing from even the highest soul but attention.'[1] He was not yet a Catholic,[2] and I had not yet begun to take his religion, already moving thither, seriously – I thought it a literary affectation. I had already founded the Rhymers' Club,[3] a weekly or was it fortnightly meeting of poets in an upstairs room at the Cheshire Cheese.[4] At one of these meetings somebody said, 'Johnson is, I am told, a neo-Catholic,' and when I asked what that was said, 'There is no God and Mary is his mother.'

It was at meetings of this club that I came to know my contemporaries, and Arthur Symons took a hold upon my friendship that became very strong in later years when Johnson, who had been advised by some doctor to take stimulant for his insomnia, had developed into a solitary drunkard. At first I was repelled by Symons because, with a superficial deduction I suppose from the chapter in *Marius* called 'Animula Vagula' – *Marius* was, I think, our only contemporary classic – he saw nothing in literature but a series of impressions. That he might have vivid impressions for his verse he had, it seemed to me, chosen deliberately a life of music halls and amorous adventure. I did not, like Johnson, who hated all thoughts of sex, object to his amorousness – I knew how hard my life was to me – but I knew the greatest kind of literature is passion. I sought passion, religious passion above all, as the greatest good of life, and always cherished the secret hope of some mysterious initiation. He thought to spend his life, in so far as it was an artistic life, in making the silver mirror without speck, and I thought to see it fused and glowing. We only understood each other in later years when he had abandoned his theory and, deeply in love at last, tried for expression of passion. Whatever I came to know of Continental literature I learned of him, for Johnson read little but the classics. He had the sympathetic intelligence of a woman and was the best listener I have ever met, but he belongs to my later life.

John Davidson, older than the rest of us and seeking to hide it

---

[1] See below, Journal, no. 194, p. 234.
[2] Johnson was received into the Catholic Church on 22 June 1891.
[3] Early in 1891. Yeats's account of the Club is given in *Letters to the New Island* and again in the Introduction to the *Oxford Book of Modern Verse*.
[4] The Old Cheshire Cheese, Fleet Street, London.

with a wig, Ernest Dowson, more intimate with Johnson and Symons than with me, Edwin Ellis came regularly to our Club – we were a dozen regular members in all.[1] But men whom we admired or tolerated would come occasionally; I remember Oscar Wilde, whom I came to know rather well, coming once, and Horne very often. We read our verses and criticized one another, but the talk had little vitality; and Symons, who knew Paris and its excellent talkers, gradually ceased to come. A movement of distrust in ideas – a form, perhaps, of my own terror of the abstract – and all those half-truths and adventitious statements that give animation had begun to arouse distrust.[2] Only when some member who was Irish – Hillier,[3] Rolleston,[4] or myself – led the talk was there animation; and [the] disapproving silence of Johnson often made us feel that we were provincials. I once heard Johnson say after a particularly heavy evening, 'Ah, yes, it is very dull, but it is interesting.'

When our evenings were over and I had gone home to bed, a more active life began; [one] day I was told that Ernest Dowson and Arthur Symons had been expelled from a cabmen's shelter because Dowson was too disreputable for the cabmen.[5]

IX

W. E. Henley was my chief employer. I had become one of that little group of friends who gathered at his house near Bedford Park – did he open his doors once a week or every fortnight? – and who were

[1] The most prominent members were Yeats, Dowson, Davidson, Rhys, Johnson, Symons, Ellis, Victor Plarr, Richard Le Gallienne and Aubrey Beardsley.

[2] The sentence is confused: the text itself is clear.

[3] Arthur Cecil Hillier. Yeats wrote to John O'Leary on 26 June 1894: 'I send you *The Second Book of the Rhymers' Club*, in which everybody is tolerably good except the Trinity College men, Rolleston, Hillier, Todhunter and Greene, who are intolerably bad as was to be expected . . .' *Letters* (Wade), p. 232.

[4] Thomas William Rolleston (1857–1920), scholar in Greek, German and Irish literature, editor of the *Dublin University Review*.

[5] Symons on Dowson, the *Savoy*, no. 4, August 1896, p. 92: '. . . an evening in which he first introduced me to those charming supper-houses, open all night through, the cabmen's shelters. There were four of us, two in evening dress, and we were welcomed, cordially and without comment, at a little place near the Langham; and, I recollect, very hospitably entertained. He was known there, and I used to think he was always at his best in a cabmen's shelter. Without a certain sordidness in his surroundings, he was never quite comfortable, never quite himself.'

afterwards the staff of his *Scots Observer* and *National Observer*. He alarmed me and impressed me exactly as he did those others who were called Henley's young men, and even today [when I meet] some one among them, showing perhaps the first signs of age, we recognise at once the bond. We have as it were a secret in common: that we have known a man whose power no others can know because it has not found expression in words. I never cared for anything in Henley's poetry except those early gay verses in the measure of Villon, and I know that their charm was the image of that other man's face. I thought his prose violent and laboured, but I was ready, as were all those others, to test myself and all I did by the man's sincere vision. I scarcely shared an opinion of his and yet afterwards when I heard that he had said to somebody, 'I do not know if Yeats is going up or going down,' I doubted myself. His hold was perhaps that he was never deceived about his taste, that he wished one well, and could not flatter. It made no difference that I dissented from his judgment of other men. He despised all of Rossetti but 'The Blessed Damozel', never spoke of Pater and probably disliked him, praised Impressionist painting that still meant nothing to me, was a romantic but not of my school, and founded [the] declamatory school of imperialist journalism. Lame from syphilis, always ailing, and with no natural mastery of written words, he perhaps tried to find his expression in us, and therefore all but loved us as himself.

He re-wrote my poems as he re-wrote the early verse of Kipling, and though I do not think I ever permanently accepted his actual words I always knew that he had found a fault. He brought into his violent politics his natural generosity, and I always felt that I suffered no loss of dignity from his opposition to all I hoped for Ireland. I remember his saying, 'It is not that I do not think Ireland fit for self-government, it is as fit as any other country' – Ireland's unfitness was the stock argument made [in] his time – 'but we have to think of the Empire. Do persuade those young men that this great thing has to go on.' There was comfort in such an attitude of mind, and he could admire as I could the folklore and folksong that Hyde[1]

---

[1] Douglas Hyde (1860–1949), poet, translator, scholar, one of the founders and first President of the Gaelic League, President of Ireland 1937–45.

had begun to discover, and he was about to write of Parnell,[1] 'He has been eighteen years before the country and we knew nothing of his character but that he was haughty,' and describe, if my memory does not deceive me, Parnell's hatred of the British Empire as 'noble'. He wanted to found a paper in Ireland and try his chances there. I was drawn to him also, I doubt not, by his aristocratic attitudes, his hatred of the crowd and of that logical realism which is but popular oratory, as it were, frozen and solidified. I did not help him in the reviews and leaders, which we believed to have created and perhaps had created such a terror among innocent sentimental writers and all flatterers of public taste, for in the puritanism of my early twenties I objected to anonymity,[2] but I wrote for him many poems and essays about Ireland, and came to feel that the necessity of excluding all opinion was my first discipline in creative prose. I forget to whom it was he said after publishing 'The Man Who Dreamed of Faeryland',[3] 'Do you see what a fine thing one of my boys has written?'

I met at his house for the first time R. A. M. Stevenson, the novelist's cousin, whom it was customary to set up as a rival to Wilde in conversation. He had no philosophic wit, his gay, fanciful wisdom had a way of fading with the sound of his voice, but he had no egotism; he charmed where Wilde compelled, and did not seem to monopolize a conversation where all were all but plotting to keep him talking. Henley himself was often content with silence, satisfied with his unanalysable gift of keeping all men near him at the stretch, of sending all away wearied out with the prolonged giving of their best. It was there I first met Wilde and afterwards he said to me, 'I had to strain every nerve to equal that man at all,' and yet Wilde himself had said all the brilliant things – Henley had done little more than listen. I was accustomed to say of him, 'He is a great actor with a bad part. Who would look at any other with Salvini upon the stage, even if he but spoke the words of some penny-a-liner?' I would say

---

[1] Charles Stewart Parnell (1846–91), leader of the Irish Home Rule Party: 'uncrowned King of Ireland'.

[2] 'Ganconagh's Apology', *John Sherman and Dhoya* (1891): 'The maker of these stories has been told that he must not bring them to you himself. He has asked me to pretend that I am the author'.

[3] The *National Observer*, 7 February 1891.

of him too that I found in him the somnambulist, and that was my test of greatness, and quote Victor Hugo's description of Napoleon, taken prisoner after Waterloo, returning in a dream to the battle-field.

X

I was twenty-three years old when the troubling of my life began. I had heard from time to time in letters from Miss O'Leary,[1] John O'Leary's old sister, of a beautiful girl who had left the society of the Viceregal Court for Dublin nationalism. In after years I persuaded myself that I felt premonitory excitement at the first reading of her name.[2] Presently she drove up to our house in Bedford Park with an introduction from John O'Leary to my father.[3] I had never thought to see in a living woman so great beauty. It belonged to famous pictures, to poetry, to some legendary past. A complexion like the blossom of apples, and yet face and body had the beauty of lineaments which Blake calls the highest beauty because it changes least from youth to age, and a stature so great that she seemed of a divine race. Her movements were worthy of her form, and I under-stood at last why the poet of antiquity, where we would but speak of face and form, sings, loving some lady, that she paces like a god-dess. I remember nothing of her speech that day except that she vexed my father by praise of war, for she too was of the Romantic movement and found those uncontrovertible Victorian reasons, that seemed to announce so prosperous a future, a little grey. As I look backward, it seems to me that she brought into my life in those days – for as yet I saw only what lay upon the surface – the middle of the tint, a sound as of a Burmese gong, an overpowering tumult that had yet many pleasant secondary notes.

She asked [me] to dine with her that evening in her rooms in Ebury Street, and I think that I dined with her all but every day during her stay in London of perhaps nine days, and there was something so exuberant in her ways that it seemed natural she should

---

[1] Ellen O'Leary (1831–89). Yeats wrote a brief Introduction to a selection of her poems in 1892, *Uncollected Prose*, I, pp. 256–8.

[2] Maud Gonne (20 December 1865–27 April 1953).

[3] 30 January 1889. O'Leary (1830–1907), the Fenian leader, had returned to Ireland in 1885 after five years' imprisonment and fifteen years' exile.

give her hours in overflowing abundance. She had heard of me from O'Leary; he had praised me, and it was natural that she should give and take without stint. She lived surrounded by cages of innumerable singing birds and with these she always travelled, it seemed, taking them even upon short journeys, and they and she were now returning to Paris where their home was.

She spoke to me of her wish for a play that she could act in Dublin. Somebody had suggested Todhunter's[1] *Helena in Troas*, but he had refused. I told her of a story I had found when compiling my *Fairy and Folk Tales of the Irish Peasantry*, and offered to write for her the play I have called *The Countess Cathleen*. When I told her I wished to become an Irish Victor Hugo, was I wholly sincere? – for though a volume of bad verse translations from Hugo had been my companion at school, I had begun to simplify myself with great toil. I had seen upon her table *Tristram of Lyonesse*[2] and *Les Contemplations*, and besides it was natural to commend myself by claiming a very public talent, for her beauty as I saw it in those days seemed incompatible with private, intimate life.

She, like myself, had received the political tradition of Davis[3] with an added touch of hardness and heroism from the hand of O'Leary, and when she spoke of William O'Brien,[4] [who] was in jail making a prolonged struggle against putting on the prison clothes, she said, 'There was a time when men sacrificed their lives for their country, but now they sacrifice their dignity.' But mixed with this feeling for what is permanent in human life there was something declamatory, Latin in a bad sense, and perhaps even unscrupulous. She spoke of her desire for power, apparently for its own sake, and when we talked of politics spoke much of mere effectiveness, or the mere winning of this or that election. Her two and twenty years had taken some colour, I thought, from French Boulangist adventurers and journalist *arrivistes* of whom she had seen too much, and [she] already had

---

[1] John Todhunter (1839–1916), poet, dramatist, man of letters, author of *A Study of Shelley* (1880) and *Life of Patrick Sarsfield* (1895).

[2] Swinburne's *Tristram of Lyonesse, and Other Poems* (1882) included the poem 'The Statue of Victor Hugo', one of Swinburne's many tributes to Hugo.

[3] Thomas Davis (1814–45), leader of the Young Ireland movement, and one of the founders of the *Nation* in 1842.

[4] William O'Brien (1852–1928), journalist, Nationalist member of Parliament, founder of the agrarian and Nationalist paper, *United Ireland*, in 1881.

made some political journey into Russia in their interest. I was full of that thought of the 'Animula Vagula' chapter, I had heard it at the feet of a young Brahmin[1] in Dublin, 'Only the means can justify the end.' She meant her ends to be unselfish, but she thought almost any means justified in their success. We were seeking different things: she, some memorable action for final consecration of her youth, and I, after all, but to discover and communicate a state of being. Perhaps even in politics it would in the end be enough to have lived and thought passionately and have, like O'Leary, a head worthy of a Roman coin.

I spoke much of my spiritual philosophy. How important it all seemed to me; what would I not have given that she might think exactly right on all those great questions of the day? All is but faint to me beside a moment when she passed before a window, dressed in white, and rearranged a spray of flowers in a vase. Twelve years afterwards I put that impression into verse: ('she pulled down the pale blossom'. Quote):

[Blossom pale, she pulled down the pale blossom
At the moth hour and hid it in her bosom.][2]

I felt in the presence of a great generosity and courage, and of a mind without peace, and when she and all her singing birds had gone my melancholy was not the mere melancholy of love. I had what I thought was a 'clairvoyant' perception but was, I can see now, but an obvious deduction of an awaiting immediate disaster. I was compiling for an American publisher a selection from the Irish novelists,[3] and I can remember that all the tribulations of their heroes but reminded me of that dread. They too, according to a fashion of the writers of early Victoria, had been so often thrown without father or mother or guardian amid a world of deception, and they too, in their different way, were incurably romantic. I was in love but had not spoken of love and never meant to speak, and as the months passed I grew master of myself again. 'What wife could

---

[1] Mohini Chatterji, the Indian sage, arrived in London in 1884 and visited Dublin, where Yeats met him, in late 1885 or early 1886. See *Collected Poems*, pp. 279–80.

[2] From 'The Arrow', in the version which appeared in *In the Seven Woods* (1903).

[3] *Representative Irish Tales, compiled by W. B. Yeats* (New York, Putnam's Sons, 1891).

she make,' I thought, 'what share could she have in the life of a
student?'

XI

On some journey to Sligo I must have lingered in Dublin; my old
circle of friends and acquaintances, once flattered by her descent
among them, had begun to criticize. Even old John O'Leary[1] was
angry. William O'Brien and John Dillon[2] had just persuaded the
townsmen of Tipperary, who had a quarrel with the landlord,[3] to
build a new town on a neighbouring plot of land, and it had been
discovered that the old landlord by some grip over the new one in
some forgotten clause in a lease could turn them out of the new town
also. O'Leary himself owned property in the old town, but if he had
not he would certainly have disliked the adventure as much, for he
hated those two politicians above others. 'They want to influence
English opinion at the moment, and they think a Home Rule Bill will
come before they are found out. They are gambling with other
people's lives,' he would say, or some such phrases. Maud Gonne
had been to some formal opening of the new town. 'She is no disciple
of mine,' he said, 'she went there to show off her new bonnets.'
Somebody else had some tale of her going to the Parnell Commission
like some sentimental English sympathizer, in a green dress covered
with shamrocks. Somebody else, a Unionist, had another tale, not
less fabulous as I discovered in my anger, of her going to an otter
hunt in a muslin dress that was soon covered with mud.

Among my Dublin family friends was an artist, Miss Sarah
Purser.[4] She was so clever a woman that people found it impossible
to believe that she was a bad painter. She carried with her the prestige
of a family which contained great scholars who had published no
books, and men of science famous for clarity of mind and greatness
of range who had made no discoveries. She herself, though kind and

---

[1] 'refused now to consider her among his disciples' deleted.

[2] John Dillon (1851-1927), Member of Parliament for Tipperary 1880-3, and for
East Mayo 1885-1918; Chairman of the Irish Nationalist Party in 1918, but withdrew
after the collapse of the Party and the victory of Sinn Féin in that year.

[3] Arthur Smith-Barry. The quarrel began in June 1889; New Tipperary was built
in 1890.

[4] Sarah Purser (1848-1943), portrait painter, wit and patroness of the arts.

considerate when her heart was touched, gave currency to a small, genuine wit by fastening to it, like a pair of wings, brutality. She had painted Maud Gonne's portrait, and the portrait seemed to symbolize the common thought. The diary of a certain[1] Marie Bashkirtseff[2] had just been made popular by the commendation of Gladstone.[3] It was the thoughts of a girl full of egotism, sensationalism, and not very interesting talent. Miss Purser's portrait, in pose and in expression, was an unconscious imitation of the frontispiece of that book. She met me with the sentence, 'So Maud Gonne is dying in the South of France, and her portrait is on sale,' and went on to tell how she had lunched with Maud Gonne in Paris and there was a very tall Frenchman there – and I thought she dwelt upon his presence for my sake – and a doctor, and the doctor had said to her, 'They will be both dead in six months.'

When I reached Sligo, I was among Unionists, and some young landlord, a dull, not unkindly man, told how he was peeping through a hotel window at a public meeting that had been called to support his tenants against him. Somebody had shouted from the audience, 'Shoot him,' and a beautiful girl upon the platform, whom he believed to be Maud Gonne, had clapped her hands. My uncle, George Pollexfen, with obvious reluctance, not wishing to speak against any friend of mine, hinted that he knew of his own knowledge something very bad about her. 'I once saw her,' and here he stopped to explain what had brought him to Dublin, 'in the hall of the Gresham Hotel speaking to Mr William Redmond.[4] What will not women do for notoriety?' He considered all Nationalist members of parliament as socially impossible. All these stories infuriated me, and [I] would murmur to myself Blake's 'Mary': (quote last lines):

[She remembers no Face like the Human Divine.
All Faces have Envy, sweet Mary, but thine;

---

[1] 'clever, egotistical, rather vulgar' deleted.

[2] Maria Bashkirtseva (1860–84): her *Journal*, published in Paris in 1887, commanded great interest mainly because of its star-crossed brilliance. The English translation appeared in 1890.

[3] 'Journal de Marie Bashkirtseff', *The Nineteenth Century*, vol. 26, no. 152, October 1889, pp. 602–7; a review of the Paris edition.

[4] William H. K. Redmond, brother of John Redmond: he was Member of Parliament for East Clare. Killed in action at Messines, 7 June 1917.

And thine is a Face of sweet Love in despair,
And thine is a Face of mild sorrow & care,
And thine is a Face of wild terror & fear
That shall never be quiet till laid on its bier.][1]

In reality, I learned that till her illness she had been doing much
work in association with various members of the National League,[2]
and especially its secretary, Tim Harrington,[3] and was becoming
influential.

XII

A few months later I was again in Ireland[4] and I heard that she was
in Dublin. I called and waited for her at a little hotel in Nassau
Street,[5] which no longer exists, in a room overlooking the College
Park. At the first sight of her as she came through the door, her
great height seeming to fill it, I was overwhelmed with emotion, an
intoxication of pity. She did not seem to have any beauty, her face
was wasted, the form of the bones showing, and there was no life
in her manner. As our talk became intimate, she hinted at some unhappiness, some disillusionment. The old hard resonance had gone
and she had become gentle and indolent. I was in love once more and
no longer wished to fight against it. I no longer thought what kind
of wife would this woman make, but of her need for protection and
for peace.

Yet I left Dublin next day to stay somewhere in Orange Ulster
with the brilliant student of my old Dublin school, Charles Johnston,[6] and spent a week or ten days with him and his elder brother,

[1] *Complete Writings* (ed. Keynes), p. 429.

[2] Founded in September 1882 to unite all the groups then competing for Nationalist
favour: its patron was Parnell.

[3] Timothy C. Harrington, Parnellite Member of Parliament, was General Secretary
of the League. Author of the famous article, 'A Plan of Campaign', *United Ireland*, 23
October 1886.

[4] July 1891.

[5] The Nassau Hotel, South Frederick Street.

[6] Charles Johnston (1867–1931), son of William Johnston of Ballykilbeg, Co. Down,
Member of Parliament for South Belfast. A Theosophist, Charles Johnston founded the
Dublin Hermetic Society. Yeats arrived at Ballykilbeg House, four miles from Down-
patrick, on 23 July 1891: 'I have been away in County Down, looking almost in vain
among its half-Scotch people for the legends I find so plentiful in the West.' *Letters to
the New Island*, p. 138; dated 12 September 1891.

making fire balloons. We made the fire balloons of tissue paper and then chased them over the countryside, our chase becoming longer and longer as our skill in manufacture improved. I was not, it seems – not altogether – captive; but presently came from her a letter touching a little upon her sadness, and telling of a dream of some past life. She and I had been brother and sister somewhere on the edge of the Arabian desert, and sold together into slavery. She had an impression of some long journey and of miles upon miles of the desert sand. I returned to Dublin at once, and that evening, but a few minutes after we had met, asked her to marry me. I remember a curious thing. I had come into the room with that purpose in my mind, and hardly looked at her or thought of her beauty. I sat there holding her hand and speaking vehemently. She did not take away her hand for a while. I ceased to speak, and presently as I sat in silence I felt her nearness to me and her beauty. At once I knew that my confidence had gone, and an instant later she drew her hand away. No, she could not marry – there were reasons – she would never marry; but in words that had no conventional ring she asked for my friendship. We spent the next day upon the cliff paths at Howth[1] and dined at a little cottage near the Baily Lighthouse, where her old nurse lived, and I overheard the old nurse asking if we were engaged to be married. At the day's end I found I had spent ten shillings, which seemed to me a very great sum.

I saw her day after day. I read her my unfinished *The Countess Cathleen*, and I noticed that she became moved at the passage, 'the joy of losing joy, of ceasing all resistance' –

> [there is a kind of joy
> In casting hope away, in losing joy,
> In ceasing all resistance.][2]

---

[1] '. . . Maud Gonne at Howth station waiting a train, Pallas Athene in that straight back and arrogant head:'

'Beautiful Lofty Things', *Collected Poems*, p. 348.

[2] The First Merchant's speech, *Variorum Plays*, p. 108. Also, from 'The Circus Animals' Desertion':

> And then a counter-truth filled out its play,
> *The Countess Cathleen* was the name I gave it;
> She, pity-crazed, had given her soul away,
> But masterful Heaven had intervened to save it.
> I thought my dear must her own soul destroy,

and thought, she is burdened by a sense of responsibility for herself.
I told her after meeting her in London I had come to understand the
tale of a woman selling her soul to buy food for a starving people
as a symbol of all souls who lose their peace, or their fineness, or any
beauty of the spirit in political service, but chiefly of her soul that
had seemed so incapable of rest.[1] For the moment she had no
political work nor plan of any, and we saw each other continually.
Suddenly she was called back to France, and she told me in confidence that she had joined a secret political society and though she
had come to look upon its members as self-seekers and adventurers
she could not disobey this, the first definite summons it had sent
to her. I stayed on in Ireland, probably at Sligo with my uncle,
George Pollexfen, finishing *The Countess Cathleen* that had become
but the symbolical song of my pity. Then came a letter of wild
sorrow. She had adopted a little child, she told me, some three years
ago, and now this child had died. Mixed into her incoherent grief
were accounts of the death bird that had pecked at the nursery
window the day when it was taken ill, and how at sight of the bird
she had brought doctor after doctor.

XIII

She returned to Ireland in the same ship with Parnell's body,[2]
arriving at Kingstown[3] a little after six in the morning. I met her
on the pier and went with her to her hotel, where we breakfasted.
She was dressed in extravagantly deep mourning, for Parnell,
people thought, thinking her very theatrical. We spoke of the child's
death. She had built a memorial chapel, using some of her capital.
'What did money matter to her now?' From another I learned later
on that she had the body embalmed. That day and on later days she

---

> So did fanaticism and hate enslave it,
> And this brought forth a dream and soon enough
> This dream itself had all my thought and love.
>
> *Collected Poems*, pp. 391–2.

[1] 'A soul incapable of remorse or rest'; a phrase in reference to Kevin O'Higgins in
'The Municipal Gallery Revisited', *Collected Poems*, p. 368.

[2] Parnell died in Brighton on 6 October 1891, and was buried in Glasnevin Cemetery,
Dublin, on 11 October.

[3] Now Dun Laoghaire, Co. Dublin.

went over again the details of the death – speech was a relief to her.
She was plainly very ill. She had for the first days of her grief lost
the power of speaking French, which she knew almost as well as
English, and she had acquired the habit, unlearned afterwards with
great difficulty, of taking chloroform in order to sleep. We were
continually together; my spiritual philosophy was evidently a great
comfort to her. We spoke often of the state of death, and it was plain
that she was thinking of the soul of her 'Georgette'.

One evening we were joined by a friend I had made at the art
school in Kildare Street.[1] This was George Russell.[2] He had given
up art and was now an accountant in a draper's shop, for his will
was weak and an emotional occupation would have weakened it still
further. He had seen many visions, and some of them had contained
information about matters of fact that were afterwards verified; but,
though his own personal revelation was often original and very
remarkable, he accepted in the main the conclusions of Theosophy.
He spoke of reincarnation, and Maud Gonne asked him, 'How soon
a child was reborn, and if [reborn], where?' He said, 'It may be
reborn in the same family.' I could see that Maud Gonne was
deeply impressed, and I quieted my more sceptical intelligence, as I
have so often done in her presence. I remember a pang of conscience.
Ought I not to say, 'The whole doctrine of the reincarnation of the
soul is hypothetical. It is the most plausible of the explanations of
the world, but can we say more than that?' or some like sentence?

I had already taken a decision that will not suggest scepticism.
She now told me of an apparition of a woman dressed in grey and
with a grey veil covering the lower part of her face, which had
appeared to her [in] childhood. Perhaps when one loves one is not
quite sane, or perhaps one can pierce – in sudden intuition – behind
the veil.[3] I decided to make this woman visible at will. I had come to
believe that she was an evil spirit troubling Maud Gonne's life
unseen, weakening affections and above all creating a desire for
power and excitement. But, if it were visible, it would speak, it would

[1] Metropolitan School of Art, Leinster House, Kildare Street, Dublin, where Yeats studied, 1884–6.

[2] George W. Russell (AE) (1867–1935), poet and mystic. At this time he was working in Pim's, South Great George's Street, Dublin.

[3] 'I have often wondered if I did great evil.' deleted.

put its temptation into words and she would face it with her intellect, and at last banish it. I made a symbol according to the rules of my Order, considering it as an inhabitant of the fifth element with another element subordinate, and almost at once it became visible. I of course saw nothing beyond an uncertain impression on the mind, but Maud Gonne saw it almost as if palpably present. It told its story, taking up what was perhaps a later event of her dream of the desert. It was a past personality of hers, now seeking to be reunited with her. She had been priestess in a temple somewhere in Egypt and under the influence of a certain priest who was her lover gave false oracles for money, and because of this the personality of that life had split off from the soul and remained a half-living shadow. I would have taken all this for but a symbolic event, expressing a psychological state or spirit (is not Rahab 'an Eternal State' in William Blake?),[1] but for a coincidence. When I had been in the Esoteric Section of the Theosophical Society, I had been taught as one of the secrets of that initiation that a just such separated, half-living personality might haunt the soul in its new life and seek a reunion that must be always refused. I had not then the evidence that I have now of the most profound knowledge of all that passes in our minds and in the minds of those with whom we are even in remote contact, upon the part of beings of whom I know nothing except that they are invisible, subtle, and perhaps full of a secret laughter.

She had come [to] have need of me, as it seemed, and I had no doubt that need would become love, that it was already coming so. I had even as I watched her a sense of cruelty, as though I were a hunter taking captive some beautiful wild creature.[2] We went to London and were initiated in the Hermetic Students, and I began to form plans of our lives devoted to mystic truth, and spoke to her of Nicholas Flamel and his wife, Pernella.[3] In a propaganda, secret

[1] 'Rahab is an Eternal State', 'Jerusalem', plate 52, *Complete Writings*, p. 681.
[2] 'I began to talk to her of my plan, which I thought she felt only less emphatically. I wished now to make her my lover.' deleted.
[3] In the Cuala Press edition of *The Green Helmet, and Other Poems* (1910) the first eight poems are linked under the title, 'Raymond Lully and his wife Pernella'. An erratum note reads, in part: 'By a slip of the pen when I was writing out the heading for the first group of poems, I put Raymond Lully's name in the room of the later Alchemist, Nicholas Flamel.'

and seeking out only the most profound and subtle minds, that great beauty would be to others, as it was always to me, symbolic and mysterious. She stayed with her sister in London. I noticed that one evening when I paid her some compliment her face was deeply tinted. She returned to Paris, and her cousin, a young girl of like age, meeting me in the street, asked me 'why I was not in Paris'. I had no money. I had spent in Ireland all my earnings, and now instead of earning more as quickly as possible I spent more than half my time writing to her. Surely if I told her all my thoughts, all my hopes and my ambitions, she would never leave me.

I knew indeed that energies would return and that I must set her to some work – a secret, mystic propaganda might be insufficient. And now the death of Parnell had shown me, as I thought, what that work would be. When I had gone to London with my father and mother, it had been with the thought of returning some day to begin some movement like that of Young Ireland, though less immediately political. I had not thought out the details and during my years in London I had come to think of societies and movements to encourage literature, or create it where it was not, as absurd – is not the artist always solitary? – and yet now I wished to found societies and to influence newspapers. I began to justify this plan to that newer, mocking self by saying that Ireland, which could not support a critical press, must find a substitute. A moment later that newer self would convict me of insincerity and show me that I was seeking to find a work that would not be demoralizing, as I thought that even the most necessary politics were, not for all, but mostly for her whose soul I partly judged from her physical beauty and partly knew to be distinguished and subtle. I knew by a perception that seemed to come into my mind from without, so sudden it was, that the romance of Irish public life had gone and that the young, perhaps for many years to come, would seek some unpolitical form for national feeling.

I had occasionally lectured to a little patriotic society of young Irish men and women at Southwark, clerks for the most part, and their sisters and sweethearts. I made an appointment with the most energetic of them to explain my new plan. He was very ready for it, for his society had ceased to meet. The women had taken to laughing at the lectures – they were always the same and they had heard them so often – and nobody would give another lecture. I invited these men to meet in my study in Bedford Park to plan a new propaganda, and invited to meet them a man I had met in Dublin when he edited the *Dublin University Review*. He had indeed been appointed at my suggestion, and I had seen his admirable translations from the German. I had been impressed also by his physical beauty, as of a Greek statue. This man, T. W. Rolleston, came to be what Russell calls 'an intimate enemy'; without passion, though in mind and in body he seemed a vessel shaped for fiery use, I came to think him, in Ben Jonson's phrase, 'a hollow image'. And yet after five and twenty years I continually murmur to myself his lyric, 'In a quiet watered land, a land of roses'.[1] He was the true founder of the Irish Literary Society,[2] though the first general idea was mine, understanding all about resolutions and amendments and the like.

I had a plan for a series of books like the old National Library of Davis, and found that Sir Charles Gavan Duffy[3] had suggested a similar scheme to one or two of the young Southwark Irishmen. We decided to amalgamate the schemes and to organize the sales through the Irish Literary Society in London and a similar society to be founded in Dublin.[4] I sent Rolleston there and he got together a group of learned [men], many our political opponents, who decided that one really necessary thing was to raise more money for a certain learned society they all belonged to. I had not set my thoughts on learned men and went to Dublin in a passion. The first man I sought out was a butter merchant, whose name I had been given in Southwark, and a society, the National Literary Society, which afflicts me now by its permanence and by its dullness, so changed it is from its fiery youth, was planned out over a butter tub.

[1] 'The Dead at Clonmacnoise'. Yeats quoted the first lines in a Senate speech, 10 June 1925, *The Senate Speeches of W. B. Yeats*, ed. Donald R. Pearce (London, Faber & Faber, 1961), pp. 88–9.

[2] The preliminary meeting which led to the foundation of the Irish Literary Society of London was held on 28 December 1891.

[3] Sir Charles Gavan Duffy (1816–1903), one of the founders of the *Nation*, designed to direct 'the sympathy of educated men of all parties to the great end of Nationality'.

[4] The National Literary Society (Dublin) was founded on 24 May 1892 and held its first public meeting at the Rotunda on 16 August 1892.

XIV

The world where I was to do my work was partly familiar to me; Nationalists I had met in my father's studio or at the Young Ireland Society[1] and at O'Leary's house before I had left Dublin, Protestants generally and many Catholic Nationalists of a slightly younger generation met now for the first time. The most important, indeed the one indispensable man, was John O'Leary himself, and I was sure of his support. His long imprisonment, his association with famous figures of the past, his lofty character, and perhaps his distinguished head had given him great authority. I was not to find him an easy ally, and perhaps I should not have had him for ally at all had he not suggested that I book a lodging in the same untidy old eighteenth-century house.[2] It often took me the whole day to convince [him] of the rightness of some resolution I wanted the Society to pass, and the desirability of some book I had hoped to have published. His once passionate mind, in the isolation of prison and banishment, had as it were dried and hardened into certain constantly repeated formulas, unwieldy as pieces of lava, but these formulas were invariably his own, the result of the experiences of his life. I seldom thought these formulas untrue, but their application wasted many days in argument.

The next in importance was his disciple, the orator J. F. Taylor,[3] a gaunt, ungainly man, whose mind was perpetually occupied with an impassioned argument, to which he brought vast historical erudition, upon the justice of the national cause. He saw the world, as it were, in mathematical forms, and, being incapable of compromise, hated and would always hate the actual leaders of Ireland. Had O'Leary not outlived all his associates and become the critic of another generation, their friendship had been impossible. He had a mystical faith, derived from Catholic orthodoxy, in logic to its last extreme.

[1] The Society met every week at 41 York Street, Dublin. Yeats attended meetings in 1885 and 1886.

[2] Lonsdale House, St Lawrence Road, Clontarf.

[3] John Francis Taylor, barrister. His defence of the study of the Irish language, in a speech to the Law Students' Debating Society on 24 October 1901, is recalled and amplified in the newsroom chapter of Joyce's *Ulysses*. On 29 January 1886, Taylor delivered the Inaugural Address to the Young Ireland Society, his theme 'Parliaments of Ireland'.

He was enraged, and he seemed at times to live in rage, at my quotation from Blake: 'It is ordained that those who cannot defend the truth shall defend an error that enthusiasm and life may not cease.'[1] Error could have no justification. He knew nothing of poetry or of painting, though he seemed to know by heart whole plays of Shakespeare and all the more famous passages in Milton, and was deeply read in eighteenth-century literature. He understood alone eloquence, an impassioned pleading. He sometimes gave me an impression of insanity.

Then there was John O'Leary's friend, Dr Sigerson,[2] who had edited a patriotic paper in his youth and lost patients through some theological opinions. At first I was impressed by him, though never without a sense of comedy. He spoke with a curious broken accent, cut his hair as if after [the] frontispiece of *Sartor Resartus*, and made upon me the impression of having played before ignorant men the part of a great savant, a great Foreign Servant. Some newspaper, indeed, had just published an essay upon some Danish Sigerson because, as the editor told me, it was a cousin of his, and he would become hot in defence of the Danish invaders of Ireland and deny that they had burned churches. His family had come to Ireland in the ninth century with those invaders, and had no other connexion with Denmark. He flew into every argument, always evading its thought, and one soon discovered that he never disclosed any conviction of his own and that he was exceedingly timid in action. 'He burned his fingers long ago with liberal Catholicism,' people would say. I always found him kind and even generous, but soon discovered that he had, whenever I could follow him, erudition without scholarship, and that he had among historical events the thoughts of a child. He thought himself a judge of art and returned always from his rare visits to the Continent with portfolios full of forgeries.

Those with whom I was to have the most lasting sympathy were

---

[1] 'That he who will not defend Truth may be compell'd to defend
  A Lie: that he may be snared and caught and snared and taken:
  That Enthusiasm and Life may not cease; arise Spectre, arise!'
        'Jerusalem', plate 9, *Complete Writings*, p. 628.
[2] George Sigerson (1839–1925): his *Bards of the Gael and Gall* was published in 1897. At the first public meeting of the National Literary Society he read a paper entitled 'Irish Literature'.

as a rule the least effective, the least honoured in the world of hard logic. There was a novelist, Richard Ashe King,[1] who gave me great help. He lived in a little cottage near Kingstown and wrote criticism for *Truth*. He was gentle and amiable, and 'the only man', O'Leary would say, 'I have ever met who acknowledges that his will is weak'. I have never heard him argue, and he gave one the impression of happiness. 'The life of a writer is the best life in the world, if one is not married,' he said. I troubled his life a good deal for I got him to write and say unpopular truths, and he seemed overwhelmed when he saw how unpopular they were. That anybody should be disliked for an idea filled him with wonder.

The man most important to the future was certainly Dr Douglas Hyde. I had found a publisher while still in London for his *Beside the Fire* and *Love Songs of Connacht*,[2] and it was the first literary use of the English dialect of the Connacht country people that had roused my imagination for these books. His faculty was by nature narrative and lyrical, and at our committees, at any rate if Taylor or O'Leary were debating, he gave me an impression of timidity or confusion. His perpetual association with peasants, whose songs and stories he took down in their cottages from early childhood when he learned Irish from an old man on a kitchen floor, had given him, though a strong man, that cunning that is the strength of the weak. He was always diplomatizing, evading as far as he could prominent positions and the familiarity of his fellows that he might escape jealousy and detraction. He once told me, when I paid a brief visit to him in Connacht, that I was the only man from Dublin who had ever stayed in his house.[3] 'They would draw me into their quarrels,' he said. He also never spoke his real thought, but unlike Sigerson perhaps could not, for his mind moved among pictures, itself indeed a premise but never an argument. In later years the necessities of Gaelic politics destroyed his sense of style and undermined his instinct for himself. He ceased to write in that delicate, emotional dialect of the people, and wrote and spoke, when he spoke in public, from coarse reasoning.

[1] King (1839–1932) was literary editor of *Truth*.
[2] *Beside the Fire: A Collection of Irish Gaelic Folk Stories* (London, David Nutt, 1890). *Love Songs of Connacht* (London, T. Fisher Unwin; Dublin, Gill, 1893).
[3] Frenchpark, Co. Roscommon.

I recall faintly the images of Dr Coffey,[1] the head of the Catholic medical school and now Chancellor of the new University, and Richard O'Donovan,[2] now a professor or officer of some kind in that University, both well-liked and respected men.

My impression is of a moment when I had proposed a certain musician for the committee. They were obviously embarrassed and made it plain that there was a reason quite final against his election, but that it was not a reason they cared to speak of. At last a member told me privately that the musician had run off with another man's wife. 'Yes,' I said, 'many years ago, and the man was impotent and out of his mind believing that his neighbours were undermining his house to blow it up.' The subject was at once changed. Even in private 'nobody wished to speak of the matter'.

Then there were two groups of young men, a political group who supported me even when I attacked the political literature they loved – O'Leary's friendship was commendation enough for them, and I was not their rival – and a literary group made up from the members of what was called 'the Pan-Celtic Society'.[3] This society had died of public derision because of a rule that its members should publish nothing without putting the name of the Society after their names. Their poems had appeared mainly in country newspapers, without exciting admiration. I had almost from the first the enmity of these poets, and had probably earned it by some needless criticism at a moment of exasperation.

Then there was C. H. Oldham, now Professor of Political Economy. He joined my Society, but took no official part. 'I have lost faith since the death of Parnell,' he said. He had many photographs of Maud Gonne upon the walls of the discussion club[4] he presided over on Saturday evenings, and was later on to take an important part as her friend in the library scheme – collecting many

[1] Denis Coffey (1864–1945), first President of University College, Dublin, 1908–40.
[2] Robert Donovan (1862–1934), Professor of English Literature at University College, Dublin, 1908–34.
[3] Founded by Gerald C. Pelly on 1 March 1888.
[4] The Contemporary Club, which Charles Hubert Oldham founded in 1885: in the same year he started the *Dublin University Review*. The members of the Club met for topical discussion every Saturday night at Oldham's rooms, 116 Grafton Street. From 1904 to 1906 the venue was 42 Upper Leeson Street; from 1906 to 1945, when the Club came to an end, members met in a room in Lincoln Chambers.

books though always refusing to join the committee. He was constantly rude, without ill-feeling or temper, from mere coarseness of nerve, and yet was himself exceedingly sensitive. When anyone would point this out, I was accustomed to reply with a quotation from a magical book, 'The toad is so timid that if you frown at it for a quarter of an hour it will die', and yet as I look back he is a pleasant memory. With a vigorous and rather handsome head, he seemed, because more lucid than those about him while sharing in all their interests, the most evenly happy in that litigious society. At moments, when blinded by hot morality and a very good heart, he had that touch of helplessness which stirs the affections.

Walking home at three in the morning from his club, he had seen an object like a blanket lying on the low roof of a neighbouring outhouse. 'The cover of my neighbour's cistern has blown off,' he said, and got a rake and began raking it down. It stood up, it was his neighbour's daughter, who had climbed out of her bedroom window onto the outhouse roof to look at the stars. Another night he had arrived to see the servant of a neighbouring house letting out a young man, and had at once written and posted her a letter of moral admonition. When he got [up] next morning about noon, confident of a good deed, he had seen a cab at the neighbour's front door and the girl's box hoisted upon it. Unable to read, she had carried the letter to her mistress. My crowning memory is from the description of a friend. My friend was in a little western seaport, in a small hotel where a number of French visitors, invited by a political society, had just arrived. My friend heard a violent dispute below at the front door, and on looking out of the window saw Oldham and a boy, and an enraged landlady was declaring that she had never been so insulted in her life. Oldham and the boy had hung over their shoulders two ropes, and from these ropes, dangling at back and front, much crockery ware of a kind that are not usually carried through the streets in broad daylight. Oldham was explaining that this sudden rush of visitors must find the hotel imperfectly provided. 'I must consider,' he said, 'the reputation of my country.'

Perhaps I do not seem friendly enough writing of men who, after all, helped to accomplish an important work, and doubtless they showed to the *habitués* of their tables virtues they did not show to me.

But looking back now after many years, and knowing how hard it [is] to keep men in their graves,[1] I will put an inscribed stone over their heads that they may not plague another generation. Their patriotism was exceedingly great, and they were by that undone, driven to form opinions on matters beyond their experience. One is not always at one's best when one says, 'I must consider the reputation of my country.' To me they were mainly hostile men, though allies for momentary reasons, and formidable because they could outface my truths by irresistible deductions from some premise everybody there but myself seemed to accept. For how could I prove by argument that certain wavering rhythms, for instance, are nearer to the soul than the resolute rhythm of political oratory, or even that such a question had any importance? I had by taking to propaganda estranged the artist's only friend, Time, who brings to his side the purified senses of men.

XV

The Parnellite newspaper [was] *United Ireland* – there I could always write, and find the discussion around any important lecture. The editor,[2] a pleasant, indolent man who had written a book of fairy stories, left the main control to John McGrath, a man of twenty-five or so, known to have written the famous article[3] that accused the anti-Parnellites of the murder of Parnell. To help me he started a controversy under the heading, 'Is Dublin the intellectual capital of the Irish race?'[4] and decided the matter not by an inquiry as to whether there the ablest Irishmen lived, but as a matter of morals. 'Was not

[1] 'Though grave-diggers' toil is long,
Sharp their spades, their muscles strong,
They but thrust their buried men
Back in the human mind again.'
From 'Under Ben Bulben', *Collected Poems*, p. 398.

[2] Edmund Leamy (1848–1904).

[3] Unsigned article, 'Done to Death', *United Ireland*, 10 October 1891: the accusation was directed against T. M. Healy, John Dillon, and William O'Brien. 'They have killed him. Under God today, we solemnly believe that they have killed him.' The charge was repeated in another unsigned article, 'The Dead Chief', in the same issue.

[4] McGrath's article appeared in *United Ireland*, 2 April 1892. A letter from Yeats on the subject was published in *United Ireland*, 14 May 1892. *Uncollected Prose*, vol. 1, pp. 222–5.

it the duty of Irishmen to consider Dublin their intellectual capital, and then always to accept its leadership?' We had the support of all the Nationalist press. A new Ireland, they told their readers, had been born; the Ireland of Mitchel and Davis had returned.

One lecture, Dr Hyde's 'Necessity of de-Anglicizing Ireland',[1] led to the formation of [a] sub-committee of the National Literary Society, and presently that sub-committee, neglected as I thought by the council, resigned and became the Gaelic League. We had dropped into the chemical solution the crystal that caused the whole mass to drop its crystals. The London society had no man of the importance of Dr Douglas Hyde, but many young journalists who were able to celebrate our work in the English and American press. There was no limit to our confidence; a few months after our first meeting a history of our movement was published in volume form,[2] and on one of my visits to London I had some difficulty in preventing our council there accepting a circular that began with these words: 'Ireland, despite the dramatic genius of our people, has had no dramatist like Shakespeare, but a sub-committee of the Irish Literary Society has decided that the time has come.'

Maud Gonne's share had been clear to me from the first. She was to found branches throughout Ireland. She had her beauty and her eloquence and enough money to travel, and who could place a limit upon her influence in those little country towns where life is so dull? 'Become the fiery hand of the intellectual movement,' I had said to her. A young man in a solicitor's office, Henry Dixon – perhaps a grandchild of his may be among my readers – had invented an excellent plan and had allowed me to take it for my own. We were to send to any group of men and women who would form a branch a collection of books of Irish literature. In return for the library, which we decided should contain besides books given by friends a couple of pounds' worth of new books, they were to arrange a public lecture and give half the gate money to the central society. In this way the scheme would be partly self-supporting, and the societies were to be centres for the sale of publications and

---

[1] Delivered to the National Literary Society, 25 November 1892.

[2] W. P. Ryan, *The Irish Literary Revival: its History, Pioneers, and Possibilities* (London, 1894).

later on they might be visited by a travelling theatre I was planning out. I had intended to begin with a play upon the life and death of Robert Emmet.

For the only time in my life I was a popular personage, my name known to the crowd and remembered in the affections of the wise. Standish O'Grady,[1] whose *History of Ireland: Heroic Period* had been the start of us all, showed me a passage in the new book he was writing[2] – a meditation before the mountain of Slieve Fuad. The young man it spoke of – who once seeming of so little account had now become strong to uphold or to strike down – was meant, he said, for a description of myself.[3] On an expedition into Ulster to found some branch there I was asked to call upon a certain work-man's wife, an author of patriotic stories in a children's paper. I found her and her four children all in their Sunday best and she made me a little speech and, turning to her children, said, 'When you are grown up and have children of your own you will tell them that you once saw this man.'

XVI

While I was working out these plans, in which there was much patriotism and more desire for a fair woman, and watching them prosper beyond my hopes, Maud Gonne had found more exciting work. After the fall of Parnell, tenants evicted during the Land War were abandoned, or so it seemed, by their leaders. There was no longer any money from America and the energies of political Ireland were absorbed in the dispute between Parnellite and anti-Parnellite. She felt responsible for certain of these tenants as she had been among those who advised them to join the Plan of Campaign,[4]

---

[1] O'Grady (1846–1928): his *History of Ireland: Heroic Period* was published in 1878.

[2] *The Flight of the Eagle* (1897).

[3] Yeats confuses Fuad with Gullion. Fuad is the Milesian Druid King referred to in *The Flight of the Eagle*, Slieve Gullion the mountain guarded by 'three dreadful queens'. The young man is described 'with his right hand he upholds the weak, and with the left prostrates powers, and tyrants tremble before the light of his mild eyes'. Standish O'Grady, *Selected Essays and Passages* (Dublin, 1917), p. 339.

[4] A plan devised during the Land War by which tenants refused to pay more than what they considered a fair rent; if the landlord refused to accept this sum, it was used to relieve evicted tenants. The plan lasted from October 1886 to December 1890.

and she began lecturing in France for their benefit. She spoke of the wrongs of Ireland and much of certain Irishmen who were in jail for attempting to blow up public buildings. Some of these men, who had already served many years, were in bad health, and seven or seventeen had, it was said, lost their reason. Neither of the Irish parties would take up their cause for fear of compromising the Home Rule movement with the English electorate. Perhaps her lectures, besides bringing in a little money for the evicted tenants, might make England anxious enough for her good name in France to release some of these men.

She lectured first in Paris and then in the French provinces, and her success was exceedingly great. Michael Davitt[1] had come to her help with certain letters: M. Magnard[2] had placed the *Figaro* at her disposal. Everywhere old journalists and young students spoke of the cruelty of England, and the English Embassy had begun to show signs of uneasiness. I was touched at her success and read with pleasure of her 'mysterious eye' that drew some journalist to say it contained the shadow of battles yet to come. I also knew that vague look in the eyes and had often wondered at its meaning – the wisdom that must surely accompany its symbol, her beauty, or lack of any thought? Looking backward now I see that a mastery over popular feeling, abandoned by the members of Parliament through a quarrel that was to last for nine years, was about to pass into her hands. At the moment I was jealous of all those unknown helpers who arranged her lectures – had she not told me too a French friend, seeing her unhappy, had suggested her first lecture? And then too I saw no sufficient gain for so much toil – a few more tenants restored, perhaps a few dynamite prisoners released – and I had begun to dream of a co-ordination of intellectual and political forces. Her oratory, by its emotional temper, was an appeal to herself and also to something uncontrollable, something that could never be co-ordinated. I also, as Hyde later on with more success, had begun to bid[3] for that forsaken leadership.

My Dublin world was even blinder. O'Leary saw but a beautiful

---

[1] Davitt (1846–1906), founder of the Land League.
[2] Francis Magnard (1837–94), editor of the *Figaro* after Villemessant's death.
[3] 'dream' deleted.

woman seeking excitement, and Miss Sarah Purser said, continuing her pictorial interpretation, 'Maud Gonne talks politics in Paris, and literature to you, and at the Horse Show she would talk of a clinking brood mare.' I always defended her, though I was full of disquiet, and said often, 'None of you understands her force of character.' She came to Ireland again and again and often to the West where, through her efforts, all the tenants who had joined some combination through her influence were restored to their houses and farms. When in Dublin, we were always together and she collected books for our country branches and founded, I think, three of the seven branches, which were all we ever attained to. But it was no longer possible for her to become that 'fiery hand'. Till some political project came into her head she was the woman I had come to love. She lived as ever, surrounded by dogs and birds, and I became gradually aware of many charities – old women or old men past work were always seeking her out;[1] and I began to notice a patience beyond my reach in handling birds or beasts. I could play with bird or beast half the day, but I was not patient with its obstinacy.

XVII

She seemed to understand every subtlety of my own art and especially all my spiritual philosophy, and I was still full of William Blake, and sometimes she would say I had saved her from despair. We worked much with symbols, and she would pass at once into semi-trance and see all very distinctly. I was always seeking to bring her mind by their means into closer union with the soul, and above all with the peace of the soul. Two visions startled me and were a prophecy of moods that had not yet shown themselves in her life. I told her that during life we were able to enter at certain moments the heavenly circles we would inhabit in eternity. I called up the appropriate angelic form and asked how many were her

[1] 'I will talk no more of books or the long war
But walk by the dry thorn until I have found
Some beggar sheltering from the wind, and there
Manage the talk until her name come round.
If there be rags enough he will know her name
And be well pleased remembering it. . . .'
    From 'Her Praise', *Collected Poems*, p. 169.

circles. She said, 'He is telling me that I am in Hell, but that some day I will be able to enter three circles, though I cannot now.' He then showed her three circles: a garden, 'the circle of almost fulfilled desire'; a place in [a] wood with a fallen tree, 'the place of peace eternal, which is very brief for every human soul'; a mountain with a winding road and a cross, 'the circle of labour from divine love'.

Months later, on another visit to Dublin, and after she had forgotten, as I found, even the number of these circles, he showed her the hells she had fallen in: a great sea with hands as of drowning men rising out of it – a memory of a drawing by Blake perhaps – the circle of unfulfilled desire; a great precipice with dragons trying in vain to climb it – a continual climbing and falling, the circle of unfulfilled aspirations; and then a vast emptiness and the falling petals of a torn rose, the circle of revenge. I read out my notes of the original vision and pointed out the correspondences. 'Peace eternal' was the opposite of unfulfilled aspiration, and revenge of 'labour from the divine love'.

Now too the grey woman showed herself as very evil; hither[to] Maud Gonne had thought her only sorrowful. Speaking suddenly to Madame ——,[1] a friend who was present while Maud Gonne was in semi-trance, she had described herself as a murderess of children. Upon another occasion this friend, a pious woman, suddenly screamed in the middle of some vision [of] Maud Gonne's. She had found herself amid the fires of Hell and for days afterwards found all about the smell of sulphur – she said that her towels smelled of it in the morning. She had a great affection for Maud Gonne, and certainly suspected neither of us of diabolic practices. She thought it a warning to herself because she had not joined the Catholic Church. She died a Catholic a few years later. I believe now that Maud Gonne had a strong subconscious conviction that her soul was lost, and that though her conscious mind repelled all its accompanying symbols, these symbols could become visible in minds in close accord with her mind. Perhaps there was also an actual contest between two

---

[1] 'Rowley' deleted. '. . . a certain Mrs Rowley, who is a friend of Miss Gonne's. . . . She is kindly and well-meaning, and ardently Irish. . . .' Yeats to John O'Leary, February 1892, *Letters* (Wade), pp. 202–3.

troops of spirits for the control of her mind, and those who were pushing toward God may [have] caused the others to take on a diabolic shape. The names I had used when the woman smelt the sulphur were divine archangel and angel names connected with the three highest of kabalist sephiroth.[1]

I heard much scandal about her, but dismissed the grosser scandal at once, and one persistent story I put away with the thought, 'She would have told me if it were true.' It had come to seem as if the intimacy of our minds could not be greater, and I explained the fact that marriage seemed to have slipped further away by my own immaturity and lack of achievement. One night when going to sleep I had seen suddenly a thimble, and a shapeless white mass that puzzled me. The next day on passing a tobacconist's I saw that it was a lump of meerschaum not yet made into a pipe. She was complete; I was not.

XVIII

I came to hate her politics, my one visible rival. One day when [she] spent all day playing with a hawk somebody had sent her from Donegal I was delighted, because she gave up for that play a political caucus. The candidate she was interested in was defeated by half-a-dozen votes. 'But for you,' she said, 'he would have been returned,' and I was scornful at the idea that an Irish member the more would have been worth spoiling our day for, when we had so few days. I thought that the forces I had myself begun to organize, and like forces, would settle all such things, give them but time. We had a quarrel, and even after she had gone to France and returned again there was a slight estrangement. I was on my side deeply moved because she seemed to take my own work, especially a quarrel that had arisen, too lightly. To her it was only, it often seemed, a troublesome dispute among her friends that she kept herself apart from out of decent tact. I believed that the intellectual future of Ireland was at stake.

Sir Charles Gavan Duffy had now arrived and, instead of finding

[1] Sephiroth: 'In the philosophy of the Cabbala, the ten hypostatized attributes or emanations by means of which the Infinite enters into relation with the finite.' *O.E.D.*

in him an assistant upon equal terms as I expected, I found a domineering obstinacy and an entire lack of any culture that I could recognize. The books he wished to publish were all books that by some chance had failed to find publication in his youth, the works of political associates or of friends long dead. After a long quarrel I got Dr Hyde and T. W. Rolleston appointed editors[1] under Gavan Duffy to represent the two societies, and began sending up many suggestions through these editors or through an advisory committee I had persuaded the London society to elect, and by chance I was myself a member. In this way Dr Hyde's *History of Gaelic Literature*[2] and Standish O'Grady's *Bog and Stars*[3] and certain lives of Swift and Goldsmith were added to a series that, had it not been killed after a couple of years by the books chosen by its editor-in-chief, would have done much for popular education. Sir Charles Gavan Duffy insisted on an excellent unpublished historical work – excellent, that is, for the proceedings of a learned society – by Thomas Davis,[4] and so successful had our plans been that we sold ten thousand copies before anybody had found time to read it. Unhappily, when they did read it, they made up their minds to have nothing more to do with us or our books.

Besides making suggestions I had an ungracious task: to stop the publication of books Gavan Duffy had set his heart on. Dr Sigerson and J. F. Taylor sided with Gavan Duffy against me and the movement was soon divided, the young men on the whole taking my side.[5] To Sigerson and to Taylor as to Duffy, Ireland was perhaps but one side in an argument. I wished to make it, by good writing, an experience, and to be able to say with Walt Whitman, 'I convince as a sleeping child convinces,' and that was so little formidable and is it not necessary for Ireland to be formidable? Besides, Taylor's

---

[1] In an article in the *Freeman's Journal*, 6 September 1892, Yeats protested against the arrangement by which Gavan Duffy would be appointed sole editor of the New Irish Publishing Company. Yeats proposed a committee of five members: his protest was supported by *United Ireland*, 10 September 1892.

[2] *The Story of Early Gaelic Literature* (London, Unwin; Dublin, Sealy, 1895).

[3] *The Bog of Stars, and Other Stories and Sketches of Elizabethan Ireland* (London, Unwin; Dublin, Sealy, 1893).

[4] *The Patriot Parliament of 1689* (1893).

[5] Specimens of the controversy appeared in the *Freeman's Journal*, 6, 7, 8, 9, 10 September 1892, and *United Ireland*, 10 and 24 September 1892. *Uncollected Prose*, vol. I, pp. 239–45.

imagination, in which there was much chivalry, was touched by the spectacle of an old man coming back at the end of his life to take up again the patriotic work of his youth. I was too full of the impatience of youth to be touched, and began an attack on the literature, above all on the poetry, of Young Ireland. At some of our committee meetings questions perhaps of [the] merits of *The Spirit of the Nation*,[1] a volume of political verse then in its fiftieth edition, would often put our proper business aside, and passion ran so high at times between Taylor and myself – O'Leary taking my side – that I have known strangers drawn by sport or sympathy to step into the room and nobody have a mind disengaged enough to turn them out.

The cleverer and better educated of those opposed to me did not think the literature of Young Ireland very satisfactory, but it was all Ireland had, they said, and if we were to admit its defects England would take advantage of the admission. The argument would rouse me to fury; England had only bound the hands of Ireland, they would silence her intelligence. Others who believed perhaps, as indeed thousands did, that *The Spirit of the Nation* was as great lyric poetry as any in the world would then say that I disliked it because I was under English influence – the influence of English decadent poets perhaps – and I would reply that it was they, whose lives were an argument over wrongs and rights, who could not escape from England even in their dreams. I took it all with a seriousness that amuses my more tolerant years, believing, as I had done years before at some school debating society, that I stood with Plato and with Socrates. To Taylor, to Sigerson perhaps, I was but an over-confident young man who had interrupted a charming compliment to an old statesman at the end of his career. Upon my side, my emotions were exasperated by jealousy, for everyone that came near Maud Gonne made me jealous, and by the strain upon my nerves of that perplexed wooing. The discussion soon reflected itself in the subcommittee that chose the books for the country libraries, and meetings that sometimes took place in her sitting-room became interminable.

[1] *The Spirit of the Nation*, ed. Thomas Davis (Dublin, 1845).

XIX

I think that Taylor and I must have often shown ourselves in no good light, and I have little doubt that I, because I was the younger and so had the least discipline, came out of it the worse. I noticed that his temper, which was notorious, only increased the vigour of his mind, whereas I, whose convictions were founded not upon any logical argument but upon a series of delicate perceptions, became confused and contradictory, or wrecked my cause by overstatement. Even O'Leary, who though his pride, which was one half his nobility, made him refuse to think his cause had any need of second-rate literature or incomplete criticism or even of a self-conscious apologetics, was against me again and again in matters of detail. It was to me a time [of] great pain and disquiet. I have found that if many people accuse one of vanity, of affectation, of ignorance, an ignoble image is created from which the soul frees itself with difficulty, an undiscerned self-loathing.

Presently Maud Gonne and I had a serious quarrel.[1] Much that preceded it or followed has grown confused in the memory, but certain mental images are very distinct. I remember her taking the lodgings that were to be for us both so unlucky. They were kept by two not very clean old women, who received her with extraordinary obsequiousness in [a] room with heavy curtains over the windows and a table with a dull, hanging tablecloth. I remember how beautiful she looked, how badly I had behaved to Taylor with whom I had just quarrelled, and that was the beginning. It was the old issue. I had objected, I think, to the great number of books of Irish oratory selected by him for the country libraries, and in his presence had pressed my objection against rhetorical writing in a way that seemed to touch upon his own gift. I had had much provocation and besides I was also jealous of him, not because I thought him a suitor, but because he seemed to influence her mind in things where I alone should have influence, I believed; but I accepted all she said and added my own accusations to hers.

A couple of days later a cold she had developed into congestion of her lungs, and I was not admitted by Dr Sigerson, with whom I

1 Summer 1893.

had recently quarrelled about Sir Charles Gavan Duffy. Meanwhile one of her objects of charity, a woman with an unhealthy clay-coloured complexion and moist, morbid hands, finding that the two old women had left the door open to save themselves the trouble of answering the bell, had climbed the stairs and taken upon herself the duties of a nurse. For want of better help the doctor had accepted her, and from her, for I had arranged to meet her nightly in a public garden, I had my daily news. Presently the news became melodramatic. I was to think no more of Maud Gonne – who was looking for some ground of quarrel – she loved another, indeed perhaps two others, for ill as she was she had decided to hurry back to France to be present at a duel between them. Maud Gonne had even forbidden them to fight before her arrival, or anywhere but in her own drawing room. On other occasions she would report that I would not see Maud Gonne again.

Presently May Gonne[1] arrived in Dublin and from her I had more reliable news. Maud Gonne was leaving – she was so ill [she] was to be carried to the train and the doctor had protested in writing. For a long time I knew nothing, and then heard, no longer rumour, that this protégée, the first of many about whom I was to somewhat fail in cordiality, had repeated some story about me, apparently less melodramatic than that she had carried to my ears, for it had been believed. Presently I found a horrible story circulated everywhere. I had been Maud Gonne's lover, and there had been an illegal operation and I had been present during the operation. The protégée was one [of] those sinister women who without stimulants are only half alive, and she found her chosen stimulants in her own mind. Maud Gonne herself afterwards told me how awaking in the middle of the night she found those eyes, which I remember as vague and always moist, bent down above her face. She had told her to go to the other end of the room. 'No, I must not,' was the answer, 'Dr Sigerson says you may die at any moment, I am waiting for the moment of death.' Once there had been another visitor, an insurrectionary, patriotic old man who in his turn, finding the front door open, had climbed the stairs also, had sat down by the sofa where the sick

---

[1] Maud Gonne's cousin.

woman lay and blabbed out his sorrow mixed up with description
of the crowds that would attend the funeral.

XX

I went to Sligo seeking to call to myself my courage once again with
the lines 'Into the Twilight': did not the dew shine though love
decayed 'Burning in fires of a slanderous tongue?'[1] Then, on arriving
from the last visit to Sligo or some earlier visit, O'Leary met me with
the sentence, 'Well, what I warned you of has happened; they are
all jealous of you now. You should have followed my advice.' He
had urged me to keep myself apart from the young men, and [I]
with my father's democratic ideas, his memories of John Stuart Mill
and Walt Whitman for half-conscious guide, had gone everywhere
with them as one of themselves. With the young politicians this had
done [no] mischief and I had their support to the end, but I found
now that those who wrote verses or essays were all against me. My
attack on Young Ireland they had welcomed, for [they] always
insisted on our need of new literature, but now without joining
Duffy they became my critics. They had refused to send on to the
country societies a number of books Maud Gonne and I had collected – what use to them were those societies? – and had voted them
to the library of [the] central society. They repeated Taylor's continuous attacks on my ignorance. I knew little his authors – Locke,
Swift, Grattan – and nothing of history, and the authors I did know –
Blake, Keats, Shelley, all the Romantic school – he ignored or
despised.

On going into some bar, where however I did not drink anything,
I believe, with a group of political young men who supported me
through all at much expense of time and out of sheer patriotism for
they [had] nothing to gain, I was horrified at the indecency of the
conversation, of their conversation in the presence of the barmaid.
The most intelligent, seemingly the most unruly and the most un-

----

[1] 'Your mother Eire is always young,
    Dew ever shining and twilight grey;
    Though hope fall from you and love decay,
    Burning in fires of a slanderous tongue.'
From 'Into the Twilight', first published in the *National Observer*, 29 July 1893.

bridled tongue,[1] seemed a part with his always unbrushed clothes and generally unshaven chin.

I brought to a small meeting of the National Literary Society, intended for literary conversation over the tea table, the three volumes of interpretation and edition of William Blake which Ellis and I had just published. I was very proud; here at last was a substantial book; perhaps even, it might seem, a little erudition. Dr Sigerson took the third volume, in which occur the reproductions of the Prophetic Books, and explained to all present that the many nude figures had been reproduced in the work for exclusively artistic reasons.

Lionel Johnson came to Ireland[2] and I brought him to the Contemporary Club, which I had described to him before my own return to Ireland as a place of excellent talk, and he refused to speak, and said that everybody, whether in it or out of it, made bad speeches to him. His own drinking habit had grown on him since I left London, and when he stayed at my lodging had soon the habit of sitting at a table with John McGrath and my fellow lodger and half a dozen more talking politics and religion to four or five in the morning. He did not seem less oratorical than the others, as I recall, at four one morning as I left him to find my bed. He was bolt upright among a group of men in various stages of lying or lounging intoxication, and as I left was saying, 'I believe in nothing but the Holy Roman Catholic Church.'

I found one night my friend[3] when I went to the Contemporary Club towards one in the morning. He was very drunk and was saying with a cordial wave of his arm to all those politicians, scarce one of whom knew any prose but of the newspapers, 'Can any of you tell me why there is no English prose after the close of the eighteenth century?'

[1] Doubtful reading.

[2] Johnson made his first visit to Ireland in September 1893; later visits in April 1894 and May 1898.

[3] After the reference to the Catholic Church, Yeats began a new paragraph: 'My friend A. H. Bullen, the Elizabethan scholar came to Ireland on nego', meaning evidently 'negotiations'. At that point he apparently thought of putting in another anecdote about Johnson; he added the words 'I found one night' in the vacant space above 'My friend', and deleted all the words from 'A. H. Bullen' to 'nego'; continuing then with, 'when I went to the Contemporary Club . . . '. It is more than probable that Johnson, rather than Bullen, is intended: only the fact that Yeats speaks elsewhere of both men in association with alcohol makes this interpretation somewhat uncertain.

XXI

I had a crystal and showed many how to see in it, and an even larger number to see visions according to the method of my Order. A very considerable proportion would pass into trance and see what I called up as vividly as ever with the eye of the body. Looking back now I recognize that these visions often repeated to me my own thoughts – often some woman would see a marriage with a beautiful woman. My own divination had not been so lucky, for the Tarot had foretold disaster, and now the young doctor[1] had a vision that was perhaps an obscure prophecy of my life for years to come. When we had set up house together, he had made me promise never to ask him to see a vision or even allow him to do so. One night I was making somebody else see and he began to beg that I would make him see also. I refused. A few days afterward I was again experimenting in his presence and suddenly discovered that he was entranced. I questioned him. He was looking at a little Greek temple and a woman, perhaps a priestess, came to him from the temple. She led him to a great door in some other building. Now he found himself in a great white room with an empty throne and at the far end a trembling door. Someone had plainly just passed through it. I said, 'Follow.' He passed through the door to find himself in another room like the first, with another trembling door, and when he passed through that door also there was a third white room, and a third trembling door. Then he turned himself in darkness and when I called for light he was before an empty tomb. The lid of the tomb with an inscription lay against the wall. I told him to read the inscription, but when he tried to he was back in the first room and saw that the throne and certain other seats were overset. All was in confusion. He awoke, and when I asked what he had seen said, 'I remember nothing after a woman came from a temple and gave me a cup of wine.' I told him what he had described and that he had not spoken of any cup of wine, and said, 'What do you think it all means?' He said, 'Perhaps the death of the reigning sovereign.' He meant

---

[1] Yeats wrote but cancelled earlier in the manuscript: 'I never spent more than a pound a week, staying at first among a group of theosophists who kept house together, and afterwards sharing rooms first with John O'Leary, then with a young doctor who undertook the housekeeping.'

Queen Victoria, but he had a different meaning to me, though neither then nor now do I understand all its meaning, for at that very time I was meeting the hysterical nurse in the public garden. But why that open, inscribed tomb? Have I sought on earth what I should seek beyond the grave?

XXII

It was growing increasingly hard to earn a living. I never spent more than a pound a week, but I could now scarcely earn so much and was growing anxious. My work was interfered with by lack of money, and I had to allow the London society to do things I objected to because I could not afford my ticket to London. As a result of the split in the Irish party that followed the fall of Parnell,[1] there were two newspapers for every one before it, and papers that had but half their old circulation could not pay for verse or even for reviews. I found on my return from some journey that a young Mayo lad was in what had been my lodging, and the young Mayo doctor had given him very plainly the affection that had once been mine. I gathered up a few books and papers, my only property, and went to London. I stayed with my people at Bedford Park for a while, quarrelling a good deal with my younger sister.

XXIII

I was tortured by sexual desire and had been for many years. I have often said to myself that some day I would put it all down in a book that some young man of talent might not think as I did that my shame was mine alone. It began when I was fifteen years old. I had been bathing, and lay down in the sun on the sand on the Third Rosses[2] and covered my body with sand. Presently the weight of the sand began to affect the organ of sex, though at first I did not know what the strange, growing sensation was. It was only at the orgasm that I knew, remembering some boy's description or the description in my grandfather's encyclopedia. It was many days before I

---

[1] After November 1890.   [2] Rosses Point, Sligo.

discovered how to renew that wonderful sensation. From that on it was a continual struggle against an experience that almost invariably left me with exhausted nerves. Normal sexual intercourse does not affect me more than other men, but that, though never frequent, was plain ruin. It filled me with loathing of myself; and yet at first pride and perhaps, a little, lack of obvious opportunity, and now love kept me in unctuous celibacy. When I returned to London in my twenty-seventh year I think my love seemed almost hopeless, and I knew that my friends had all mistresses of one kind or another and that most, at need, went home with harlots. Henley, indeed, mocked at any other life. I had never since childhood kissed a woman's lips. At Hammersmith I saw a woman of the town walking up and down in the empty railway station. I thought of offering myself to her, but the old thought came back, 'No, I love the most beautiful woman in the world.'

XXIV

At a literary dinner[1] where there were some fifty or sixty guests I noticed opposite me, between celebrated novelists, a woman of great beauty. Her face had a perfectly Greek regularity, though her skin was a little darker than a Greek's would have been and her hair was very dark. She was exquisitely dressed with what seemed to me very old lace over her breast, and had the same sensitive look of distinction I had admired in Eva Gore-Booth.[2] She was, it seemed, about my own age, but suggested to me an incomparable distinction.[3] I was not introduced to her, but found that she was related to a member of the Rhymers' Club and had asked my name.

I began to write *The Land of Heart's Desire* to supply the niece of a new friend, Miss Florence Farr,[4] with a part, and put into it my

---

[1] Early in 1894.

[2] The younger of the sisters celebrated in 'In Memory of Eva Gore-Booth and Con Markiewicz': 'both beautiful', one (Eva) 'a gazelle'. Eva (1870–1926) devoted her life to the women's suffrage movement. Yeats did not meet her until late in 1894, but he had already seen her at Sligo.

[3] 'and the hat she came in was known as Margaret Vernon.' deleted.

[4] Florence Beatrice Farr, born 7 July 1860, in Bromley, Kent: actress, wife of Edward Emery. She played Aleel in the first production of *The Countess Cathleen* in 1899. Yeats first met her in 1890 when she was acting in Todhunter's *A Sicilian Idyll*. She

own despair. I could not tell why Maud Gonne had turned from me unless she had done so from some vague desire for some impossible life, for some unvarying excitement like that of the heroine of my play. Before it was finished I went to Paris[1] to stay with MacGregor Mathers, now married to Bergson's sister. The decay of his character that came later had not set in, though I noticed that his evocations were a dangerous strain. One day a week he and his wife were shut up together evoking, trying to influence the politics of the world, I believe now, rearranging nations according to his own grandiose phantasy, and on this day I noticed that he would spit blood. He had a small income, three or four hundred a year, allowed him by a member of the Order,[2] and there was some provision for some frater or soror, as we are called, staying with him.

Maud Gonne was of course my chief interest; she had not left France for a long time now and was, I was told, ill again. I saw her, and our relations, which were friendly enough, had not our old intimacy. I remember going with her to call upon some friend and noting that she mounted the stairs slowly and with difficulty. She had not gone on with her work in the Order, and was soon to withdraw altogether, disliking, she said, our absorption in biblical symbolism, but MacGregor Mathers was her firm admirer. I remember little of the time but that I went here and there murmuring the lines of my play, and Bergson came to call, very well dressed and very courteous. He was but an obscure professor and MacGregor Mathers was impatient. 'I have shown him all that my magic can do and I have no effect upon him.' Sometimes in the evening we would play a curious form of chess at which there should be four players. My partner would be Mrs Mathers, and Mathers would declare that he had a spirit for his. He would cover his eyes with his hands or gaze at the empty chair at the opposite corner of

---

was a senior member of the Golden Dawn. In later years she gave up the theatre and went to Ceylon, where she taught in a Vedantist seminary: she died there on 29 April 1917. Yeats's tribute to her is given in 'All Souls' Night'. George Yeats has written, in a Foreword to *Florence Farr, Bernard Shaw and W. B. Yeats*, ed. Clifford Bax (Dublin, Cuala Press, 1941), of the relation between Yeats and Florence Farr: 'Their brief love affair came to an end because "she got bored".'

[1] February 1894.

[2] Annie E. F. Horniman (1861–1937): the allowance was £449 a year.

the board before moving his partner's piece. I found him a gay, companionable man, very learned in his own subject, but [without] the standards of a scholar. He would sometimes come down to breakfast with a Horace in his hands and sometimes with Macpherson's *Ossian*, and it made him angry to doubt the perfect authenticity of *Ossian*.

XXV

On my return from France came a performance of my play[1] and it had a measure of success, keeping the stage in part perhaps from the kindness of the management, my friend Florence Farr, for nearly seven weeks. Presently the member of the Rhymers' Club introduced me to the lady I had seen between the two famous novelists, and a friendship I hope to keep till death began. In this book I cannot give her her real name – Diana Vernon sounds pleasantly in my ears and will suit her as well as any other.[2] When I went to see her she said, 'So-and-so seemed disinclined to introduce us; after I saw your play I made up my mind to write to you if [I] could not meet you otherwise.' She had profound culture, a knowledge of French, English, and Italian literature, and seemed always at leisure. Her nature was gentle and contemplative, and she was content, it seems, to have no more of life than leisure and the talk of her friends. Her husband,[3] whom I saw but once, was much older and seemed a little heavy, a little without life. As yet I did not know how utterly estranged they were. I told her of my love sorrow, indeed it was my obsession, never leaving by day or night.

---

[1] *The Land of Heart's Desire*, first performed in the Avenue Theatre, London, on 29 March 1894. The role of the Faery Child was played by Dorothy Paget, Florence Farr's niece.

[2] Mrs Olivia Shakespear, née Olive Tucker, a cousin of Lionel Johnson. A letter, undated but franked 30 May 1894, from Johnson to Yeats has a note added: 'I shall be so glad to see you – Olivia Shakespear.' Mrs Shakespear published several novels, including *Love on a Mortal Lease* (1894), *The Journey of High Honour* (1895), *The False Laurel* (1896) and *The Devotees* (1904). She died in 1938. Diana Vernon is the heroine of Scott's *Rob Roy*.

[3] Hope Shakespear, a solicitor.

XXVI

I had not solved the difficulty of living. I went to Sligo and spent six months there with my uncle[1] at Thornhill. At, I imagine, the outset of my visit, I was able to do him [a service] and to increase my own confidence in those unknown forces. There was a rumour of smallpox 'somewhere on the mountain', a false rumour as it turned out, and my uncle, always in a panic about his health, decided upon re-vaccination. Out of curiosity, for I did not believe the rumour or indeed care if it was true, I was vaccinated also. The vaccine was bad, it seems; my uncle got blood poisoning and I had rather a slow recovery but no serious illness. Presently my uncle became delirious and the family doctor called into consultation the other principal doctor. One night when all was at its worst, about eleven, I went into my uncle's room and sat at his bedside. He was in delirium and with a high temperature, and when I asked what he saw said 'red dancing figures'. Without saying what I was doing I used the symbol of water and the divine names connected in the kabalistic system with the moon. Presently he said that he saw a river flowing through the room and sweeping all the red figures away. I then told him what I had done and stayed till he said he felt now that he could sleep. I then told him if the figures returned to banish them by the name of the archangel Gabriel who, as moon archangel, could control the waters. I had not the right to give him the name I had used as, though he had entered my Order, he had but taken as yet some lower degrees. In the morning the family doctor came to see me. My uncle had told him of his good night, and that I had given him 'a secret word' that had banished a return of the red figures. 'I suppose', he said, 'it is a kind of hypnotism.'

When my uncle was better or before his illness, a young bank clerk, or my cousin Lucy, or a rough young man, clerk in the work-house, would come in after dinner and I used all three as seers. A vision of the bank clerk, of the Garden of Eden, is described in an essay on Magic,[2] but not his refusal to call any more. 'If a man were

---

[1] George Pollexfen. Yeats was at Thornhill in November 1894, and stayed there until early summer 1895.

[2] First published in the *Monthly Review*, September 1901; included in *Ideas of*

to believe that,' he said, 'it would ruin his whole life. If a man's in business he has to do queer things and, if he believed that, he could not do them.' 'But you are a Christian,' I said. 'Oh yes, but Christianity is figurative.'[1] He had perhaps, as so often happens in Ireland, a purity of the imagination and refined feeling that made it possible for the guardian spirits to approach him in moments of vision, combined with a crude rationalism and commonness of the conscious mind. The clerk from the workhouse saw easily, but nothing of any value – he seemed common throughout; and my cousin Lucy with less lofty symbolism than the bank clerk – who yet in his daily self did [not] know what a symbol was – had a clairvoyance that moved more among verifiable things. Her chief power was an occasional pre-vision. I got with her my first proof of the old magical claim that names have a power apart from our associations with them, at any rate from our obvious associations. I was trying to call up 'the last incarnation of George Pollexfen' and all there expected some event in the eighteenth century at latest. She saw an obvious Anglo-Indian, and my uncle remembered that there was one other George Pollexfen in the world, a retired Anglo-Indian. Lucy Middleton had never to her knowledge heard of this man, and [he] belonged to a branch of the family from whom the Sligo Pollexfens had separated a century ago, and George had never met or seen any member of this branch.

I found I had the reputation of a magician; there was a story among the country people of my being carried five miles in the winking of an eye, and of my sending my cousin from her house at the First Rosses to the rocks of the Third in a like eye-wink – I had indeed sent her there in vision. I do not remember if it was now or at some later visit that a servant at her house gave notice after a water evocation of mine, begun long after she was in her bed. She had seen mermaids in the night who soaked her in sea water. I remember hearing as I went upstairs after an evening of evocation my uncle's old, second-sighted servant[2] moaning in the midst of some terrifying

---

Good and Evil (1903). *Essays and Introductions*, p. 45, recounts the bank clerk's vision.
[1] '. . . a young Church of Ireland man, a bank-clerk in the West of Ireland', *Essays and Introductions*, p. 45.
[2] Mary Battle, *Autobiographies*, p. 70.

dream. Certainly our thoughts, and we were not yet sure if it was more than this, affected all neighbouring sensitive minds.

I was re-writing *The Countess Cathleen* as a result perhaps of my practical stage experience with *The Land of Heart's Desire*, elaborating the death scene, filling it with the old Irish mythology as that was getting an always greater mastery over my imagination. It may have been now that I paid a visit to Lissadell[1] where Sir Henry Gore-Booth, his wife and son,[2] and his two daughters lived. My uncle had always had faith in my talent, but I think that now for the first time the few others that remained of my mother's people began to think I had not thrown away my life. In my childhood I had seen on clear days from the hill above my grandmother's house or from the carriage if our drive was towards Ben Bulben or from the smooth grass hill of Rosses the grey stone walls of Lissadell among its trees. We were merchant people of the town. No matter how rich we grew, no matter how many thousands a year our mills or our ships brought in, we could never be 'county', nor indeed had we any desire to be so. We would meet on grand juries those people in the great houses – Lissadell among its woods, Hazelwood House by the lake's edge, and Markree Castle encircled by wood after wood – and we would speak no malicious gossip and knew ourselves respected in turn, but the long-settled habit of Irish life set up a wall. One man, indeed, a merchant at the other end of the town, did sometimes drift a little into such society, but we despised him for it as for the gay, pleasant-looking unsubstantial look of his house, the only house in the neighbourhood that had been changed; certain gay verandahs giving the windows where they faced the lake an indecorous look. But my going to the Gore-Booths was different. I had written books and it was my business to write books and it was natural to wish to talk to those whose books you liked, and besides I was no longer of my grandfather's house. I could no longer say, 'We do so-and-so or we think so-and-so.'

I have no memory of when I first met the Gore-Booth girls or

---

[1] 'I have been staying at Lissadell for a couple of days', Yeats to Lily Yeats, 23 November 1894, *Letters* (Wade), p. 239. Lissadell is ten miles from Sligo, and five from Drumcliffe.

[2] Josslyn Gore-Booth.

how I came to be asked. Con Gore-Booth[1] all through my later
boyhood had been romantic to me, and more than once as I looked
over to the grey wall and roof I had repeated to myself Milton's
lines:

> Bosomed deep[2] in tufted trees,
> Where perhaps some beauty lies,
> The cynosure of neighbouring eyes.

She had often passed me on horseback, going or coming from some
hunt, and was acknowledged beauty of the county. I heard now and
then [of] some tom-boyish feat or of her reckless riding, but the
general impression was always that she was respected and admired.
To the country people she was always Miss Gore, for they never
spoke the name Booth which had brought with it English merchant
blood, I believe, and it was a Gore always their fathers had served
and obeyed. She surprised me now at our first meeting by some small
physical resemblance to Maud Gonne, though so much shorter and
smaller, and by a very exact resemblance in voice. In later years her
voice became shrill and high, but at the time I write of it was low
and soft. I was perhaps the first to give her any detailed account of
one[3] in imitation of whom, perhaps, she was to earn the life-sentence
she is now serving.[4]

I was at once in closer sympathy with her sister, Eva, whose
delicate, gazelle-like beauty reflected a mind far more subtle and
distinguished. Eva was for a couple of happy weeks my close friend,
and I told her all of my unhappiness in love; indeed so close at once
that I nearly said to her, as William Blake said to Catherine Boucher,
'You pity me, there[fore] I love you.' 'But no,' I thought, 'this house
would never accept so penniless a suitor', and, besides, I was still
deeply in love with that other and had but just written 'All Things
Uncomely and Broken'.[5] I threw the Tarot, and when the Fool

_____

[1] Constance Gore-Booth (1868–1927). In 1898 she went to Paris to study painting,
there met and married the painter Count Casimir de Markiewicz. In 1916 she commanded the revolutionary forces which held St Stephen's Green in Dublin during
Easter Week.

[2] Should read 'high'. 'L'Allegro', lines 78–80.   [3] Maud Gonne.

[4] Countess Markiewicz was arrested on 30 April 1916, sentenced to penal servitude
for life on 6 May 1916, but released on 18 June 1917.

[5] 'The Lover Tells of the Rose in His Heart', first published as 'The Rose in My
Heart', *National Observer*, 12 November 1892.

came up, which means that nothing at all would happen, I turned my mind away. And yet I longed to rid my mind of an obsession that was eating into my mind and beginning to affect my health.

It was during this long visit that my friendship with my uncle became very close. He never treated me quite as a grown man and had the selfishness of an old bachelor – I remember still with a little resentment that if there was but one kidney with the bacon at breakfast he always took it without apology – and he complained continually of his health. I took all this as part of [a] character I could not imagine different, and began to think of his house very much as one thinks of home. In a sense Sligo has always been my home.

XXVII

I returned to London in the midst of the Wilde case, and my father said the moment I arrived that I should go to see Wilde and ask if I could be of any help. 'He was very kind to you, perhaps he may wish to call [you] as a witness to something or other.' I went to Oakley Street[1] the day after I arrived and brought some letters – George Russell and others had written to me – of sympathy with his trouble. He had increased my admiration by his courage at the first trial which was just over,[2] and I was soon to discover that my world, where historical knowledge had lessened or taken away the horror or disgust at his form of vice prevalent elsewhere in England, had many stories of his courage and self-possession. I myself on hearing the first rumours at Sligo had said to an old man, Cochrane of the Glen, while I was drinking his excellent port, 'He will prove himself a man.' I had always felt the man in him and that his wit was, as [it] were, but the sword of the swashbuckler. When I arrived at Oakley Street I was let in by a very grave servant and found Oscar's brother, Willy Wilde, alone. I handed him the letters. He said, 'Before I give him this, you must tell me what is in it. Are you telling him "to run away"? All his friends are telling him that, and we have made up

---

[1] Wilde was staying at his mother's house, 146 Oakley Street, Chelsea.
[2] 1 May 1895. Wilde was released on bail on 7 May, and the second trial began on 20 May.

our minds that he must go to prison if necessary.' I said, 'No, I certainly would not advise him to run away.' I doubt if he was sober and I noticed presently that the tears were wetting his cheeks. 'Oh yes, he could escape,' he said. 'There is a yacht anchored there in the Thames and £5000 to pay his bail. Well, if not anchored there in the Thames, still he can escape – yes, if I had to inflate a balloon in the back garden myself. But he is resolved to face the music, like Christ.' He then told me that Wilde considered that it was his duty for the sake of his wife and children to take whatever chance there was, however small, of getting off. If acquitted, he could live out of England for a time and then return 'and gather friends about him again', and if condemned he would have purged his offence.

I was not [to] see him, he was at Mrs Leverson's,[1] a witty Jewess who wrote for *Punch* and gathered artists and men of letters about her, and while I was there Willy Wilde's wife came in just having seen [him] and sat down with an air of relief saying, 'It is all right now, he has resolved to go to jail if necessary.' Willy Wilde seemed pathetically grateful for my visit. My packet of letters – letters [from] his countrymen, he would say – would encourage Wilde. 'He and I were not good friends,' he said, 'I need not say more, you will understand. But he came to me like a wounded stag and I took him in.' He then told how Wilde had been turned out of hotel after hotel at the close of the libel action against Lord Queensberry. There was no pretence that he was innocent. 'It was all his vanity; they swung incense before his heart.' I left, followed by Willy Wilde to the door with offers to get me work on his paper the *Daily Telegraph*. I got another bundle of letters and these I carried to the court, but I never saw Wilde again.

XXVIII

Was it now that Henley's little daughter died?[2] Henley and his wife had not been on very good terms, and the child had brought them together, and now a disease that [had] its source in Henley's vicious youth destroyed it. Henley was broken by it. 'She had the

---

[1] Ada Leverson (1862–1933). Her friendship with Wilde is defined in *Letters to the Sphinx from Oscar Wilde* (London, Duckworth, 1930).

[2] Henley's daughter Margaret, his only child, died on 11 February 1894, aged six.

genius of the mind and the genius of the body,' he said to me. One
night a number of us were gathered at his house at Mortlake. His
ne'er-do-well brother[1] was there, now but recently set up as picture-
framer and to fail in that as in all else. I remember Henley saying,
'When I was young, syphilis was the terror that walked by night,'
and the picture-dealer, who was always the family moralist, answering, 'and quite right too.' He said that night as we sat round a square
table, 'Listen to this, Yeats here believes in magic – ridiculous.'
Henley said, 'Oh no, not ridiculous, black magic is all the go in
Paris now.' And then to me he said, 'It is just a game, isn't it?' I said,
wishing to put the question [aside] and timid as always in his
presence, 'Oh, one has a vision and one wants to have another.' A
moment later we were all hushed by Henley's comment, 'I want to
know how I am to get to my daughter. I was sitting here the other
night and she came in and played round the room, and it was only
when I saw that the door was shut that I knew it was a vision.'

XXIX

I met T. W. Rolleston in some café in the Strand. We had for some
time been on distant terms. I had sent to him an offer of a seat in
Mayo believed to be safe for the Parnellite party – my friend the
young Mayo doctor had influence there. He had refused, as he hoped
by Gavan Duffy's influence 'to be returned to Parliament by a combination of parties'. The two parties were at the time in a frenzy for
one another's destruction. I had been full of derision of this man
who, because he had himself no passion, was blind to all the force of
life. A little later he had, I considered, betrayed me. When I left
London to found the National Literary Society, I had made arrangements with a publisher, Mr Fisher Unwin, through his reader,
Edward Garnett, to publish for me a series of Irish books if my
negotiation with Gavan Duffy failed. I had told Rolleston, my fellow
worker in the London society. While I was in Ireland, I heard un-
expectedly that he had brought Gavan Duffy to this publisher. I
went to London, getting the money together with difficulty, to find
that Duffy's proposal had been accepted, Mr Unwin's reader

[1] Anthony Henley.

believing it to be my scheme. Having no passion, I thought, he is incapable of belief, and an established person seemed more solid to his imagination than any promises. Yet now, as in earlier life, I believed in him again, noticing his courteous manners and his beautiful classic face.

He told me of 'the new movement', as it was called.[1] A secret organization was being founded to continue both the Fenian propaganda and the parliamentary movement. He invited me to join. I had begun to dread a revival of Fenianism. Hitherto, whenever the constitutional party had been weakened, Fenianism had revived, and we spoke always of the swing of the pendulum, using a phrase used in England for a mere change between Conservatism and Liberalism. But with us that swing brought death, defeat, and long discouragement. When I had taken advantage of that swing to found my own movement, I had hoped [for] a revival of Young Ireland politics that, as ready as Davis would have been for any dangerous hope, would set itself against hopeless danger. I had failed, defeated as I believed by a combination of old men and perhaps because Maud Gonne was absorbed in her own projects.

In accepting Rolleston's offer I acted for the first time without any thought of her. I too had come to need excitement, forgetfulness. I remember that I saw clearly that such a movement as he described might possibly be swept from its path by ignorant men and involve us all in some wild conspiracy. I thought myself ready for the sacrifice. Rolleston introduced me to a Dr Mark Ryan,[2] a London doctor who was head of the new organization; through his hands the American money which went no longer to the members of Parliament

---

[1] The Irish National Alliance, sometimes known as the Irish National Brotherhood, an organization which broke away from the Irish Republican Brotherhood about 1895. Yeats was a member of the Irish Republican Brotherhood *circa* 1886. On 30 November 1936 he wrote to Ethel Mannin: 'Some day you will understand what I see in the Irish National Movement and why I can be no other sort of revolutionist – as a young man I belonged to the I.R.B. and was in many things O'Leary's pupil.' *Letters* (Wade), p. 869.

[2] Mark F. Ryan (1844–1940), author of *Fenian Memories*, posthumously published (Dublin, Gill, 1945). He brought Rolleston into the I.R.B. A police report in Dublin Castle, dated 7 October 1899, reads: 'W. B. Yeats is known as a literary enthusiast, more or less of a revolutionary, and an associate of Dr Mark Ryan, to which description by the Inspector General [of the Royal Irish Constabulary] Major Gosselin can add nothing.' $\left(\text{Dublin Castle Papers } \dfrac{76s}{24838}\right)$.

would pass. He brought me to see another doctor whose name I forget. As we sat in this man's little dispensary near Tottenham Court Road, he told us of a working man who had just gone out. The working man, coming out of a music hall with his wife, had been arrested on a charge of drunkenness. He had chaffed the policeman. It had all happened that moment and he asked for a certificate of sobriety. 'Was he sober?' said Dr Ryan. 'Oh, perfectly.' 'And did you give him the certificate?' 'Oh no, the police are the best friends I have.' I did not feel that he would go far with us in our work, but in Dr Mark Ryan I discovered a very touching benevolence. He was not an able man but had great influence because during his long life he had befriended many Irishmen, often giving them the money to set them up in business. Lionel Johnson, my most intimate friend through these years, came with me to see him and felt the charm of that man who tolerated fools too gladly because of a nature naturally indulgent. I found he had a naïve and touching faith in men who were better educated, and as yet he had not, as a little later, fallen under the influence of a clever, rather mad rogue.[1] His associates in this new secret society were almost all doctors, peasant or half-peasant in origin, and none had any genuine culture. In Ireland it was just such men, though of a younger generation, who had understood my ideas. Rolleston and Johnson and I had perhaps the instrument we had been looking for.

A few weeks, however, after my initiation – not a very ceremonious matter – Rolleston resigned. A young poetess, a Miss Alice Milligan,[2] had dreamed one night that he was in danger of arrest – no doubt his handsome face had set her dreaming. He had not much belief in dreams, but then it was plain that his belief in his cause was even fainter, and I had even to return to him every scrap of writing I had ever had of him for fear that his pleasant, innocent correspondence contained anything which [the] government might use against him.

At the debates of the Irish Literary Society I made violent speeches. The Society was supposed to be non-political; that had been my own decision, for I had thought that whereas the Dublin

[1] See p. 110, n. 1, on Frank Hugh O'Donnell.
[2] Novelist, poet, playwright (1866-1953), a friend of George Russell (AE) who edited her *Hero Lays* (Dublin, Maunsel, 1908).

Society would stagnate without politics the London Society could best hold together as an Irish meeting-place in a strange land. I never broke the rule, which applied to the politics of the hour only, but politics was implied in almost all I said. Besides my quarrel with the older men, I had a blind anger against Unionist Ireland. They had opposed to our movement their mere weight and indifference, and had written and spoken as if the finest literature of Ireland – certain old ballads in English, the Gaelic heroic tales, the new literature of AE and Johnson, Standish O'Grady, or myself – was itself provincial and barbarous. They had done this not in the interest, I repeated again and again, of Shakespeare and Milton, but of those third-rate English novelists who were almost their only reading. What was happening in literature, I repeated again and again, was happening through the whole life of the country. An imitation of the habits of thought, the character, the manners, the opinions – and these never at their best – of an alien people was preventing the national character taking its own natural form, and this imitation was spread by what I called a system of bribery. Appointments, success of all kinds, came only to these; the springs of national life ran dry.

I found myself unpopular, and suffered, discovering that if men speak much ill of you it makes at moments a part of the image of yourself – that is your only support against the world – and that you see yourself too as if with hostile eyes. I remember some judge resigning from the committee after some speech of mine. I had not come to understand that fine things cannot be torn out of the hostile netting, but must be slowly disentangled with delicate fingers. What made things worse was that I had, a romantic in all, a cult of passion. In the speech that made the judge resign I had described the dishonest figures of Swift's attack on Wood's half-pence and, making that my text, had argued that, because no sane man is permitted to lie knowing[ly], God made certain men mad, and that it was these men – daimon-possessed as I said – who, possessing truths of passion that were intellectual falsehoods, had created nations.

In private conversation if politics were the theme, or above all any of those ideas of my own movement which implied politics, I would lose my temper, and [be] miserable afterwards for hours.

In committee meetings, on the other hand, where the technical forms gave me time to deliberate, I had great influence and was generally the governing mind. I asked Lionel Johnson to criticize my manner there, and he said, 'It has but one defect; it is somewhat too suave.'

XXX

I had received while at Sligo many letters from Diana Vernon, kind letters that gave me a sense of half-conscious excitement. I remember after one such letter asking some country woman to throw the tea leaves for me and my disappointment at the vagueness of the oracle. (I think Mary Battle, my uncle's second-sighted servant, was again ill and away.) She was to tell me later on that my letters were unconscious love-letters, and I was taken by surprise at the description. I do not know how long after my return the conversation that was to decide so much in my life took place. I had found the Rhymer who had introduced me under the influence of drink,[1] speaking vaguely and with vague movements, and while we were speaking this recent memory came back. She[2] spoke of her pagan life in a way that made me believe that she had had many lovers and loathed her life. I thought of that young man so nearly related. Here is the same weakness, I thought; two souls so distinguished and contemplative that the common world seems empty. What is there left but sanctity, or some satisfying affection, or mere dissipation? – 'Folly the comforter,' some Elizabethan had called it. Her beauty, dark and still, had the nobility of defeated things, and how could it help but wring my heart? I took a fortnight to decide what I should do.

I was poor and it would be a hard struggle if I asked her [to] come away, and perhaps after all I would but add my tragedy to hers, for she might return to that evil life. But, after all, if I could not get the woman I loved, it would be a comfort even but for a little while to devote myself to another. No doubt my excited senses had their share in the argument, but it was an unconscious one. At the end of the fortnight I asked her to leave home with me. She became very gay and joyous and a few days later praised me [for] what she thought

---

[1] 'drugs' deleted.   [2] Diana Vernon.

my beautiful tact in giving at the moment but a brother's kiss. Doubtless at the moment I was exalted above the senses, and yet I do not [think] I knew any better way of kissing, for when on our first railway journey together – we were to spend the day at Kew – she gave me the long passionate kiss of love I was startled and a little shocked.

Presently I told something of my thoughts during that fortnight, and she [was] perplexed and ashamed that I should have had such imagination of her. Her wickedness had never gone further than her own mind; I would be her first lover. We decided that we should be but friends till she could leave her home for mine, but agreed to wait until her mother, a very old woman, had died. We decided to consult each a woman friend that we might be kept to these resolutions, as sponsors of our adventure, and for nearly a year met in railway carriages and at picture galleries and occasionally at her house.[1] At Dulwich Gallery she taught me to care for Watteau – she too was of Pater's school – and at the National Gallery for the painter who pleased her best of all, Mantegna. I wrote her several poems, all curiously elaborate in style, 'The Shadowy Horses',[2] and ——— and ———,[3] and thought I was once more in love. I noticed that she was like the mild heroines of my plays. She seemed a part of myself.

I noticed that she did not talk so well as when I had at first known her, her mind seemed more burdened, but she would show in her movements an unforeseen youth; she seemed to have gone back to her twentieth year. For a short time, a few months I think, I shared a flat with Arthur Symons in the Temple.[4] Symons knew I had such a friend and plan, but did [not] know her name. He indeed met my friend somewhere in society and asked if he might call, and came back with her praises. At last she and her sponsor were to come to tea. I do not think I had asked Symons, for I went myself to buy the cake. As I came home with the parcel I began to think of Maud Gonne till my thought was interrupted by my finding the door

[1] 18 Porchester Square, Hyde Park.
[2] 'He Bids His Beloved Be at Peace', *Collected Poems*, p. 69.
[3] 'He Gives His Beloved Certain Rhymes' and 'A Poet to His Beloved', *Collected Poems*, pp. 71, 70.
[4] 2 Fountain Court, Middle Temple: in autumn 1895.

locked. I had forgotten the key and I went off in a great fuss to find a locksmith and found instead a man who climbed along the roof and in at an attic window.

That night at twelve o'clock I said to Symons, who had just come in, 'Did I ever tell you about Maud Gonne?' and till two or three in the morning I spoke of my love for her. Of all the men I have known he was the best listener; he could listen as a woman listens, never meeting one's thought as a man does with a rival thought, but taking up what one said and changing [it], giving it as it were flesh and bone.[1] A couple of days later I got a wild letter from Maud Gonne, who was in Dublin. 'Was I ill? Had some accident happened?' On a day that was, I found, the day I had had those guests and lost the key, I had walked into the room in her hotel where she was sitting with friends. At first she thought I was really there, but presently on finding that no one else saw me knew that it was my ghost. She told me to return at twelve that night and I vanished. At twelve I had stood, dressed in some strange, priest-like costume, at her bedside and brought her soul away, and we had wandered round the cliffs [of] Howth where we had been together years before. I remember one phrase very clearly, 'It was very sad, and all the seagulls were asleep.'[2] All my old love had returned and began to struggle with the new.

Presently I was asked to call and see my friend's sponsor. She condemned our idea of going away from home. There were various arguments that I cannot recall without perhaps, against my will, revealing Diana Vernon's true name. My sponsor came to see me and used the same arguments, and both, people of the world, advised us to live together without more ado. Then Diana Vernon tried to get a separation from the husband who had for her, she believed, aversion or indifference. 'He ceased to pay court to me from

---

[1] Cf. the poem 'On Woman', *Collected Poems*, pp. 164–6:
> 'May God be praised for woman
> That gives up all her mind,
> A man may find in no man
> A friendship of her kind
> That covers all he has brought
> As with her flesh and bone,
> Nor quarrels with a thought
> Because it is not her own.'

[2] 'All my old love had now come back to me. Years afterwards she told me that she had wished, during those days, to take me for her husband.' deleted.

the day of our marriage,' she had said. He was deeply distressed and became ill, and she gave up the project and said to me, 'It will be kinder to deceive him.' Our senses were engaged now, and though we spoke of parting it was but to declare it impossible. I took my present rooms at Woburn Buildings[1] and furnished them very meagrely with such cheap furniture as I could throw away without regret as I grew more prosperous. She came with me to make every purchase, and I remember an embarrassed conversation in the presence of some Tottenham Court [Road] shop man upon the width of the bed – every inch increased the expense.

At last she came to me in I think January of my thirtieth year,[2] and I was impotent from nervous excitement. The next day we met at the British Museum – we were studying together – and I wondered that there seemed no change in me or in her. A week later she came to me again, and my nervous excitement was so painful that it seemed best but to sit over our tea and talk. I do not think we kissed each other except at the moment of her leaving. She understood instead of, as another would, changing liking for dislike – was only troubled by my trouble. My nervousness did not return again and we had many days of happiness. It will always be a grief to me that I could not give the love that was her beauty's right, but she was too near my soul, too salutary and wholesome to my inmost being. All our lives long, as da Vinci says,[3] we long, thinking it is but the moon that we long [for], for our destruction, and how, when we meet [it] in the shape of a most fair woman, can we do less than leave all others for her? Do we not seek our dissolution upon her lips?

---

[1] 18 Woburn Buildings, which later became 5 Woburn Walk, now incorporated in the New Ambassador's Hotel. Yeats took the rooms about 25 March 1896.

[2] Thirty-first, if 1896: the reference to January is apparently inaccurate if the venue is Woburn Buildings.

[3] 'Behold now the hope and desire of going back to one's own country or returning to primal chaos, like that of the moth to the light, of the man who with perpetual longing always looks forward with joy to each new spring and each new summer, and to the new months and the new years, deeming that the things he longs for are too slow in coming; and who does not perceive that he is longing for his own destruction. But this longing is in its quintessence the spirit of the elements, which finding itself imprisoned within the life of the human body desires continually to return to its source.

'And I would have you to know that this same longing is in its quintessence inherent in nature, and that man is a type of the world.' *The Notebooks of Leonardo da Vinci*, trans. Edward MacCurdy (London, Cape, 1938), vol. I, pp. 80–1. Cf. Yeats's poem 'The Wheel', *Collected Poems*, p. 237, and *Mythologies*, pp. 301–2.

My liaison lasted but a year, interrupted by one journey to Italy upon her part and by one of mine also to Paris.[1] I had a struggle to earn my living, and that made it harder for me, I was so often pre-occupied when she came. Then Maud Gonne wrote to me; she was in London and would I come to dine? I dined with her and my trouble increased – she certainly had no thought of the mischief she was doing. And at last one morning instead of reading much love poetry, as my way was to bring the right mood round, I wrote letters. My friend found my mood did not answer hers and burst into tears. 'There is someone else in your heart,' she said.[2] It was the breaking between us for many years.

XXXI

A year before I went to Woburn Buildings, while Diana Vernon and I were meeting at Dulwich Picture Gallery and in railway trains, and while I was still sharing a flat with Arthur Symons, the *Savoy* magazine had been founded.[3] The condemnation of Wilde had brought ruin upon a whole movement in art and letters. The Rhymers were not affected; we had all written for the smaller public that has knowledge and is undisturbed by popular feeling. We were a little more unpopular with those [who] did not read us; it was necessary to avoid a little more carefully than before young men studying for the army and the imperfectly educated generally, but our new books would still sell out their editions of perhaps three hundred copies. There were, however, a number of novelists and essayists and artists who had caught the ear of the great public, many in the pages of the *Yellow Book*, and who made war by auda-cious stories or the inversions of a mainly mechanical wit upon the Victorian conventions, and their public was to turn firmly against them. We spoke of them among ourselves much as young poets and essayists today speak of their abler successors, Bennett and Wells, who have floated into popularity upon the returning seriousness of the public.

[1] December 1896–January 1897, the trip to Paris.
[2] Cf. 'The Lover Mourns for the Loss of Love', *Collected Poems*, p. 68.
[3] The first issue appeared in January 1896.

Two men more or less permanently upon the *Yellow Book* staff excited our admiration, Aubrey Beardsley and Max Beerbohm, and it was especially against Aubrey Beardsley that public indignation was most fierce. He had been dismissed from the art editorship of the *Yellow Book* under circumstances that roused us to fury. Mr Edmund Gosse tells how Mrs Humphry Ward showed him a letter, which she was about to post to John Lane, the publisher, demanding his dismissal. Edmund Gosse pointed out that because the British public considered Beardsley's art immoral was not sufficient reason for an act that would connect him in the public mind with a form of vice with which he had no connection whatever. She said that William Watson, the poet – whose periodical fits of insanity are his sufficient excuse – had asked her to write, and she added, 'My position before the British public makes it necessary for me to write.' He believed that he dissuaded her, but Aubrey Beardsley's sister, whom I saw of late constantly when she was dying, insisted that she did post the letter.[1] Watson certainly wrote, and the result was Aubrey Beardsley's dismissal, and though he had not been for some time on speaking terms with Wilde, and had never liked him, his name had become infamous. He had lived before some public always. 'When I was a child,' he would say, 'I was a musical genius, and when I came to a room people stared at me. I still wish to be stared at.' He could not work without that stimulant and fell into despondency, his sister has told me, and took to the dissipation that was to bring him to his death.

Leonard Smithers,[2] a most disreputable man, came one morning to Fountain Court and asked Arthur Symons to edit a magazine for him. He wished, he explained, even at some loss if the loss were not too great, to improve his status. Symons made two conditions: that Smithers should drop his secret trade in lascivious books, and appoint Aubrey Beardsley, whom Symons had I think never met, art editor. Both conditions were accepted, and we began a warfare on the British public at a time when we had all against us. Our publisher's name was certainly against us, but after all outlaws, whether

---

[1] Mabel Beardsley: cancer was diagnosed in 1912, she died in 1916. Cf. *Letters* (Wade), pp. 574–5, and the sequence of poems, 'Upon a Dying Lady'.
[2] Leonard Charles Smithers (1861–1907), solicitor turned publisher.

they have offended through their virtues or their vices, soon discover that if they do not support one another no one else will. Symons asked my help and I did so on the condition that, the supper to celebrate our first number finished, I should never meet the publisher nor enter his house. Symons had found Beardsley on a sofa, spitting blood, evidently very ill, but at the promise of work he seemed to return to life and vigour.

I had in my pocket at the supper two letters remonstrating with me for writing in such a magazine, one by AE calling it 'the organ of the incubi and the succubi,'[1] and one from T. W. Rolleston. Symons borrowed them and read both in a spirit of mischief to the publisher. I heard the publisher shouting, 'Give me that letter; I'll prosecute him. I tell you I will prosecute him.' It was Rolleston's, but Symons backed away and hid the letter in his pocket and began to read out AE's. It was even more violent, but reduced everyone [to] silence. Presently Beardsley came up to me and said, 'You will be surprised at what I am going to say to you. I agree with your friend. I have always been haunted by the spiritual life. When I was a child, I saw a bleeding Christ over the mantelpiece. But after all I think there is a kind of morality in doing one's work when one wants to do other things far more.'

After the supper was over I wanted to go away. Symons said, 'No, we must go on to Smithers's flat. He will be offended if we do not; you need never go there again.' Smithers and Beardsley had gone on ahead of us, and when we arrived Beardsley was lying on two chairs in the middle of the room and Smithers was sweating at his hurdy-gurdy piano. His piano was at ordinary times worked by electricity, but at the moment his electricity had been cut off or he had not paid the bill and could only make music by turning the handle. Beardsley was praising the beautiful tone, the incomparable touch – going into the lavatory at intervals to spit blood – and Smithers, flattered, sweated on.

[1] There is also an undated letter (? September 1896) from AE to Yeats: 'I never see the *Savoy* and never intend to touch it. I will wait until your work is published in other ways. I don't want to get allied with the currents of people with a sexual mania like Beardsley, Symons or that ruck. It is all "mud from a muddy spring" and any pure stream of thought that mingles must lose its purity.' *Some Passages from the Letters of AE to W. B. Yeats* (Dundrum, Cuala Press, 1936), p. 4.

In Beardsley I found that noble courage[1] that seems to me at times, whether in man or woman, the greatest of human faculties. I saw it in all he said and did, in the clear logic of speech and in [the] clean swift line of his art. His disease presented continuously before his mind, as one of its symptoms, lascivious images, and he drew them in their horror, their fascination, and became the first satirist of the soul English art has produced. I once said to him, 'Beardsley, I was defending you last night in the only way possible by saying that all you draw is inspired by fury against iniquity.' 'If it were so inspired,' he said, 'it would be no way different.'[2] So great was his pride in his own sincerity. And yet certainly at the time I write [of] there was no fury, nothing but an icy passion for all reality. He had had a beautiful mistress, and I remember his coming to our flat of a morning with some painted woman with whom he had, I suppose, spent the night. And yet sexual desire under the pressure of disease became insatiable, and I was told at the time of his death that he had hastened it by masturbation. It was natural, perhaps, that so much of his nature should be uncontrollable, for I had in his presence a greater sense of power than has come to me from any young man of his age. I cannot imagine to myself the profession where he would not have made himself a foremost man.

Dowson came in from time to time, but was for the most part at Dieppe or in some Normandy village near; he was writing poems for the *Savoy* and translations for Smithers, and received with two or three others, who had, it was half-understood, no duties but to associate with Smithers – a task nobody liked – two pounds a week. Dowson, vague and drifting, gave me always [a] sense of that weakness that seems to go with certain high virtues of sweetness and of courtesy. I cannot imagine the world where he would have succeeded. At best, if best it should be called, he might have escaped that

---

[1] 'And how should her heart fail her
Or sickness break her will
With her dead brother's valour
For an example still.'
From 'Upon a Dying Lady', *Collected Poems*, p. 179. Aubrey Beardsley died in 1898 at the age of twenty-six.
[2] 'She said of her brother, "He hated the people who denied the existence of evil, and so being young he filled his pictures with evil. He had a passion for reality."' Yeats to Lady Gregory, 11 February 1913, *Letters* (Wade), p. 575.

unlucky passion for the restaurant-keeper's daughter and the drink
and dissipation that were soon to bring him to his death, and lived
a harmless, sheltered, and probably inarticulate life. As it was he
was burning to the socket, in exquisite songs celebrating in words
full of subtle refinement all those whom he named with himself 'us
the bitter and gay'.[1] While I was at Fountain Court, Symons, who
had sent him proofs of his too-candid essay,[2] received a letter of
remonstrance. 'I am living an industrious and innocent life in a
small Norman village,' the letter said.[3] But before the letter,
though it had been dispatched later, came a telegram. 'Sell my ring
and send money: arrested.' There was a ring he had left with Symons
for such an occasion. He had got drunk and fought the village baker.
His money proved unnecessary, for the French magistrate on being
told by some sympathetic villager that he had 'an illustrious English
poet' before him had said, 'Quite right, I will imprison the baker.'

When he was sober, Symons would say, for I have no intimate
knowledge of Dowson but through him – I avoided the haunts
where he could be best known – he would not look at a woman; did
he not belong to the restaurant-keeper's daughter? But, drunk, any
woman, dirty or clean, served his purpose. Living as often as not in
some common lodging-house, where he paid perhaps threepence for
his bed, less from poverty than indifference, he was content with
coarse fare. Could not a glass of wine, absinthe perhaps, transfigure
all? 'Symons,' he had cried, taking Symons by the coat as he had

[1] 'Villanelle of the Poet's Road': Dowson, *Poetical Works*, ed. Desmond Flower
(London, Cassell and John Lane, The Bodley Head, 1934), p. 74.

[2] Arthur Symons, 'A Literary Causerie: On a Book of Verses', *Savoy*, no. 4,
August 1896, pp. 91–3. Symons does not name Dowson, but the reference is clear: 'a
young poet whom I have the privilege to know somewhat intimately . . . a look and
manner of pathetic charm, a sort of Keats-like face, the face of a demoralized Keats . . .
a gradual slipping into deeper and steadier waters of oblivion . . . the swift, disastrous,
and suicidal energy of genius . . . I liked to see him occasionally, for a change, drinking
nothing stronger than coffee or tea. At Oxford, I believe, his favourite form of intoxication had been haschisch; afterwards he gave up this somewhat elaborate experiment in
visionary sensations for readier means of oblivion; but he returned to it, I remember, for
at least one afternoon, in a company of which I had been the gatherer, and of which I
was the host. The experiment was not a successful one. . . .'

[3] Dowson did not remonstrate: the letter merely suggested that Symons might
consider toning down a few phrases which would 'give an erronous & too lurid account
of me'. Otherwise, Dowson was content that Symons's text should stand. *The Letters of
Ernest Dowson*, edited by Desmond Flower and Henry Maas (London, Cassell, 1967),
letter dated 5 July 1896, p. 371.

passed in some Dieppe restaurant, and pointing to the harlot he was drinking with, 'she writes poetry. It is like Browning and Mrs Browning.' Just before I had come to stay at Fountain Court he had arrived one evening with a woman, perhaps the woman Symons called 'Penny plain and twopence coloured' or, for short, 'Penny plain.'[1] One or two other young men of letters had dropped in and sat round the fire, and presently the harlot, having taken off all her clothes to enjoy the better the pleasant blaze of the fire, began to tell her life history: her first perception of sex – she had tried to rub away the first hair from her body – her seduction, and then accounts of this or that man, especially of one old man who got his sexual excitement by watching her wring the necks of two pigeons, which he always brought in a basket. Two or three times she interrupted her story to go into the bedroom with one or other of the men of letters, Symons alone, who prided himself on his fastidiousness, scorning her. That scene comes into my memory very constantly in connexion with my memory of Dowson never choosing, taking whatever life brought in his vague hands. Under the pressure of wayward emotions, he produced a music with no rhetoric, no emphasis, no egotism of any kind – a pure music.

I had also heard much of Dowson from Lionel Johnson, who was even more his friend than Symons. Symons and Johnson did not like each other, for Johnson could forgive a mere sinner but not a heretic, and the poetry of Symons was a commendation of the sexual desire Johnson knew nothing of, in accomplished, passionate verse. Symons once said to me, 'Johnson believes, I am told, that he has done Dowson good. I can imagine them staggering along Oxford Street, Johnson expounding the Fathers of the Church; or sitting in Gray's Inn where Johnson has his rooms. Dowson, very bored, gets up and says, "I'm going to the East End to have a ten-penny whore," and [Johnson] gently pressing him down again with, "No, no, have another glass."'

Johnson and I were drifting apart. If he came to see me, he sat in gloomy silence if I refused him drink, and if I gave it became drunk,

---

[1] 'who would appear during my time there with Beardsley or with a message from Smithers perhaps' deleted. The incident is ascribed to Beardsley, not Dowson, in *Autobiographies*, p. 329.

and if I went to see him got drunk as a matter of course. I felt that
if I saw him I shared his responsibility, and once when I tried to get
him to sign away his liberty in some Scottish institution he had said,
'I do not want to be cured.' He had been a great influence for a while
among our Irish societies, that stately English, full of the cadence of
the eighteenth century, carrying their minds, I thought, to Grattan
and the Irish parliament. At first he had disliked Maud Gonne, but
had changed when he sat next her at some public dinner. He said
to me when it was over, 'I had thought she did her work, perhaps,
from love of notoriety, but no, it is sense of duty. I saw while she
was speaking that her hand was trembling. I think she has to force
herself to speak.' Probably these committees and lectures and public
dinners I had brought him to were all he ever saw of active life. He
had given up the world for a library. 'Yeats', he would say, 'needs
twenty years in a library, and I need twenty years in the wilderness.'

I think he had applied in too literary a form the philosophy of
Pater in the Epilogue to the *Renaissance* and in the 'Animula
Vagula' chapter,[1] and finding that for him the most exquisite impressions came from books he thought to be content with that. Seldom
leaving his bed till after sundown, he worked and read through the
silence of the night only to discover that we cannot live without
accident, the unexpected, the confusions of nature. The only accident, the only event as it were that remained, for like the poet in
Mallarmé he had 'read all the books', came from his own moods
during intoxication. Under some censored need to people that solitude, he invented innumerable conversations with people he had
never met, and would tell them for truth, and at the end, I do not
doubt, to believe their truth. It began at the university with imaginary conversations with Gladstone, and when I knew him first [he]
would quote continually what we believed, on his word, to be words
with Cardinal Manning.[2] 'When I saw him first,' he would say, 'he
asked me if I thought of choosing the religious life. I said, no, I
shall be a man of letters. "Well," he said, "I have always considered
letters a lower order of the priesthood."' These Manning conversa-

[1] Of *Marius the Epicurean*.
[2] Cardinal Newman, in *Autobiographies*, p. 305. Newman died in 1890, Manning in
1892.

tions became so famous that at Manning's death the editor of the *Nineteenth Century* asked for an essay of reminiscence, and yet I believe Johnson and Manning had never met. Johnson puzzled me at the time by his indignation at the publication of private conversation. He would not allow that Manning's death made any difference.

At last it was scarcely possible to mention a notable man but he would say, 'I knew him intimately,' and begin some reminiscence that seemed always appropriate and enlightening. His dislike for the publication of private conversation was partly genuine, a part of his indifference to all personal life, for like Sebastian van Storck[1] he refused after his sixteenth or seventeenth year to have any portrait made. He knew, before the gloom that followed upon intoxication separated him almost entirely from his kind, many artists who wished to draw that small distinguished head so like a certain archaistic Greek head at the British Museum. So far as theory went, he was an extreme ascetic, and early in our acquaintance I dined with him at some inexpensive restaurant where various courses in the *table d'hôte* seemed to me very fine after our Bedford Park joint and pudding, and noticed that as he emptied each glass of wine his doctrine became more exalted, winding up with a eulogy upon St Jerome who, that he might live undisturbed the life of the soul, had unmanned himself. And once too he had read me a story, never to be published, of some scholar led at last to suicide by his longing for what may be beyond death. I remember nothing of it now but that the scholar's dying words were in Latin, and ecstatic praise of those splendours.

I learned from him certain nobilities of style and to love in life all that can, in a favourite word of his, be called 'hieratic'. His thought seemed, as it were, to eternize and de-mortalize the soul, and certainly at moments of religion he attained to the imagery of a state of ecstasy. In him more than all others one can study the tragedy of that generation. When the soul turns from practical ends and becomes contemplative, when it ceases to be a wheel spun by the whole

[1] One of Pater's characters in *Imaginary Portraits* (1887): 'Thomas de Keyser, who understood better than any one else the kind of quaint new Atticism which had found its way into the world over those waste salt marshes, wondering whether quite its finest type as he understood it could ever actually be seen there, saw it at last, in lively motion, in the person of Sebastian van Storck, and desired to paint his portrait. A little to his surprise the young man declined the offer; not graciously, as was thought.' (London, Macmillan, 1905 reprint), p. 84.

machine, it is responsible for itself, an unendurable burden. Not yet ready for the impression of the divine will, it floats in the unnatural emptiness between the natural and the supernatural orders. Johnson had refused rather than failed to live, and when an autopsy followed his accidental death[1] during intoxication it was found that in him the man's brain was united to a body where the other organs were undeveloped, the body of a child.

Symons who was now my most intimate friend at first at Fountain Court and afterwards at Woburn Buildings consulted me over all he did and was my counsellor. He alone seemed to me, to use a favourite meaningless word of that time, 'decadent'. He seemed incapable of excess and better than any of us lived the temperate life Pater had commended. All about us were so little temperate that I can remember gloomily discussing some possible lack in ourselves. We decided to take two whiskies every night at twelve o'clock to see if we began to desire a third, and when at the fortnight's end we returned to our tumblers of hot water I said, half seriously, 'Symons, if we had felt a tendency to excess, we would be better poets.' I used to say to Symons, 'You are a perfectly moral man, but they are the morals of Thessaly.' He had always a mistress, some lady of the ballet, chosen as deliberately as if she were a contribution for the magazine, and we were troubled occasionally as to whether or not he had a bad influence. He desired a little too obviously to speak with all famous, interesting men, and I have heard him say after a visit to some theatre of varieties, 'Oh Yeats, I was never in love with a serpent charmer before.'

He had come to London in his twentieth year and had for ten years lived a life in which women were the one constant adventure, without emotion. He lived in the sentiment of the moment and with a self-conscious temperance that made it easy to cherish it, and then was surprised by a fanciful love, like that of a girl, and by a passion. The fanciful love was for a chorus girl he had never spoken to. He went night after night to watch her, and for long tried to meet her, in vain. She refused, even after all the chorus knew of the romance, because she was illegitimate, had been brought up by some old woman who taught girls to dance, and believed that she must establish

---

[1] In 1902.

herself in society by a marriage made doubly legitimate by many children. 'No, no,' the other girls would say to her, 'you will not have many children by Arthur Symons.' Even when they did meet, one drive in a hansom cab was all that came of it. Then came a real devotion to a girl of the ballet who was his mistress for a couple of years and very fond of him. One night he came to see me in great distress. Some rich man had made her an offer of marriage and she had left him to decide upon his fate. A friend of his came to see me to urge my using my influence to get him to marry. I would not take the responsibility, for I knew little of her, though that little was to her credit. He set her free and she is now the wife of some country gentleman. At some parting after a quarrel I had written out in a series of rough headings his talk with me over the unhappiness of love, and gave this to him as he went off to the train at three or four in [the] morning. In the country village he had fled to he made them into 'Amoris Victima'. Upon the patching up of this or some other quarrel he said to me, 'She has such nice feeling, Yeats. You know she must have somebody. She knew I would be jealous of a man, so she chose a woman.'

More intelligently sympathetic than any man I have known, his criticism had its foundation, but its foundation only, in the conversation of his friends. From every visit to France he would bring spoken words, at first by Goncourt and later by Mallarmé, and [I] can sometimes recognize, as for instance in his essay on Beardsley,[1] some conversation I have listened to or taken part in. After he was shut off by marriage from the old resorts, his work lost in curiosity and animation. His poetry was only charming when a criticism or the emotion of a learned connoisseur, and I doubt if mere life ever moved him deeply. He alone of all that circle, if indeed he wrecked himself, did so from no passionate need but, as it were, casually.

XXXII

Word came from time to time of Wilde, lately released,[2] and now drifting about France and Italy. He had sent this word to all his

---

[1] *Aubrey Beardsley* (London, Unicorn Press, 1898).
[2] Released on 19 May 1897.

friends, 'I will live to redeem my name,' but his health was shattered and he gave up the struggle. Dowson claimed to have attempted to reform him [at] Dieppe, to give him wholesome tastes. They had between them enough money to send one to a house of ill fame, and it was decided that Wilde was to go. He had gone, accompanied through the streets by Dowson and a cheering crowd. Dowson and the crowd had waited till he came out. 'No,' he had said, 'it has been the first for ten years and it will be the last. It was like cold mutton. But tell this in England. It will entirely restore my character.'

Note. Go on to describe Althea Gyles.[1]

XXXIII

While the *Savoy* was being published, he[2] and I went to Ireland, staying a few days upon the slopes of Ben Bulben in Sligo, and then settling down for a long stay, interrupted by a visit to the Aran Islands,[3] with Edward Martyn[4] at Tulira Castle, a new friend met probably through Symons's friend, George Moore. Before we set out Diana Vernon had been questioned by me while in a state of semi-trance. She had no knowledge of any of the popular mysticism of the day, but was powerfully affected by my symbols. When under that influence, she could approach some source of knowledge that had plain affinities with that of my Order. The first sign I had of her genuine clairvoyance was certain Greek words. I remember her calling Apollo[5] 'euceladon' and explaining it as 'justified'. 'Justified' was applied in my Order to an Egyptian sun god,[6] but when I consulted the Greek dictionary for 'euceladon' I found it meant 'harmonious'. My Order made little use of Greek.

---

[1] Yeats did not go on to describe Althea Gyles. He had already commented on her art on two occasions, the first an essay, the second a very brief note: both are reprinted as Appendixes B and C, pp. 283–7. Althea Gyles was a book-designer and poet (1868–1949). Friend of Symons and of Dowson: she became Smithers's mistress in November 1899.

[2] Symons.

[3] August–September 1896. Symons's account of the trip appeared in the *Savoy*, nos. 6, 7, 8: October, November, December 1896.

[4] Edward Martyn (1859–1924), playwright, one of the founders of the Irish Literary Theatre.

[5] Doubtful reading.

[6] 'Osiris' deleted.

I had for some time been troubled about my work. I had written 'Rosa Alchemica' and many slow-moving, elaborate poems, and felt I had lost my old country emotion [of] *The Countess Cathleen* and of the early poems. My new work would not help me in that spiritualization of Irish imagination I had set before me. I did not know what to do. Perhaps after all I was to write an elaborate mysticism without any special birthplace. Instead of plunging as I would now into the abyss of my own mind, perhaps in sleep, taking first upon me the form perhaps of some symbolic beast or bird, and only using the seership of another as subsidiary, I sought the advice of Diana Vernon. She obtained these sentences, unintelligible to herself: 'He is too much under solar influence. He is to live near water and to avoid woods, which concentrate the solar power.'

With these sentences in mind I arrived at Tulira. Edward Martyn's clumsy body, where one already saw that likeness to a parish priest now so plain, the sign of his mother's peasant blood, had not suggested to me a house where, for all the bad Gothic of the modern part, there is spaciousness and state. In the train I had described to Symons the rough two-storeyed house I expected, where some bare-foot servant would wait upon us full of capacity and good will. The many rookeries, the square old tower, and the great yard where medieval soldiers had exercised touched our sense of romance. Symons lectured me on my bad manners because, when Martyn showed us two rooms and said we were to choose, I proposed tossing a halfpenny. The place he thought, I suppose, should move one to ceremony.

It was at Tulira I decided to evoke the lunar power, which was, I believed, the chief source of my inspiration. I evoked for nine evenings with no great result, but on the ninth night as I was going to sleep I saw first a centaur and then a marvellous naked woman shooting an arrow at a star.[1] She stood like a statue upon a stone pedestal, and the flesh tints of her body seemed to make all human flesh in the contrast seem unhealthy.[2] Like the centaur she moved

---

[1] Yeats described this vision also in a letter to William Sharp, August 1896, *Letters* (Wade), pp. 266-7.

[2] 'Passages in [Balzac's] *Séraphita* suggest familiarity with a state known to me in youth, a state transcending sleep when forms, often of great beauty, appear minutely articulated in brilliant light, forms that express by word or action some spiritual idea

amid brilliant light. At breakfast Symons, who knew nothing of my
vision, read me a poem, the first he had written to a dream. He had
been visited by a woman of great beauty, but clothed. 'O source of
the songs of all poets,' he called her, or some like thing. In the house
stayed Florimond de Basterot, an old French count who had land on
the seashore. He had dreamed a couple of nights before – I was now
too excited by my vision to keep it to myself – of Neptune so vividly
that he had got out of bed and locked his door. A dream so vivid
might perhaps be solid enough to find a locked door an obstruction.
A pious Catholic, he was very serious.

Martyn was really angry, for some of my invocations, I admitted,
I had made in the waste room in the old tower of the castle where he
lived, and this waste room was directly over the chapel. I had not
known that a room over a chapel must be left empty, and that an
action such as mine might be considered to obstruct the passage of
prayer. I was forbidden even to speak of invocation, and I was sorry,
for I knew I must have much in common with Martyn, who spent
hours after we had all gone to bed reading St Chrysostom. My
invocations were a form of prayer accompanied by an active desire
for a special result, a more conscious exercise, perhaps, of the human
faculties.

A few days afterwards a new friend, Lady Gregory,[1] called and
invited me to stay at Coole, and even before I arrived began collecting for me stories of faery belief. At moments I have believed or half
believed – we cannot judge the power of those shadows – that she
came in reply to those evocations, for are not the common people
and their wisdom under the moon, and her house is at the edge of [a]
lake. But why those woods? Was I not warned against woods? I had
evoked only the moon and water. I found at last what I had been
seeking always, a life of order and of labour, where all outward
things were the image of an inward life. At my grandmother's[2] I
had learned to love an elaborate house, a garden and trees; and those

and are so moulded or tinted that they make all human flesh seem unhealthy.' From
'Louis Lambert', *London Mercury*, July 1934, reprinted in *Essays and Introductions*,
p. 439.
    [1] Augusta, Lady Gregory (1852–1932), playwright; with Yeats and Synge, co-director
of the Abbey Theatre.
    [2] Elizabeth Pollexfen's house at Merville, now Nazareth House, Sligo.

grey country houses, Lissadell, Hazelwood House, and the far, rarely seen tower of Markree, had always called to my mind a life set amid natural beauty and the activities of servants and labourers who seemed themselves natural, as bird and tree are natural. No house in a town, no solitary house even not linked to vegetable and to beast by seasonal activities, has ever seemed to me but as 'the tent of the shepherd'. My grandmother's house was a new house; the sailing ship had foundered that was bringing my great-grand-father's[1] possessions to Sligo, among them his sword and a clock so remarkable my grandfather would say there was 'only one other like it in the world'. But here many generations, and no uncultivated generation, had left the images of their service in furniture, in statuary, in pictures, and in the outline of wood and of field. I think I was meant not for a master but for a servant, and that it has been my unhappiness to see the analytic faculty dissolve all those things that invite our service, and so it is that all images of service are dear to me.

Of Lady Gregory herself as yet I knew little; women feared her, I was told by old Mrs Martyn. She was certainly kind and able, that I saw, but to what measure? She asked me, when I had been but a few minutes [in] her library,[2] where from [the] third decade of the eighteenth century her husband's family have left books, fine editions of the classics bound in calf, books on tree planting and on agriculture, the favourite English books of four generations – she asked me if I could set her to some work for our intellectual movement. She sometimes banters me by reminding me that I could see nothing for her to do but read our books. My own memory is that I said, 'If you get our books and watch what we are doing, you will soon find your work.' While I was there, and indeed upon a later visit, I did little work; I was in poor health and she brought me much into the cottages of the people. I found afterwards that it was a disappointment to her that I had written nothing.

Symons on his return to London found a story from William Sharp (or 'Fiona MacLeod' as we thought), called in his books, I think, 'The Archer'. Somebody sees in vision a woman shooting an

---

[1] William Middleton.
[2] Described in Lady Gregory's *Coole* (1931).

arrow into the sky, and then some other archer shooting at a fawn. The arrow pierces the fawn and, with the transfixed heart clinging to it, strikes into the tree.[1] It seemed impossible that Sharp could have heard of my vision in time, and part of it was new. I went to see the kabalist Dr Wynn Westcott,[2] and asked about the symbolism. He opened a drawer and showed me two drawings, one of a woman shooting at a star and one of a centaur. They were the symbolism of a kabalistic grade I had not yet attained to, a secret imagery. Then he showed me that what seemed a star was a little burning heart, and he said this heart was Tiphereth, the centre of the kabalistic tree, the heart of Christ also. The archer woman and the centaur were the higher and lower genii respectively of the path Samek, which leads from Yesod to Tiphereth, from sun to moon.[3] I remembered that Christ was sometimes the mystic fawn.

Presently a soror of my Order told me that her child had said, 'Oh Mother, I have seen a woman shooting an arrow into the sky, and I am greatly afraid she has killed God.' Diana Vernon, when I questioned her, announced, 'There were four that saw; the child will die; they will attain to a wisdom older than the serpent.' Did the child die? I do not know; by a strange inattentiveness I forgot its mother's name. Was the child that died a symbolic child – Iacchus perhaps?[4] Who were the three? The meaning of the serpent was plain enough, though I did not see it till some kabalist showed me. Samek is the straight path, that straight line which Séraphita calls the mark of man, the way of the intellectual will, and the serpent is the

[1] William Sharp (1855–1905), Scottish poet; from 1894 he wrote under the name 'Fiona MacLeod'. The relevant passage from 'The Archer' reads: 'While he watched, amazed, he saw a tall shadowy woman pass by. She stopped, and drew a great bow she carried, and shot an arrow.... The arrow went right through the fawn.... The fawn leapt away sobbing into the night: while its heart suspended, arrow-pierced, from the white stem of a silver birch.... But I have this thought of my thinking; that it was only a vision I saw, and that the fawn was the poor suffering heart of Love, and that the Archer was the great Shadowy Archer that hunts among the stars. For in the dark of the morrow after that night I was on Cnoc-na-Hurich, and I saw a woman there shooting arrow after arrow against the stars.' *Tragic Romances* (Edinburgh, Geddes, 1897), pp. 253–4. Cf. also Yeats, *Autobiographies*, pp. 576–9.

[2] London coroner: with MacGregor Mathers and William Woodman, he founded the Order of the Golden Dawn.

[3] The ten Sephiroth include Yesod (the Foundation) and Tiphereth (Beauty). Samek is one of the lines or paths connecting the Sephiroth on the Tree of Life.

[4] Iacchus, identified with Bacchus (Dionysus) and in that character venerated, especially at Delphi, as a child.

kabalistic serpent – winding nature.[1] Did the shadows accept me with
that vision, make with me as it were their painful bond? The gods,
Henry More says, throw their lines as we throw ours for the fish,
and they bait the lines with dreams, and how can we help but leap
at them?[2] Certainly it was no part of myself, armed with supernatural
knowledge or what must seem so, that created a thought [which]
stood still, as it were, in the midst of the stream of my daily thought,
so little did it resemble it; or, if it was, I prefer to [think] that the
identity is no closer than between a man and his daimon. It was no
mind, no will that I knew that warned me in vain to leave this ceaseless wandering from myself.

XXXIV

I went to Paris,[3] the old lure, and stayed for a time at the Hôtel
Corneille near the Luxembourg, and there met John Synge for the
first time. I liked him, his sincerity and his knowledge, but did not
divine his genius. Some chance caller introduced us. 'There is an
Irishman', he said, 'living on the top floor.' He was reading French
literature, Racine mainly, and hoped to live by writing articles upon
it in English papers. I persuaded him that Symons would always

[1] 'Many years ago I saw, between sleeping and waking, a woman of incredible beauty
shooting an arrow into the sky, and from the moment when I made my first guess at her
meaning I have thought much of the difference between the winding movement of
Nature and the straight line, which is called in Balzac's *Séraphita* the "Mark of Man",
but is better described as the mark of saint or sage.' 'Anima Hominis' (dated 25 February
1917), reprinted in *Mythologies*, p. 340.
[2] Yeats is recalling, somewhat vaguely, a passage in *The Immortality of the Soul*:
'And so these Daemons, though they bear us no good will, by bodily conflict they can
hurt none of us (it being so difficult a thing to come at us) and very few of us by their
Art and Industry.
'For this fancyfull Philosopher (Cardan) will have them only attempt us as we do the
Fishes, by Baits, and Nets, and Eel-spears, or such like Engines which we cast into the
bottom of the Water: So, saith he, these Aëreal Genii, keeping their station above in
the third Region of the Aire (as we do on the bank of the River, or in a Boat on the Sea,
when we fish) by sending down Dreams and Apparitions may entangle some men so,
that by affrightments and disturbances of mind at last, though at this distance, they
may work their ruine and destruction.' (Book III, ch. III, sect. iv) *A Collection of Several
Philosophical Writings of Dr Henry More* (London, 1662), p. 156. Cardan is Geronimo
Cardano (1501–76), physician and physiognomist, author of *Metoposcopia*, in which
astrology and physiognomy are related.
[3] December 1896.

be a better critic, and that he should go to Ireland – [he] knew Irish; I told him of Aran where I had just been – and find expression for a life that lacked it. 'Style comes from the shock of new material' was his own phrase later on. A little later I stayed with the MacGregors;[1] under the impact of 'the Celtic movement', as our movement was called in England, they had cast off Mathers and become plain Mac-Gregor.

I saw much now of Maud Gonne and my hope revived again. If I could go to her and prove by putting my hand into the fire till I had burned it badly, would not that make her understand that devotion like mine should [not] be lightly thrown away? Often as I went to see her I had that thought in mind, and I do not think it was fear of pain that prevented me, but fear of being mad. I wondered at moments if I was not really mad. Then one morning [I] began telling myself a different story, what I do not remember, but my arm suffered some other injury, was broken perhaps, for I pictured myself as carrying it in a sling. I had got up before breakfast to get a newspaper and when I returned found the MacGregors on the doorstep. 'What has happened to your arm?' Mrs MacGregor said. 'But it is all right; the *bonne* said it was in a sling.' For a moment my concentration of thought had created a magical illusion.

These events have no very precise date to me. I made many visits to Paris, and I cannot be certain always in which visit some event took place. One morning at breakfast MacGregor said to me, 'I saw a man standing in an archway last night, and he wore a kilt with the MacLeod and another tartan.' In the afternoon I began to shiver, and the shivering went on at intervals for a couple of hours, and was associated in my mind with William Sharp and Fiona MacLeod. I told MacGregor and [he] made himself clairvoyant. Sharp was in need. 'It is madness,' he said, 'but it is like the madness of a god.' We were all under the shadow of the Fiona myth, the beautiful, inspired woman living in remote islands. He then said, 'It is my wife's business,' and I went into [the] inner room with her. As I passed its door I said, 'It is strange, but my mind was full of Sharp

---

[1] Mathers and his wife moved to Paris in 1894, living first at 121 Boulevard Saint Michel, then at 1 Avenue Duquesne near the Champ de Mars, and later at 87 Rue Mozart, Auteuil. At this time Mathers assumed the title of Count MacGregor of Glenstrae.

and Fiona till this moment, but now it seems quite empty.' 'I have used a formula', she said, 'to send your soul away.' I was fool enough to write to Sharp, and [received] an unbelievable letter from a seaside hotel about the beautiful Fiona and himself. He had been very ill, terrible mental suffering, and suddenly my soul had come to heal him and he had found Fiona to tell her [he] was healed – I think I had come as a great white bird. I learned, however, from Mrs Sharp years afterwards that at the time of my experience he was certainly alone, but mad. He had gone away to struggle on with madness.

MacGregor himself lived in a world of phantoms. He would describe himself as meeting, perhaps in some crowded place, a stranger whom he would distinguish from living men by a certain tension in his heart. These strangers were his teachers. I said, 'How do you know you are not hallucinated?' He said, 'The other night I followed one of these strangers down that passage', pointing to a narrow passage from his garden to the street, 'and fell over the milk boy. The boy said, "It is too bad to be fallen over by two of you."' The break-up [of] his character that was soon to bring his expulsion from my Order had begun.[1] He was slowly demoralized by 'the Celtic movement' and Sir Walter Scott. He had taken to wearing Highland costume, though he had, I believe, never been in the Highlands, and his Scotch ancestor was ——[2] and called every young man 'lad', and drank much brandy, which he spoke of always as whisky is spoken of in Anglo-Scottish poetry. He wished to play some part in the manner of Rob Roy, and dreamed of a restoration of the Stuarts to some Highland kingdom. He was always expecting, as indeed all the visionaries of his time were, a universal war, and had made his wife learn ambulance work that they might join together some roving band. He showed me the wound of a sabre on his wrist, and explained that he and his wife had been in some student riot, hoping that general bloodshed had begun.

To help Maud Gonne in her work I had suggested and was now helping to found in Paris a 'Young Ireland Society', and had brought

[1] 'He had much industry at setting out,
      Much boisterous courage, before loneliness
      Had driven him crazed;'
            'All Souls' Night', Collected Poems, pp. 256–9.
[2] Page torn; a word or two missing.

Synge[1] into it, but presently he resigned. Maud Gonne was giving it a Fenian turn, and I remember his saying he thought England would only do Ireland right when she felt herself to be safe, the only political sentence I ever heard on his lips.

XXXV

For years now Maud Gonne had been occupied with a movement for the amnesty of the Irish political prisoners[2] who were serving, most of them, life sentences in Portland and, I think, Dartmoor. They had brought to light the woman in her, for instead of 'Mother Ireland with the crown of stars upon her head' she had these seven and twenty[3] prisoners to brood over her. I noticed an increased simplicity, a surrender of self; if she hated England, and I do not think it was as yet a bitter hatred, her charity was greater than her hate. Her visits to any prisoner moved her deeply. Once, pity seems to have given a very precise pre-vision. She told me the tale at the time, and I have gone over the details again lately. There is, unhappily, no contemporary record. She had gone to Portland prison where there were a large number of prisoners; she had seen three or four, and then came a man[4] who had lost one eye, and now the other was going. She had been placed in a kind of cage and the prisoner was in another, two or three feet off, and a warder sat between. She had with her an English artist connected with some newspaper, she thinks. She had brought him to enable her to give the prisoners political information without answering forbidden questions, as the prison authorities could not interfere with the conversation of visitors among themselves. The convict was in great pain and tried to tell her how he had lost his eye. The warder said this was forbidden, and that if he spoke of it he would be taken back to his cell, but, clinging to the bars, the man began his story – some piece of prison mismanagement or carelessness, seemingly. Maud Gonne said suddenly,[5]

[1] Yeats invited Synge to come to the Society as an 'Associate'.
[2] 'some 27 in all' deleted.
[3] The Souvenir Journal of the Committee of the Amnesty Association, dated 6 June 1893, lists 23 prisoners.
[4] Peter Callaghan, from Edinburgh; sentenced to life imprisonment in December 1883.
[5] Yeats's numbering of the pages ends at this point.

not knowing why she spoke, 'Do not say anything; I know how your eye was injured, but [do] not trouble [yourself], you will be released in six months.' Then other prisoners were brought to see her, and apparently in a kind of dream, for it was only afterwards she knew what had happened, she told each man that he would be released, and when.

Coming away the artist said, 'I am sure you did it out of kindness, but you have done a very cruel thing. You told those men they would all be released, and you told each man how soon, and they are all life-sentences.' She answered, 'I hardly remember anything, but I know it will all come true.' He then told her after what periods – one year, two years, six months, or whatever might be – she had told each man he would be free. Every prophecy was fulfilled and, she tells me, to the letter. Certainly she worked hard to bring that fulfilment about. Morley,[1] who had failed to keep a pledge, lost his seat, for she put up a Labour candidate[2] against him, cast the Irish vote in favour [of] the Labour candidate, and split the Liberal majority. I remember her telling me that her correspondence at one time took up eight hours a day.

XXXVI

We had already begun a work together that was for me to be most wasteful. She had told me that she wished to go to America to collect for a proposed monument to Wolfe Tone in Dublin,[3] but found some unexplained difficulty in getting the needed authorization from the Dublin body. I offered an authorization, and called a meeting of the principal men of 'the new movement' at my rooms. We passed the authorization, and I should have considered my work done, but I discovered a situation that interested me. For some time I had paid little attention to the new movement. I found in it only one man

[1] John Morley (1838–1923), Chief Secretary for Ireland 1892–5. Member of Parliament for Newcastle-on-Tyne, he lost his seat in 1895. He was understood to have pledged his support for the amnesty of the Irish political prisoners, but on 29 October 1894, when he received a deputation from the Dublin Corporation on the matter, he declined to act.

[2] F. Hamill. The seat was won by C. F. Hamond (Conservative).

[3] Maud Gonne addressed her first meeting in America on 24 October 1897, asking for funds for a Wolfe Tone monument and for the Irish Amnesty Association.

sufficiently educated to interest me or understand what I was talking about. His name was, I think, Sellers, and [he] was a member of the Primrose League, an extreme Unionist body, but satisfied some love of disguise by combining it with Fenianism, and he had ceased to attend our meetings. It was only now that I discovered that it represented one of two violently opposed sections into which Irish–American revolutionists had split. One was the Triangle, as it was called,[1] and the other was that of Devoy.[2] They were split because Devoy [and] his party accused the Triangle of the murder of a certain Dr Cronin. The Dublin committee represented Devoy, and my friends the supposed murderers. It was years ago; the court had acquitted Sullivan,[3] the accused man, and we could not with the sea between re-try the case. Perhaps if I allowed myself to be elected President of the English committee, I could keep the movement from dividing up into its elements. I was elected,[4] and found the task heavy.

Presently I formed a grandiose plan without considering the men I had to work with, exactly as if [I] were writing something in a story. The Dublin committee on which we, who came gradually to speak for many societies scattered through England and Scotland, had the right to send so many representatives was a large body – two or three hundred perhaps. It was soon to have a vast organization behind it, and the actual laying of the stone would be, I had heard rumours, attended by twenty thousand Irish-Americans – special ships were being chartered. The Spanish American War had not yet

[1] 'with its centre in Chicago' deleted.

[2] 'with its centre in New York' deleted. John Devoy (1842–1928), a leader of Clan na Gael, the Irish–American Fenian organization. Editor of the *Gaelic American*, a weekly paper devoted to the independence of Ireland. *Devoy's Post-Bag*, vol. II, ed. William O'Brien and Desmond Ryan (Dublin, Fallon, 1953), pp. 232 ff., gives an account of the Triangle controversy.

[3] Alexander Sullivan, arrested in May 1889 for the alleged murder of Dr Patrick Cronin. Yeats's letter to Katharine Tynan, 25 July 1889, refers to Mrs Sullivan: 'She is coming this evening to meet York Powell, Sydney Hall and Miss Purser. I wrote an article for her a day or two ago – something about Dr Cronin. She is not yet sure that he is dead at all. He seems to have been a great rascal. It was really a very becoming thing to remove him – if he be dead and the man found at Chicago be not someone else. A Spy has no rights.' *Letters* (Wade), p. 131. Yeats's article has not been found. That Dr Cronin was a spy has not been established.

[4] Of the Executive of the Centenary Association (for Great Britain and France) Yeats was elected President, Mark Ryan Treasurer, and Geoffrey Lavelle Secretary.

come to engage their thoughts or their plans elsewhere. Why could we not turn this council into something like an Irish Parliament? There were then four parties in Ireland: the Parnellites and anti-Parnellites, the official Unionist and the New Unionist Party, headed by Lord Castletown, which wished to secure a fairer fiscal arrangement with England. Why not, after the laying of the stone, invite all these parties to make a statement before us? The first two parties dare not refuse, and Castletown would come, I knew, for I soon had a half-promise. The official Unionists we would only ask for form's sake. I will then, I thought, bring forward my own policy, if possible as the official policy of the English Wolfe Tone Associations. It was this. After some more careful and formal system of elections, our council should sit permanently, and the representatives of the various Irish parties should agree to sit in Westminster only as a deputation from us, and only when we decided that a vital Irish issue had arisen. They would be less expense to the nation and, as English parties would polarize in a new way, the occasional attendances, never to be foreseen, would produce great disturbance. The council could let it be understood that it was ready to adopt unconstitutional means if it should seem at any time that success lay that way, and so get the whole nation, Fenian and constitutional alike, behind it. I should have checked that swing of the pendulum I so dreaded.

A series of detailed memories floats up. The first shows that I was only reliably courageous in my thoughts. I went to Dublin with a certain mad rogue[1] for my fellow delegate. He made some unseemly row there, and when I got up in the council to put matters right I was suppressed by O'Leary, who was in the chair and did not understand my intentions. When I came back I allowed the rogue to make his report, a perversion of the facts, to our small central committee without protest or explanation. He was still new to me and I am cowed by new personalities. I did nothing but correct the impression in the minutes.

I remember noticing an elderly man who came in for a moment at the close of each of our weekly committee meetings and said some-

---

[1] 'Frank Hugh O'Donnell' deleted. O'Donnell (1848–1916) Member of Parliament for Galway in 1874, and for Dungarvan in 1877. Vice-President of the Home Rule Confederation in Great Britain.

thing to the secretary and went out. I asked who he was. I was told
that he was a schoolmaster who early in life had made a vow neither
to smoke nor drink but to give the money saved to the Irish cause.
His weekly half-crowns haunted me continually and accused us of
extravagance.

I remember a proposal for a silver medal, which was to contain
upon it the usual round tower and wolf-dog and cross and harp. Our
committee, all good Catholics outside politics, decided that the cross
had been so detrimental to the national cause – the fall of Parnell
was a recent event – that it was to be taken out. A deputation was
sent to the artist, but we accepted his explanation that the cross
could not be left out as that would leave the harp with nothing to
lean on.

I remember an intoxicated man coming on Derby Day to apolo-
gize for some rudeness by some young men who had not recognized
us, and his looking at us all, hesitating, and then saying, 'No, no, I
will not. I care for nobody now but Venus and Adonis and the other
planets of heaven.'[1]

I remember Maud Gonne reading out a series of most excellent
proposals for rousing popular enthusiasm, and our accepting most
of these, and her saying to me afterwards, 'A voice came to me this
morning as I lay in bed and dictated that paper to me. I noticed
afterwards that the clock stopped when it began to speak.'

I remember going into the office of the Dublin committee in
D'Olier Street and finding the front door open and the office door
open and the cupboard door open and the room empty and eighteen
pounds in gold on the shelf.

I have a memory, full of self-mockery, of the Jubilee riot of 1897.
Maud Gonne had promised a then small Labour leader, James
Connolly,[2] since executed for his part in the rebellion of 1916, to
speak at his Socialist society, meaning one of the small regular
meetings. When we arrived in Dublin for some meeting of the council, she found the streets placarded with an announcement of a

---

[1] In *The Player Queen* Septimus says (lines 101-2), 'What do I care for any one now
except Venus and Adonis and the other planets of heaven?'

[2] James Connolly (1870-1916) founded the *Irish Worker*, organized the Citizen Army,
and became one of the leaders of the Easter Rising. He is celebrated in Yeats's 'Easter
1916' and 'The Rose Tree', *Collected Poems*, pp. 202-5, 206.

Socialist meeting in Dame Street, and her name as that of the principal speaker. She was not a Socialist, and had never spoken in Dublin to an open-air meeting, and wrote to refuse. I was with her when Connolly called. If she refused, he was ruined, for nobody would believe that he had ever had a promise. She was firm and he went away, but his despair was so deep that I softened her heart afterwards. She drove to the house he lived in on a car, and came back with a pathetic account of his wife and his four children and their one room.

The next day there was a great crowd in Dame Street, and while Maud Gonne was speaking an old woman kept waving a miniature before her face, a portrait of a martyr of the great rebellion, a treasure of some household in a shrine, and calling out, 'I was in it before she was born.' Maud Gonne told how the day before was the anniversary, when she was accustomed to decorate the graves of the martyrs, and that the custodian of some graveyard – St Michan's[1] perhaps – had refused her admission because it was Queen Victoria's Jubilee.[2] She said then, speaking slowly in a low voice that yet seemed to go through the whole crowd, 'Must the graves of our dead go undecorated because Victoria has her Jubilee?' and the whole crowd went wild.

That evening there was a meeting of our council in the City Hall, and when we came out after it the crowds were waiting for us all round the Hall. We were going to the National Club in Rutland Square,[3] and they came too. Outside the National Club a magic lantern was to show on a white screen statistics of evictions, deaths from starvation, etc., during Victoria's reign. Somewhere in front of us was a mock funeral Maud Gonne devised, a coffin with 'The British Empire' printed upon it, and black flags with the names of all those who had been hanged for treason during Queen Victoria's reign. Presently they began breaking windows where there were decorations. Maud Gonne was walking with a joyous face; she had taken all those people into her heart. I knew she would not interfere. I knew her principle. If a crowd does anything illegal and you try to

[1] In Church Street, Dublin; John and Henry Sheares and William Orr, the United Irishmen, are buried in the vaults of the church.
[2] 22 June 1897.
[3] Now Parnell Square.

stop it, you may succeed, but you are certain to seem to have done it
to keep from danger yourself. I tried to speak and could only whisper.
I had spoken too much through a disorderly debate at the council,
and my voice had gone. Then I too resigned myself and felt the
excitement of the moment, that joyous irresponsibility and sense of
power.

At the National Club she and I were given tea, and I settled down
to a long table, as I believed, on which I had been writing all day
upon some subject in no way connected with politics. Thereupon a
man more excited than I have ever seen anybody or ever shall see
anybody ran in calling out, 'Oh, it is awful; it is awful. Police are
batoning the people outside. It is awful,' and so on. Maud Gonne
got [up] and said she was going out and somebody else said she would
be hurt. I told them to lock the door and keep her in. My brain was
not working quickly; I remember regretting my tea, which was
getting cold. She was perhaps right to be angry when I refused to let
her out unless she explained what she meant to do. 'How do I
know till I get out?' she said. I offered to go out myself if she would
not try to get out when the door was opened, though what I could
have done with my whisper I do not know, but she would make no
promise. Later on she told me that I had made her do the only
cowardly thing of her life. That night I went to all the newspaper
offices and took responsibility for my action.[1] My memory is that
two hundred people were taken to hospital and that one old woman
was killed.[2]

XXXVII

I remember some meeting, I think it was that very Jubilee meeting,
of the council at which she succeeded in winning so much support
among our opponents – we had only a handful among the two
hundred or three hundred delegates – that she limited the weekly
spending power; there had been great extravagance. Passions had

[1] 'and asked the editors not to attack the police. I had an idea that the police could be
won over.' deleted.

[2] *United Ireland*, 3 July, has a full report of the inquest on Mrs Fitzsimons, who died
in Jervis Street Hospital following injury at a baton charge by police at Rutland Square
on Jubilee night. The *Irish Times*, 23 June, reported that 'as many as two hundred people'
were treated for injuries.

been very high, those secret societies undermining all, and yet so gracious had she been, her voice always low and sweet, that she was applauded by friend and enemy alike. The foundation stone was laid a year after the riot, and a procession[1] passed through Dublin greater than anything since O'Connell's centenary[2] – was it twenty years before? – and that procession was, I have always believed, the immediate cause of the reunion of the Irish Party. At the head of the procession went the majority of the Dublin council and their friends. I was with Maud Gonne in a wagonette behind them, and then came the Irish parties walking side by side like cattle in a storm. I heard John Redmond[3] say to John Dillon,[4] leader of the anti-Parnellites, 'I went up to the head of the procession just now, and one of the marshals said to me, "Your place is further back, Mr Redmond." I said, "I will stay where I am." He said then, "In that case, Mr Redmond, I will lead you back."' At the laying of the stone I said, thinking of the procession as a silent protest of the people at the quarrels of Irish public life, 'The people themselves made this movement.' But a cry rose all over the great crowd, 'No, no, it was Maud Gonne that made it.'

My own conclusion from it all, however, had been not contempt of the quarrelling party – their quarrels, though mean and unrestrained in manner, had a worthy cause – but that they alone had any political training. No, certainly my grandiose project would not do; the Dublin council would not make an Irish parliament.

XXXVIII

I asked a Dublin newspaper to place at the disposal of 'the new movement' a weekly column, and this was granted. On the way home I mentioned this to the fellow delegate I shall call, for I have no good to say of him, but the Mad Rogue. Within a few days, and before I had brought it before the committee, there appeared in this column a very remarkable and romantic report of the activities of

[1] 15 August 1898.   [2] 6 August 1875.
[3] John Redmond (1856–1918), Nationalist Member of Parliament and, in 1900, Chairman of the reunited Irish Party. A leader of the Home Rule movement, he was opposed to violence or revolution, and was shocked by the Easter Rising.
[4] 'to certain of his late enemies', *Autobiographies*, p. 365.

an unknown secret society. It was certainly not the new movement, and nobody could tell if it had any existence. Presently I was asked to go and see the Rogue, who was in hospital after a gas explosion in his flat, and next week my conversation was published as the report of, I think, 'Court Shannon', one of the imaginary branches. These phantoms were so impressive that he kept the column in his hands for months.[1] He was to become my enemy, and to fix upon me a charge of anti-Catholic bias I have not yet cast off.[2]

I had been shown in London some months before a leaflet attacking Michael Davitt in disgraceful language, slandering, if I recollect rightly, his mother or some near relation, and noticed that it was signed with a *nom de plume* used by the officials of the new movement. I was going to Paris and brought it with me and found that Maud Gonne had already seen it and had decided also that it must be repudiated. We both stated that we would never attend a meeting organized by the new movement if it was not withdrawn and publicly apologized for. While we were urging this, a second leaflet appeared, signed by the Dublin *nom de plume*, and attacking, I think, the mother or other near relation of a London doctor supposed wrongly to have written the first leaflet. Our London friends said 'nothing can be done now,' but I was in a rage and wrote a repudiation describing both as unworthy of men of honour, and got O'Leary to force it upon the Dublin body while Maud Gonne got it through and formally accepted in London. We were promised that it would be circulated wherever the leaflets had been, and we did not inquire too closely as to whether this was done, satisfied to have got the two secret societies to sign and print at their own expense a

[1] A typescript of autobiographical material which Yeats dictated to his wife in 1927 has the following passage: 'I had been asked to obtain for certain influential members of the English organization a column or so in every week's *United Ireland*, the fighting Nationalist paper of the moment. On the boat to Holyhead I told O'Donnell, who had been my fellow-delegate to some meeting or other, and a week or so later found that the column, instead of containing my friends' news of the meeting of the association, contained reports of the branches of a vast secret society, each branch being named a court, and the whole, or some part, being signed by the supposed head in imitation of the Pope, "servant of servants". I saw whose handiwork it was, but the thing was so precise and confident that I might have believed in it were it not that a couple of weeks later I found some words of mine as the report of "Court Shannon".' (Typescript in Senator Michael Yeats's possession.)

[2] 'But now a charge of heresy became public. I had offended Frank Hugh O'Donnell; [he] saw his chance.' deleted.

document eating words they had accepted as their own. I have still that trophy.

When we had almost finished we discovered that[1] the Mad Rogue was the author. A sinister man, he was very able when not dominated by some evil passion, but nearer to the traditional idea of a ruined soul than anybody I have ever met. He had once been conspicuous in public life, but had been driven out of it by Parnell, and one could not tell what old score he wished to pay off on Michael Davitt. He was less man than a machine, whose wheels turned always with calculable certainty from an impulse of hate or jealousy. He was soon to have his vengeance on me. Later on he was convicted of a charge of purloining, probably in part to his private purse and certainly to what he believed the gain of his political influence, two thousand pounds sent by the Boer Republic to help, during the Boer War, revolutionary activity in Ireland;[2] and of selling to Delcassé[3] a French officer sent by the French War Office – which had a policy not that of the Ministry of Foreign Affairs – partly as a spy and partly to negotiate with our people.[4] When he began to print [a] series of slanders upon Maud Gonne, I was able to prevent his getting a seat in the Irish Party, where he would have been a more dangerous slanderer, by laying some of the evidence before John Dillon. Dillon was a stranger to me, but he acted very honourably. The Irish Party returned a subscription of one hundred pounds, Boer money sent by our Rogue to the Party fund.

[1] 'Frank Hugh O'Donnell was author of the first pamphlet.' deleted. O'Donnell later accused Davitt of 'inveracity', *A History of the Irish Parliamentary Party* (London, Longmans, Green, 1918), vol. II, p. 246.
[2] This incident is described in Maud Gonne MacBride, *A Servant of the Queen* (Dublin, Golden Eagle Books, 1950 edition), pp. 292–3, though O'Donnell is not named. Reference is made to 'a British agent', but O'Donnell is clearly intended.
[3] Théophile Delcassé (1852–1923), French Foreign Minister 1898–1908, 1914–15. An article in the *United Irishman*, 12 August 1899, discusses one of his diplomatic missions.
[4] This passage is clearer in a later version which Yeats dictated to his wife in 1927: 'He had committed certain other offences of which the most serious was the betrayal of a French officer. Ireland at that time had considerable influence at the French War Office, and without the knowledge of Delcassé, who was at the Foreign Office, they sent an officer to do a little espionage and he asked our people in London to supply him with a secretary. . . . [O'Donnell] had long been a reputed Austrian agent, and now we were to discover that he was a French agent for he informed Delcassé and the officer was disgraced.' (Typescript in Senator Michael Yeats's possession.)

XXXIX

I sometimes came to these meetings from Lady Gregory's, where I spent the summers of 1897 and 1898 as every summer since, and returned there. Some time in 1897, I think, I spent an afternoon with Count de Basterot. He arrived from Paris in the early summer of every year, and lived in a little two-storeyed house[1] close to the sea eight or nine miles from Coole. On his arrival a great flock of ducks and hens and chickens ran about in front of his door, and when he went to Rome in the autumn there would be none left. Paralysed from the waist down through sexual excess in youth, he was spending his old age in the duties of religion and in attending chapel. Lady Gregory was, I think, his principal Irish friend. In his house I explained an old project for an Irish theatre, but said I had given it up, for where in Ireland could the money be found? I had, however, some hopes of getting a little subscription theatre in London. If I wrote well, my plays would reach Ireland in the end. Count de Basterot was a Unionist and had, I think, at our meeting at Tulira disliked me, but we became good friends. Lady Gregory had written a pamphlet against Gladstone's Home Rule Bill and was, I think, still a Unionist.[2] Lady Gregory offered to collect the money for some first performance.

Legal difficulties arose, a law had to be changed,[3] and so a year passed by. Meanwhile Edward Martyn's *Heather Field* and my *Countess Cathleen* were decided upon. Lady Betty Balfour tried to help our plans by *tableaux vivants* from *The Countess Cathleen* at the Chief Secretary's Lodge.[4] She asked me if I would rehearse them and, when I explained that I could not enter an official house, asked if I thought a certain Nationalist antiquarian[5] and T. W. Rolleston,

[1] At Duras, Co. Galway.

[2] The pamphlet was published anonymously under the title *A Phantom's Progress, or Home Ruin* (London, Ridgway, 1893). The Phantom (Gladstone) returns to this world to seek, in Ireland, one person of any class whose condition has been improved by Home Rule. The argument of the fable is Unionist and anti-Catholic.

[3] On 11 July 1898, an amendment to the Local Government (Ireland) Bill was accepted, giving the Lord Lieutenant power to grant occasional licences, on the application of Dublin County Council, for theatrical performances in any approved building. (Hansard, 4th series, vol. 61, 6–15 July 1898, p. 523.)

[4] January 1899.

[5] George Coffey (1857–1916), author of *The Origins of Prehistoric Ornament in Ireland*

who had come to live in Ireland, [would] be good demons. I said they had good looks and she invited them. They accepted, thinking I had consented and that it would [be] safe politically, for I lived among the violent. In a few months they had both official posts. The antiquarian was head of a museum, and nobody accused [him] of breach of principle – his politics were an irrelevant enthusiasm; but nobody defended Rolleston, who seemed to earn his post with a pamphlet urging Dublin to give an enthusiastic reception to Queen Victoria.[1] I alone, perhaps, believed him unconscious of a bargain. He had discovered his real politics. His Nationalist convictions had never been more than the toys [of] a child, and were put away when the bell rang to meals. And 'In a quiet watered land, a land of roses'! And I once thought him a possible leader of the Irish race.

I came to see much of George Moore, whose knowledge of acting was very useful. He was Edward Martyn's close friend, having succeeded a certain charming, lascivious Count Stenbock,[2] lately dead of drink. I have observed in other abnormally virtuous men a tendency to choose friends for the sins they themselves had renounced. Martyn has a good intellect, moderate and sensible, but it seems to me that this intellect has been always thwarted by its lack of interest in life, religious caution having kept him always on the brink of the world in a half-unwilling virginity of the feelings imaging the virginity of his body. He had no interest in women, and Moore would accuse him of a frustrated passion for his own sex.[3] 'I

(1897) and *The Bronze Age in Ireland* (1913). Yeats's charge against Coffey is untrue. Coffey, a most distinguished archaeologist, had already been appointed Curator and Keeper of Irish Antiquities, the Royal Irish Academy's collection within the National Museum of Science and Art. He was appointed to this post on 6 July 1897, and held office until his resignation on 31 March 1914.

[1] The pamphlet, *Ireland, the Empire and the War* (Dublin, Sealy, Bryers & Walker, 1900) generally accords with Yeats's account of it, but does not refer specifically to Queen Victoria's visit. A review of the pamphlet (*United Irishman*, 24 March 1900) signed 'Cuguan' (i.e. Arthur Griffith) begins: 'Mr Rolleston's pamphlet is a recantation of the principles he professed up to the date of his visit to the Viceregal Lodge.' Rolleston's new post in 1900 was that of Organizer for the Department of Agriculture.

[2] Count Stanislaus Eric Stenbock (1860–95), poet, author of *The Shadow of Death* (1893). He died on 26 April 1895 at Brighton. Yeats recalls, in the Introduction to *Oxford Book of Modern Verse* (1936), 'a supper with Count Stenbock, scholar, connoisseur, drunkard, poet, pervert, most charming of men . . .'. The same meeting is the basis of an episode in Yeats's unfinished novel *The Speckled Bird*.

[3] In a typescript version of 'Dramatis Personae' the following sentence appears in the

believe,' he said to him once, 'you think sexual intercourse between men more natural than between women.' I wonder if Moore invented the answer, 'Well, at any rate it is not so disgusting.' Moore's mind upon the other hand suffered a perpetual conquest. He gave himself up to every new impression and quarrelled with everybody within reach who did not share his conviction of its importance. As a woman will speak evil of the lover who has left her, he would scorn all other impressions, those of his past life as energetically as the rest. Law, decency, social code, science, religion, his own past were but enemies. Nothing mattered but that he should be carried off – somewhere.

He and Martyn had no delusions about each other; each was more gifted than anybody else to know the other to the bone. 'No, Yeats,' Martyn once said to me when I had explained that Moore had good points, 'I've known Moore much longer than you. He has no good points.' 'Martyn is the most selfish man,' said Moore to me in I think the same week, 'the most selfish man alive. He thinks that I am damned and he does not care.' They dined together constantly and made long Continental journeys in one another's company.

Suddenly all our plans threatened to come to nothing.[1] A rumour against the orthodoxy of *The Countess Cathleen* was spreading and a priest had pronounced it heretical, and Martyn, who was paying the preliminary expenses (he ultimately paid all) withdrew. I had now met George Moore several times, and Lady Gregory and I saw at once that [he] was now the danger. I went to see him and exacted a promise that he would not see Martyn or write him without showing his letter to Lady Gregory, for nothing could help us but two priests. The play must be declared orthodox by a majority of votes and that would take several days. I got letters from Father Finlay[2] of the

---

passage on Martyn: 'He once said the majority of lost souls are lost through sexuality, had his father's instincts through repression or through some accident of birth turned, as Moore thought, into an always resisted homo-sexuality.' (Morris Library, Southern Illinois University, Carbondale.)

[1] March 1899. *The Countess Cathleen* was performed in the Antient Concert Rooms, now the Academy Cinema, Pearse Street, Dublin, on 8 May 1899, by professional actors under the management of Florence Farr. Some of the context of Yeats's difficulties is given in *Letters* (Wade), pp. 315 ff.

[2] Rev. T. A. Finlay.

Society of Jesus and Father Barry, a well-known author,[1] and sent them to Martyn, who was in Ireland. Martyn wrote that all was well again, and I went to see Moore. That incoherent face darkened. 'O Yeats,' he said, 'what an opportunity I have lost! I had almost finished my article for the *Nineteenth Century*. I called it "The Soul of Edward Martyn". It would have made a sensation all over Europe. Nobody has ever written so about his most intimate friend. What an opportunity!'

Florence Farr – who had been chosen manager – and I went that night to Dublin to engage the Antient Concert Rooms, and while we were finishing our breakfast in the Nassau Hotel, Maud Gonne's old lodging, Edward Martyn came in to tell us he had resigned again. There were large drops of sweat upon his forehead, which he was wiping with his pocket handkerchief. Moore had sent him the article in the form of a letter. However, we made light of Moore and talked him round.

This was the moment chosen by the Mad Rogue. He had been trying to return to public life through 'the new movement', but was now turning to the Church, which he was to attack a few months later in one of the ablest Irish anti-clerical books. An attack on *The Countess Cathleen* would be both vengeance and a good speculation. He wrote a pamphlet called *Souls for Gold*,[2] quoting as my own words the words of the demon merchants, and representing the scene where the women barter their souls as an attack on Irish womanhood. I do not know if it was all sheer dishonesty, or if controversy did not stir him to a kind of delirium, to a series of deductions where all had withered to a single premise as though one began again at Adam. Has not every living truth, like every living man, an infinite number of forefathers? The pamphlet was dropped into letter-boxes all over residential Dublin, and a newspaper had long violent leaders.

At last Cardinal Logue, a dull, pious old man, who had been stirred by some intrigue, published a naïve letter saying that if the play, which he admitted he had not read, was fairly represented by the pamphlet no Catholic should witness it.[3] Edward Martyn was

[1] Rev. William Barry, author of *The New Antigone*.
[2] *Souls for Gold! Pseudo-Celtic Drama in Dublin* (London, 1899).
[3] 9 May 1899. Yeats replied in the *Morning Leader*, 13 May 1899.

not disturbed – the Cardinal had not read the play, and that deprived his opinion of ecclesiastic authority, and he cared nothing for mobs and newspapers. Other Catholic friends, however, began to melt away. There was nothing to be done. Letters to the press only led to more misrepresentation and, even if one answered everything, who would have read the answers? Besides, there were real differences that looked very dark now they were exaggerated by malice. I had talked of our apprehension of the invisible by symbol, so I must have said the Virgin Mary was a symbol. And then somebody in my play as it was printed had crushed a shrine with his foot.[1] I had indeed but wished to show him for a wicked man. I had not known that to many simple Catholics such an impiety, whatever the motive, was as shameful as a naked man. Certainly I, to whom the studio and the study had been the world, had used as mere picturesque decoration what was sacred to these medieval believers.

I had to ask for police protection, and on the night of the first performance I found about twenty drawn up in the hall. The officer explained to me that they could not act until I told them that the moment had come. I turned to my friend the Mayo doctor and said, 'You must help me; I have no experience,' and a smile ran along the faces of the twenty policemen. I remembered that there had been a rumour among them that I had got up the Jubilee riots, bringing two hundred pounds from London for the purpose. We had not to use them, for though the performance took place in tumult there was no attempt, as later at the *Playboy*, to stop the performance, for a majority of the not very large audience was entirely upon our side and the opposition did not wish to altogether prevent themselves from hearing; and a number of anti-clerics from somewhere on the quayside had been sent by a revolutionist[2] with the direction, 'Applaud everything that sounds as if it might be disagreeable to the clergy.' The real opposition stayed at home. Quite new topics sounded disagreeable[3] in every act. When the demon tells the Countess Cathleen to sign the renunciation of her soul with a certain pen because it is a feather from the cock that crowed when Peter denied

---

[1] Shemus Rua in the version of the play printed in *Poems* (1895).
[2] 'Arthur Griffith', *Autobiographies*, p. 416.
[3] 'New points of objection came' deleted.

his Master, he was hissed. That too was perhaps an attack on the Catholic Church. 'It is', said a Catholic friend to me, 'as if you were to cry out after a prosperous merchant, a member of the Corporation – Lord Mayor perhaps – "I mind the time when you tumbled for halfpence behind the long car."'[1]

It was impossible to say if the play succeeded, for the question was its blasphemy. Martyn's play, *The Heather Field*, was however an undoubted success, and we began to look upon him as our genius. We had made arrangements for our second set of performances, and engaged a theatre, so confident were we in that play of his that we had not seen. I was at Coole with Lady Gregory when the manuscript came. It was very like the work of a child – not even a clever child – crude and violent. It could not be produced, and while we were wondering what we should do Moore wrote asking us not [to] condemn it. He would get Martyn to revise it; and a little later he went to Tulira and came from there to say that Edward was writing a masterpiece. One passage especially was the most powerful dialogue in modern drama. Again he came in with the same story; all would soon be worthy of that incomparable scene. And then again, but now he was gloomy and I must see him alone. The truth was it was he who was rewriting that incomparable scene. He had been led by it into too great fervour, and Martyn had taken alarm and said [he] would write his own play. 'He can't write a play,' said Moore, 'he can find subjects, which I can't do, but he will never write. I constructed *The Heather Field* for him, and I am ready to write a lot of plays for him and tell nobody. Come over and try and persuade him or he is ruined.'

I tried to persuade Martyn, but his honesty was alarmed, and Moore had to sign the play after a long struggle in which he wanted to and swore he would not as his faith in the play waxed and waned. And a very bad play it was.[2] I, however, had helped in the writing, going to Tulira for the purpose, for local and topical knowledge was necessary. Our work was disturbed by quarrels between Moore and Martyn about Moore's stories of his love adventures, perhaps

[1] A 'long car' was a horse-drawn vehicle, predecessor of the bus. 'Mind' is Anglo-Irish for 'remember'.

[2] *The Tale of a Town*; rewritten and finally acknowledged by Moore as *The Bending of the Bough*, it was first produced at the Gaiety Theatre, Dublin, on 20 February 1900.

imaginary, and about going to Mass. Martyn had only invited him on the understanding that he went to Mass and he disliked this greatly, especially as he had to go a long drive to a distant church. He was afraid to go to the neighbouring church, for years before the parish priest, because Moore had put him into a novel, had promised to have him ducked if they ever got within reach. Moore tried oversleeping himself, forgetting the hour, and plain refusal, all in vain. 'Yeats does not go to church,' I remember his saying, and the answer, 'No, Moore, you must go. I am not responsible for Yeats; he is a Protestant.' 'But I am not a Catholic.' 'Yes, you are.' 'My God, is there no way of leaving that Church?' 'Turn Protestant.' 'Is there no other way?' 'None.' These conversations, reported by the old butler, were known in the cottages for miles round.

The theatre has found its own record, and I am little concerned with it here. I remember meditating during a dress rehearsal of *Diarmuid and Grania*,[1] by Moore and myself, on the life-wasting folly of it all, and I had just said to myself that an unperturbed goat waiting to take its place in some pastoral scene was the only sensible creature among us when I heard an actor say, 'Look at that goat eating the property ivy.'[2]

XL

On a visit to Dr Hyde I had seen the Castle Rock, as it was called, in Lough Key.[3] There is this small island entirely covered by what was a still habitable but empty castle. The last man who had lived there had been Dr Hyde's father who, when a young man, lived there for a few weeks. All round were the wooded and hilly shores, a place of great beauty. I believed that the castle could be hired for little money, and had long been dreaming of making it an Irish Eleusis or Samothrace. An obsession more constant than anything but my love itself was the need of mystical rites – a ritual system of evocation and meditation – to reunite the perception of the spirit, of the divine, with natural beauty. I believed that instead of thinking of Judea as holy we should [think] our own land holy, and most holy

[1] First performed on 21 October 1901 by the F. R. Benson Company at the Gaiety Theatre, Dublin.
[2] Cf. *Letters* (Wade), pp. 355-6.
[3] Yeats stayed at Frenchpark from 13 April to 1 May 1895.

where most beautiful. Commerce and manufacture had made the world ugly; the death of pagan nature-worship had robbed visible beauty of its inviolable sanctity. I was convinced that all lonely and lovely places were crowded with invisible beings and that it would be possible to communicate with them. I meant to initiate young men and women in this worship, which would unite the radical truths of Christianity to those of a more ancient world, and to use the Castle Rock for their occasional retirement from the world.

For years to come it was in my thought, as in much of my writing, to seek also to bring again in[to] imaginative life the old sacred places – Slievenamon, Knocknarea – all that old reverence that hung – above all – about conspicuous hills. But I wished by my writings and those of the school I hoped to found to have a secret symbolical relation to these mysteries, for in that way, I thought, there will be a greater richness, a greater claim upon the love of the soul, doctrine without exhortation and rhetoric. Should not religion hide within the work of art as God is within His world, and how can the interpreter do more than whisper? I did not wish to compose rites as if for the theatre. They must in their main outline be the work of invisible hands.

My own seership was, I thought, inadequate; it was to be Maud Gonne's work and mine. Perhaps that was why we had been thrown together. Were there not strange harmonies amid discord? My outer nature was passive – but for her I should never perhaps have left my desk – but I knew my spiritual nature was passionate, even violent. In her all this was reversed, for it was her spirit only that was gentle and passive and full of charming fantasy, as though it touched the world only with the point of its finger. When I had first met her I had used as a test the death symbol, imagining it in my own mind, but not wishing to alarm her had asked that it should take the form not of a human but of a dog's skull. She said, 'I see a figure holding out its hand with a skull on it. No, there is a bruise[1] on the hand, but I was compelled to say it was a skull.' I, who could not influence her actions, could dominate her inner being. I could therefore use her clairvoyance to produce forms that would arise from both minds, though mainly seen by one, and escape therefore from what is

[1] Doubtful reading.

mere[ly] personal. There would be, as it were, a spiritual birth from the soul of a man and a woman. I knew that the incomprehensible life could select from our memories and, I believed, from the memory of the race itself; could realize of ourselves, beyond personal pre-dilection, all it required, of symbol and of myth. I believed we were about to attain a revelation.

Maud Gonne entirely shared these ideas, and I did not doubt that in carrying them out I should win her for myself. Politics were merely a means of meeting, but this was a link so perfect that [it] would restore at once, even [after] a quarrel, the sense of intimacy. At every moment of leisure we obtained in vision long lists of sym-bols. Various trees corresponded to cardinal points, and the old gods and heroes took their places gradually in a symbolic fabric that had for its centre the four talismans of the Tuatha de Danaan, the sword, the stone, the spear and the cauldron, which related them-selves in my mind with the suits of the Tarot. George Pollexfen, though already an old man, shared my plans, and his slow and difficult clairvoyance added certain symbols. He and Maud Gonne only met once – in politics he was an extreme Unionist – but he and she worked with each other's symbols and I did much of the work in his house. The forms became very continuous in my thoughts, and when AE came to stay at Coole he asked who was the white jester he had seen about the corridors. It was a form I associated with the god Aengus.

It was a time of great personal strain and sorrow. Since my mistress had left me, no other woman had come into my life, and for nearly seven years none did. I was tortured by sexual desire and disappointed love. Often as I walked in the woods at Coole it would have been a relief to have screamed aloud.[1] When desire became an unendurable torture, I would masturbate, and that, no matter how moderate I was, would make me ill. It never occurred to me to seek another love. I would repeat to myself again and again the last confession of Lancelot, and indeed it was my greatest pride, 'I have loved a queen beyond measure and exceeding long.' I was never before or since so miserable as in those years that followed my first visit to Coole. In the second as during the first visit my nervous

---

[1] 'It was the most miserable time of my life.' deleted.

system was worn out. The toil of dressing in the morning exhausted me, and Lady Gregory began to send me cups of soup when I was called.

Instead of the work which I could not make myself do, I began with her that great collection of faery belief which is now passing through the press.[1] I lived amid mystery. It seemed as if these people possessed an ancient knowledge. Ah, if we could but speak face to face with those they spoke to. 'That old man,' Lady Gregory said to me of an old man who passed us in the wood, 'may have the mystery of the ages.' I began to have visions and dreams full of wisdom or beauty. Much of my thought since is founded upon certain sentences that came in this way. Once I asked when going to sleep what was the explanation of those curious tales of people 'away', of which Lady Gregory [and] I had so many. In all these tales some man, woman, or child was believed to be carried off bodily by the faery world, a changeling, some old man or woman perhaps, or perhaps [a] mere heap of shavings bewitched into their likeness, being left instead. I awoke enough to know that I lay in bed and had the familiar objects round, but to hear a strange voice speaking through my lips: 'We make an image of him who sleeps, and it is not him who sleeps but it is like him who sleeps, and we call it Emmanuel.'[2]

I was crossing one afternoon a little stream, and as I leaped I felt an emotion very strange to me – for all my thoughts were pagan – a sense of utter dependence on the divine will. It was over in an instant, and I said to myself, 'That is the way Christians feel.' That night I seemed to wake in my bed to hear a voice saying, 'The love of God for every soul is infinite, for every soul is unique; no other soul can satisfy the same need in God.' At other times I received fragments of poems, partly hearing and partly seeing. I saw in a dream a young shepherdess among many goats and sheep.

[1] *Visions and Beliefs in the West of Ireland* was not published until September 1920. Lady Gregory's Preface is dated February 1916. Of Yeats's contributions to the book, 'Witches and Wizards and Irish Folk-Lore' is dated 1914, and 'Swedenborg, Mediums and the Desolate Places' 14 October 1914.

[2] 'I awoke one night when a young man to find my body rigid and to hear a voice that came from my lips and yet did not seem my voice saying, "We make an image of him who sleeps, and it is not he who sleeps, and we call it Emmanuel." ' *A Vision* (1937; 1962), p. 233 n.

Somebody passed and spoke the name of some young man whom she had never seen. In my dream she stood up and said good-bye to each goat and sheep by name, and set out upon a journey. While I saw I seemed to hear also at moments the words [of] the poem, but only one sentence remained with me: 'She had but just heard his name, and yet it seemed as if he had long lain between her arms.'

Sometimes as I awoke marvellous illuminated pages seemed to be held before [me], with symbolic pictures that seemed profound, but when I tried to read the text all would vanish or but a sentence remain. I remember, 'The secret of the world is so simple that it could be written on a blade of grass with the juice of a berry'; and 'The rivers of Eden are in the midst of our rivers.' Sometimes when I lay in bed seeming awake, but always on my back as one lies when in nightmare, but with a feeling of wonder and delight, I would see forms at my bedside: once a fair woman who said she was Aedain, and both man and woman; and once a young boy and a young girl dressed in olive green, with sad, gentle faces; once my mother holding a cup in her hand; once a woman with an Elizabethan ruff.

A sexual dream was very rare, I neither then nor at any other time told the woman I loved to come to me [in] such a dream; I think I surrounded her with too great reverence and fear. One night I heard a voice, while I lay on my back, say I would be shown a secret, the secret of life and of death, but I must not speak of it. The room seemed to brighten and as I looked towards the foot of the bed I saw that it was changed into precious stones and yet these stones had a familiar look – they reminded me of the raised glass fruit on the bottles of lime-juice in my childhood. I never associated this growing brightness with sex, until all became suddenly dark and I found I had emitted seed.

I dreamed that I was lying on my back in a great stone trough in a great round house. I knew it was an initiation, and a wind was blowing over [me], I think from the feet up. Round me stood forms I could not see, and certain currents of influence were being directed through my eyes and various points of my body. These influences were painful. I heard a voice say, 'We are doing this to find out if it is worth going on doing this.' I knew my fitness for initiation was being questioned. Another night I thought I was taken out of my body and into a world of light, and while in this light, which was also complete happiness, I was told I would now be shown the passage of the soul at its incarnation. I saw the mystic elements gather about my soul in a certain order, a whole elaborate process, but the details vanished as I awoke. Little remained but a sentence I seemed to have spoken to myself: 'Beauty is becoming beautiful objects, and truth is becoming truths.'

I found I could call dreams by my symbols, though I think the most profound came unsought, and I would go to sleep, say with a spray of apple blossoms[1] on my pillow. Sometimes, when I had gone to sleep with the endeavour to send my soul to that of Maud Gonne, using some symbol, which I forget, I would wake dreaming of a shower of precious stones. Sometimes she would have some corresponding experience in Paris and upon the same night, but always with more detail. I thought we became one in a world of emotion eternalized by its own intensity and purity, and that this world had for its symbol precious stones. No physical, sexual sensation ever accompanied these dreams and I noticed that once the excitement of the genital ceased, a visionary form, that of Aedain, approached.

I tried to describe some vision to Lady Gregory, and to my great surprise could not. I felt a difficulty in articulation and became confused. I had wanted to tell her of some beautiful sight, and could see no reason for this. I remembered then what I had read of mystics not being always [able] to speak, and remembered some tale of a lecturer on mysticism having to stop in the middle of a sentence. Even to this moment, though I can sometimes speak without difficulty, I am more often unable to. I am a little surprised that I can write what I please.

XLI

William Sharp came to Tulira.[2] I feel that I never properly used or valued this man, through whom the fluidic world seemed to flow, disturbing all; I allowed the sense of comedy, taken by contagion

[1] Yeats associated Maud Gonne with apple blossoms; as in 'The Shadowy Waters' and several early poems. Cf. p. 40.
[2] In the late summer of 1897.

from others, to hide from me my own knowledge. To look at his big body, his high colour, his handsome head with the great crop of bristly hair, no one could have divined the ceaseless presence of that fluidic life.[1] When I walked with him I would say in my own mind, 'When we come to the third bush, let us say, a red spirit will rush out of it.' We would come to the bush and [he] would say, 'Some red thing has come out of the bush.' I once took him to a faery rath and evoked, but when I tried to speak to him I got no answer. He was entranced with his arms round a great elm tree. When he awoke he declared that his soul had flowed in the sap through the elm. I had as yet no suspicion that the beautiful Fiona was but a secondary personality,[2] elaborated by a conscious or half-conscious mystification (see letter in appendix),[3] excited it would seem at first by the presence of some woman. When I stayed at Tulira to meet him, I found Martyn full of derision over some tale he had told after dinner the night before to Martin Morris, now Lord Killanin, an unsympathetic hearer, and himself. He had been somewhere abroad when he saw the sideral body of Fiona enter the room as a beautiful young man, and became aware that he was a woman to the spiritual sight. She lay with him, he said, as a man with a woman, and for days afterwards his breasts swelled so that he had almost the physical likeness of a woman.

[1] Yeats to Katharine Tynan, 1 July 1887: 'I was introduced to Sharp of the *Sonnets of This Century* and hated his red British face of flaccid contentment.' *Letters* (Wade), pp. 42–3.

[2] Elizabeth A. Sharp writes in *William Sharp: A Memoir by His Wife* (London, Heinemann, 1910), p. 424: 'In a lecture given by Mr Yeats to the Aberdeen Centre of the Franco-Scottish Society in 1907 the Irish poet referred to his friend. He considered that "Sharp had in many ways an extraordinarily primitive mind. He was fond of speaking of himself as the representative of the old bards," and the Irish poet thought there was really something in the claim. . . . He continued that W.S. was the most extraordinary psychic he had ever encountered. He really believed that "Fiona Macleod was a secondary personality – as distinct a secondary personality as those one reads about in books of psychical research. At times he [W.S.] was really to all intents and purposes a different being."'

[3] Yeats does not give the letter: the manuscript does not contain an appendix. The letter may be the one described on p. 288, where Elizabeth A. Sharp quotes from a letter which accords fairly well with Yeats's account.

XLII

AE (George Russell), a visionary of another type, stayed both at Coole and at Tulira while I was there. The fluidic world flowed less through him than before him, and left his mind unclouded and untroubled. I had a little while before introduced him to Sir Horace Plunkett,[1] and he was becoming the dominant influence in the Agriculture Organization Society. He had taken up the question of the agricultural banks, and in six months had founded more than had been founded in ten years. And yet he had said to me, 'How can I do this work, who never yet read a book through that is not in verse?' He had at first refused Horace Plunkett's offer, though it more than trebled his income in the large shop where he was accountant, because his followers had need of him. He only consented when I brought them in deputation to say – the thought and wording were their own – that they were becoming his shadows, and would find themselves, perhaps, if he went away. Of recent years our friendship, that began in the Dublin art school, has been strained rather than broken. He has the religious genius, and it is the essence of that genius that all souls are equal in its eyes. Queen or apple woman, it is all one, seeing that none can be more than an immortal soul. Whereas I have been concerned with men's capacities, with all [that] divides man from man. I seem to him harsh, hypercritical, overbearing even, and he seems to encourage in all the arts the spirit of the amateur.

Our relations were now strained by something else, and more temporary. He saw constantly before him in vision an extraordinary world, the nature spirits as he believed, and I wished him to record all as Swedenborg had recorded, and submit his clairvoyance to certain tests. This seemed to him an impiety, and perhaps the turning towards it of the analytic intellect[2] checked his gift, and he became extremely angry; and my insistence on understanding

---

[1] Sir Horace Plunkett (1854–1932). Member of Parliament 1892–1900. In 1894 he founded the Irish Agriculture Organization Society.

[2] 'But I, whose virtues are the definitions
   Of the analytic mind, can neither close
   The eye of the mind nor keep my tongue from speech.'
                        'The People', *Collected Poems*, p. 170.

symbolically what he took for literal truth increased his anger. Presently he softened and gave a detailed account of the light that rayed from the ascending degrees of the nature spirits and my three worlds, that of the nature spirits or watery world, that of the heavens, and that of the gods. My neighbourhood disturbed him, making his visions take on a form he disliked, an obviously symbolic form – there were even winged angels. His vision was probably higher, I thought, than any that came to me except in sleep, and of his sleep I knew nothing. He believed that every night, as before birth, the soul hung as upon a cross and saw its life and all its sorrow and willed that life, knowing it for just.

I thought his waking vision higher than mine from an experiment. Once while we were seeing at the same time without telling each other what we saw, I could but see a savage man prostrate before an idol while he saw a man's soul hovering in mid-air before a vast divinity. I saved him once from morbid melancholy and temptation. He was painting a stagnant deep pool in a clump of trees at Coole, and was morose and melancholy. I divined that something was wrong, for with men of his kind all is an evocation, and not daring to give him a symbol, persuaded him to paint the garden in hot sunlight. At once he became cheerful again and told me that he had seen in the stagnant pool figures that promised him all wisdom if he would but drown himself. It was not at the pool side he was worst tempted, but at night: they stood perpetually beside his bed.

XLIII

I joined Maud Gonne from time to time, once at Belfast, where she [had] gone on some political mission, sometimes at Paris, often in Dublin. In Dublin I never went to the same hotel, fearing to compromise her, though she often laughed at my scruple. Once she complained that she saw too much of me. 'I do not say', she said, 'that the crowds are in love with me, but they would hate anybody who was.' But I never failed to get my letter saying when we could meet. One morning I woke in my hotel somewhere near Rutland Square with the fading vision of her face bending over mine and the knowledge that she had just kissed me. I joined her after breakfast in the Nassau Hotel. We were to spend the day together and visit in the afternoon the old Fenian leader, James Stephens. She said, 'Had you a strange dream last night?' I said, 'I dreamed this morning for the first time in my life that you kissed me.' She made no answer, but late that night when dinner was over and I was about to return home she said, 'I will tell you now what happened. When I fell asleep last night I saw standing at my bedside a great spirit. He took me to a great throng of spirits, and you were among them. My hand was put into yours and I was told that we were married. After that I remember nothing.' Then and there for the first time with the bodily mouth, she kissed me.

The next day I found her sitting very gloomily over the fire. 'I should not have spoken to you in that way,' she said, 'for I can never be your wife in reality.' I said, 'Do you love anyone else?' and she said 'No' but added that there was somebody else, and that she had to be a moral nature for two. Then bit by bit came out the story of her life, things I had heard all twisted awry by scandal, and disbelieved.

She had met in the South of France the French Boulangist deputy, Millevoye,[1] while staying with a relative in her nineteenth year, and had at once and without any urging on his part fallen in love with him. She then returned to Dublin where her father[2] had a military command.[3] She had sat one night over the fire thinking over her future life. She longed to have control over her own life, and chance discovery of some book on magic among her father's books had made her believe that the Devil, if she prayed to him, might help her. He was rather a real personage to her, for in her earlier girlhood she had wanted to join a convent. She asked the Devil to give her control of her own life and offered in return her soul. At that moment the clock struck twelve, and she felt of a

[1] Lucien Millevoye, French political journalist, editor of *La Patrie*.

[2] The words from the beginning of the present paragraph up to this point are deleted, but they are required by the narrative.

[3] Colonel Thomas Gonne was Assistant Adjutant-General in Dublin. Sean O'Casey has the following passage in *Inishfallen, Fare Thee Well*: 'There she sits stonily silent, once a sibyl of patriotism from whom no oracle ever came; now silent and aged; her deep-set eyes now sad, agleam with disappointment; never quite at ease with the crowd, whose cheers she loved; the colonel's daughter still.' O'Casey, *Autobiographies II* (London, Macmillan, 1963 edition), pp. 152–3.

sudden that the prayer had been heard and answered. Within a fortnight her father died suddenly, and she was stricken with remorse.

She had control of her life now, and when she was of age settled in Paris, and after some months became Millevoye's mistress. She was often away from him, for sexual love soon began to repel her, but was for all that very much in love. Then he failed her in various ways. But [she] gave me no coherent account and when I asked some questions clenched her hands together and said it was not well to speak of such things. He had, I discovered, at one time urged her to become the mistress of one man to help his political projects, and that she had refused. Then a little boy was born, the adopted child I had been told of – she thought that sexual love was only justified by children. If the boy had not died, she would have broken with Millevoye altogether and lived in Ireland. As it was, after its death she had thought of breaking with him, and had engaged herself for a week to someone else – I thought, I may have had that poor betrothal for my reward – but had broken it off. The idea came to her that the lost child might be reborn, and she had gone back to Millevoye, in the vault under the memorial chapel. A girl child was born, now two years old.[1] Since the child's birth, I understood her to say amid so much broken speech, she and Millevoye had lived apart.

But she was necessary to him, 'She did not know what would happen to him if her influence was not there.' I wonder as I write these words if I rightly understood, if she had not [in] mind some service he might fall from, to a political ideal. I thought at the time that [she] was appeasing a troubled conscience by performing to the last tittle every duty, and Lady Gregory confirmed me later in this thought. And in all that followed I was careful to touch [her] as one might a sister. If she was to come to me, it must be from no temporary passionate impulse, but with the approval of her conscience. Many a time since then, as I lay awake at night, have I accused myself of acting, not as I thought from a high scruple, but from a dread of moral responsibility, and my thoughts have gone round and round, as do miserable thoughts, coming to no solution.

[1] Iseult Gonne (1895-1954).

A little later, how many days I do not remember, we were sitting together when she said, 'I hear a voice saying, "You are about to receive the initiation of the spear."' We became silent; a double vision unfolded itself, neither speaking till all was finished. She thought herself a great stone statue through which passed flame, and I felt myself becoming flame and mounting up through and looking out of the eyes of a great stone Minerva. Were the beings which stand behind human life trying to unite us, or had we brought it by our own dreams? She was now always very emotional, and would kiss me very tenderly, but when I spoke of marriage on the eve of her leaving said, 'No, it seems to me impossible.' And then, with clenched hands, 'I have a horror and terror of physical love.' Lady Gregory was in Venice, but had come home at once on receiving from me an incoherent letter. She offered me money to travel, and told me not to leave Maud Gonne till I had her promise of marriage, but I said, 'No, I am too exhausted; I can do no more.'[1]

---

[1] On the last leaf of the manuscript there is a working draft, barely decipherable, of the opening lines of 'Lines Written in Dejection', as follows. (× before a line means that the entire line is deleted in the manuscript):

× No longer can the moon

× The round green eyes, the long wavering bodies
× of the dark leopards of the moon
× No longer the moon
× Can send me no longer the green eyed leopards and the wavering bodies
× The green eyed leopards of the moon
× Now die the old hares in the grass and all the wild witches and lovers
   That

'Lines Written in Dejection' was first published in *The Wild Swans at Coole* (Cuala Press, 1917). Richard Ellmann gives October (?) 1915 as the date of composition. Another draft of the poem appears in the 'Maud Gonne' Notebook. The definitive text is *Collected Poems*, pp. 163-4.

Journal

Journal

W. B. Yeats

Abbey Theatre Dublin
and
18 Woburn Buildings, Euston Road, London

Private

1

Why should I blame her that she filled my days
With misery, or that she would of late
Have taught to ignorant men most violent ways
Or hurled the little streets upon the great
Had they but courage equal to desire?
What could have made her peaceful with a mind
That nobleness made simple as a fire,
With/And beauty like a tightened bow, a kind
That is not natural in an age like this
Being high and solitary and most stern
Why what could she have done being what she is?
Was there another Troy for her to burn?[1]

December 1908

2

The other day in Paris[2] I found that for days I lost all social presence
of mind through the very ordinary folly of a very ordinary person. I
heard in every word she spoke ancient enemies of vanity and senti-
mentality, and became rude and, according[ly], miserable. This is my
worst fault, rooted in ♂ ♀ ☽.[3] I must watch myself carefully, recording

---

[1] 'No Second Troy', *Collected Poems*, p. 101.
[2] Yeats spent December 1908 in Paris, working on *The Player Queen*, taking French
lessons and seeing Maud Gonne.
[3] Mars in opposition to Moon.

errors that I may become interested in their cure. Perhaps I should seek out people I dislike till I have conquered this petulant combativeness. It is always inexcusable to lose one's self-possession. It always comes from impatience, from a kind of spiritual fright at someone who is here and now more powerful, even if only from stupidity. I am never angry with those in my power. I fear strangers; I fear the representatives of the collective opinion, and so rage stupidly and rudely, exaggerating what I feel and think.

3

Dec. 13 [1908]. Have been looking through *Collected Works*, volume VII.[1] I now see what is wrong with 'Tables of the Law'. The hero must not seem for a moment a shadow of the hero of 'Rosa Alchemica'. He is not the mask but the face. He realizes himself. He cannot obtain vision in the ordinary sense. He is himself the centre. Perhaps he dreams he is speaking. He is not spoken to. He puts himself in place of Christ. He is not the revolt of multitude. What did the woman in Paris reveal to the Magi?[2] Surely some reconciliation between face and mask? Does the narrator refuse this manuscript, and so never learn its contents? Is it simply the doctrine of the Mask? The choosing of some one mask? Hardly, for that would but be the imitation of Christ in a new form. Is it becoming mask after mask? Perhaps the name only should be given, 'Mask and Face'. Yet the nature of the man seems to prepare for a continual change, a phantasmagoria. One day one god and the next another.

The imitation of Christ as distinguished from the self-realization of the 'Tables of the Law'. What of it? Christ is but another self, but he is the supernatural self.

4

Jan. 14 [1909]. Last night there was a debate on a political question at the Arts Club.[3] I was for a moment inclined to use arguments

[1] Published in December 1908.   [2] In 'The Adoration of the Magi'.
[3] Yeats became a member of the United Arts Club, Dublin, on 28 May 1908, and a Vice-President on 29 June 1910.

merely to answer something said by one speaker or the other. In pursuit of the mask I resolved to say only fanciful and personal things, and so to escape out of mere combat. I did so, and I noticed that all the arguments which had occurred to me earlier were said by someone or other. Logic is a machine; one can leave it to itself; unhelped it will force those present to exhaust the subject. The fool is as likely as the sage to speak the appropriate answer to any assertion. If an argument is forgotten, somebody will go home miserable. You throw your money on the table, and you receive so much change. Style, personality (deliberately adopted and therefore a mask), is the only escape from all the heat of the bargaining, from all but the sight of the money changers.

5

To keep these notes natural and useful to me in my life I must keep one note from leading on to another. To do that is to surrender oneself to literature. Every note must first have come as a casual thought, then it will be my life. If Christ or Buddha or Socrates had written, they would have surrendered life for a logical process.[1]

6

Jan. 22 [1909]. I have been talking to one of the group around George Russell, typical of the new class which is rising in Ireland: often not ill-bred in manner and therefore the more manifestly with the ill-breeding of the mind. Every thought made in some manufactory, and with the mark upon it of its wholesale origin – all those thoughts which were never really thought out in their current form in any individual mind, being the creation of impersonal mechanism – of schools, of textbooks, of newspapers, these above all. There thus was that confidence which the first thinker of anything never has, for all thinkers are alike in this, they approach the truth full of hesitation and doubt, the timidity of the laboratory. Confidence comes from

[1] This sentence is clearer in a later version: 'Neither Christ nor Buddha nor Socrates wrote a book, for to do that is to exchange life for a logical process.' *Autobiographies*, p. 461.

repetition, from the breath of many mouths. This ill-breeding of the mind is far more destructive than the mere bad manners that spits on the floor. Is not all charm inherited? – whether of the intellect, of the manners, or of character, or of literature? A great lady is as simple as a good poet. Both possess nothing that is not ancient and their own, and both are full of uncertainty about everything but themselves, about everything that can be changed, about all that they merely think. They assume certainties, to the one fashions, to the other opinion, and re-mould all slightly.

7

A conversation. I was telling Miss Young[1] how Nevinson[2] had said to me that no European army would fight again even as well as those of France and Prussia fought in 1870. He said, 'It is not that Wellington's peasants believed in another life. They were not aware enough to know what they believed. They fought well because the personal imagination had not been aroused by education. Today we all (I admit to it myself among the rest) have realized that the worst thing that could happen us would be to be dead.' He has been in more danger than any man I know, in practically every European war for years. Miss Young replied with an air of immeasurable patronage, 'Once upon a time men thought dishonour was worse than death.'

8

I have had a curious breakdown of some sort.[3] I had been working hard, and suddenly I found I could not use my mind on any serious subject. Yet at this moment I cannot tell if the whole thing was not a slight indisposition brought on by too much smoking heightened by that kind of nervous fright I get from time to time: the fear of losing my inspiration by absorption in outer things. The poet's enemies are those industries that make a good citizen. A poet is a

[1] The poetess Ella Young (1867–1956).

[2] Henry W. Nevinson (1856–1941), war correspondent. His account of his friendship with Yeats appeared in the *London Mercury*, vol. 39, no. 233, March 1939.

[3] Yeats mentions this breakdown in a letter (? March 1909) to Florence Farr. *Letters* (Wade), p. 526.

good citizen turned inside out. I do not know whether these attacks of nerves are a sign from within telling me that I should leave this theatre at all cost, or only old combativeness disguised because I feel that I was sacrificed to Fay, who should have been sternly dealt with when he showed himself insubordinate.[1] It was he who made the present arrangement necessary. If it is this last, I must resist it. If Lady Gregory, who has done so much for me, made, as I believe, this one mistake, I must endure the results with patience and good will.

9

The reviews of *The Miser*[2] in papers today – an article in Thursday's *Sinn Féin* – showed the old dislike of farce and dialect. Written by men who are essentially parvenus in intellectual things, they shudder a little at all that is not obviously and notoriously refined. It is the objection to the word 'shift' in a new form.[3] Our own secretary,[4] I can see, has a deep hatred of Molière. None of these people can get out of their heads the idea that we are exaggerating the farce of Molière. We really reduce it. Years ago Dr Sigerson said of the last verse of my 'Moll Magee', 'Why candles? Surely tapers.' For the same reason the writers – I notice particularly in this the younger men – generally put into their articles every name of a foreign writer they happen to think of.

10

Today the thought came to me that PIAL[5] never really understands my plans, or nature, or ideas. Then came the thought, what matter?

[1] W. G. Fay demanded that the Directors of the Abbey Theatre appoint him manager and producer: this was refused, and he resigned on 13 January 1908. (Fay gives his side of the row in W. G. Fay and Catherine Carswell, *The Fays of the Abbey Theatre* (1935), pp. 223 ff.) His resignation led to one of the most quarrelsome periods in the history of the Abbey.
[2] Lady Gregory's translation was first performed on 21 January 1909.
[3] In the performance of Synge's *The Playboy of the Western World* on 26 January 1907, Christy Mahon's reference to 'a drift of chosen females standing in their shifts' was deemed offensive.
[4] W. A. Henderson, Secretary of the Abbey Theatre 1906–12.
[5] Maud Gonne's initials as a member of the Order of the Golden Dawn: she was initiated on 1 December 1891. The present thought is turned into verse in no. 12, a draft of 'Words', *Collected Poems*, pp. 100–1. See also entry no. 15, p. 144.

How much of the best I have done and still do is but the attempt to explain myself to her? If she understood, I should lack a reason for writing, and one never can have too many reasons for doing what is so laborious.

11

To oppose the new ill-breeding of Ireland, which may in a few years destroy all that has given Ireland a distinguished name in the world ('Oh Ireland, mother of the bravest soldiers and the most beautiful women,' cried Borrow when he thought of the hospitality shown to him, a distributor of Bibles, by the Irish monks in Spain), I can only set up a secondary or interior personality created by me out of the tradition of myself, and this personality (alas, to me only possible in my writings) must be always gracious and simple. It must have that slight separation from immediate interests which makes charm possible, while remaining near enough for fire. Is not charm what it is, perhaps, because it is an escape from mechanism? So much of the world as is dominated by the contest of interests is a mechanism. The newspaper is the roar of the machine. Argument, the moment acknowledged victory is sought, becomes a clash of interests. One should not, above all not in books, which sigh for immortality, argue at all if one is not ready to leave to another apparent victory. In daily life one becomes rude the moment one grudges to the clown his perpetual triumph.

12

I had this thought an ~~hour/~~while ago
×   I thought of this a while
    I suddenly thought an hour ago
    My darling cannot understand
    What I have done, or what would do
    In this blind bitter land
×   And I was dashed to think of it
    And I grew sorry thinking it
×   I had grown sorry at the thought
    Until my thought ~~grew clear/~~cleared up again
    Remembering that the best I have writ

Was ~~but~~/writ to make ~~it~~/all plain
~~That/How~~/That every year ~~I have said~~/I've cried at length
~~She'll~~/She can but understand it all
Because ~~I've~~/I have come into my strength
And words obey my call
× ~~But~~/And had she done so He can say
× Who shook me from his sieve
× If I'd have thrown poor words away
× And been content to live.
               or else this verse
× ~~But/And/How~~/That had she done so ~~He~~/who can say
× ~~Who~~/But he that shook me from his sieve
× ~~Whether~~/If I'd have thrown poor words away
× And been content to live.

That had she done so – who can say
What would have shaken from the sieve –
I might ~~then~~/have thrown poor words away
And been content to live.[1]

                                January 22 [1909]

13

I have just had a letter telling me that poor W. Fay and his wife are close to starvation in London. They got home from America with savings, £40 it seems, but this money is now almost gone. I keep asking myself if we could have him back in the Abbey. To do so is to endanger the whole discipline of the Theatre, and to spend on paying him money which the actors who have stuck to us have a right to feel they have earned. And yet he is an actor of genius. His whole generation were either useless to the arts, or almost so. He, like most of the actors who have left us for one reason or other, grew up at a time when nothing outside the ordinary business of life in Ireland was taken seriously but politics. He for all his genius could not take his own art seriously. He could not make himself work at it. He prided himself instead upon management, which made him

       [1] 'Words', *Collected Poems*, pp. 100–1.

important in the eyes of his friends, and he had not the self-control for that. Miss Quinn,[1] Miss Walker,[2] and the others were the same. Politics had made them sterile. They could not work seriously at their art, and they could not see it with pure eyes and love it for its own sake. We got no good writers until we got to a generation which more or less grew up under the influence of our own movement. To the rest, the arts were merely a necessary part of a programme of national life. Even those who were not consciously politicians were influenced by the general way of looking at things. Even the highest political motives will not make an artist.

14

My sister says that my father says, 'A man does not love a woman because he thinks her clever or because he admires her, but because he likes the way she has of scratching her head.'

15

Jan. 23 [1909]. The second and third stanzas of poem written yesterday should read:

> I had grown weary of the sun;
> Until my thoughts cleared up again
> Remembering that the best I~~'ve~~/have done
> Was done to make it plain;
>
> That every year I have cried 'At length
> My darling understands it all
> Because I have come into my strength
> And words obey my call.'

16

It seems to me that love, if it is fine, is essentially a discipline, but it needs so much wisdom that the love of Solomon and Sheba must

---

[1] Máire T. Quinn, Abbey actress, left the Company in 1903 following a dispute about *The Shadow of the Glen.*

[2] Marie Walker Abbey actress, better known as Máire Nic Shiubhlaigh.

have lasted for all the silence of the Scriptures. In wise love each divines the high secret self of the other and, refusing to believe in the mere daily self, creates a mirror where the lover or the beloved sees an image to copy in daily life. Love also creates the mask.

17

My dear is angry that of late
I cry all base blood down
As though she had not taught me hate
By ~~kindness~~/kisses to a clown.[1]

18

Our modern poetry is imaginative. It is the poetry of the young. The poetry of the greatest periods is an expression of the appetites and habits. Hence we select where they exhausted. Jan. 24 [1909].

19

Something brings to mind that I forgot out of 'The Pathway'[2] this saying of Mohini's.[3] 'When I was young I was very happy. I thought truth was something that could be conveyed from one man's mind to another's. I now know that it is a state of mind.'

20

A conversation. Last night I met Birrell.[4] There was some rich man there, and some person spoke of the great power that wealth might have for good. The rich man was talking of starting a deer forest in Connacht. Birrell said, 'Wealth has very little power, it can really do

---

[1] The marriage of Maud Gonne and John MacBride, which took place in Paris on 21 February 1903, ended in 1905. This poem was not published.

[2] An essay, first published as 'The Way of Wisdom', in the *Speaker*, 14 April 1900, and reprinted as 'The Pathway' in *Collected Works*, vol. 8 (1908).

[3] Mohini Chatterji, a Bengali Brahmin whom Yeats met in Dublin in 1885 or 1886. 'Mohini Chatterji', *Collected Poems*, pp. 279–80.

[4] Augustine Birrell (1850–1933), Chief Secretary for Ireland from 1907 to 1916.

very little.' I said, 'Yet every now and then one meets some charming person who likes all fine things and is quite delightful and who would not have had these qualities if some great-grandfather had not sold his country for gold.' Birrell answered, 'I admit that wealth occasionally – Darwin was an example – enables someone to write a great book.' I answered, 'Oh, that was not what I was thinking of. I meant that it creates the fine life which we look at with affectionate eyes out of our garret windows. We must not leave our garrets, but we could not write well but for what we see from the windows.' Then Birrell answered, 'Then writers are parasites.'[1] I noticed that most of the other guests, two or three judges among them, seemed, beside Birrell and the rich man, too sympathetic and anxious to please; I myself among the rest. Birrell and the rich man did not care a bean for any of us. We talked, they were talked to.

21

Dean Bernard[2] was there too, a charming and intelligent man, but with the too ingratiating manner of certain highly educated Catholic priests, a manner one does not think compatible with deep spiritual experience. We discussed self-realization and self-sacrifice. He said that classic self-realization had failed and yet the victory of Christian self-sacrifice had plunged the world into the Dark Ages. I reminded him of some Norse god, who was hung over an abyss for three days, 'a sacrifice to himself', to show that the two were not incompatible, but he answered, 'Von Hartmann[3] discusses the question whether the soul may not sacrifice itself, even to the losing of itself, for some good end.' I said, 'That is the problem of my *Countess Cathleen*,' and he said, 'It is a further problem whether a nation may make this sacrifice.' He must have been thinking of Ireland.[4]

[1] Cf. no. 188, pp. 230.

[2] John Henry Bernard (1860–1927), Dean of St Patrick's Cathedral 1902–11, Protestant Archbishop of Dublin 1915–19, Provost of Trinity College, Dublin, 1919–27.

[3] Karl Robert Eduard von Hartmann (1842–1906), German philosopher, author of *The Philosophy of the Unconscious* (1869).

[4] Across nos. 20 and 21 Yeats later wrote:
Augustine Birrell dreams he has found a trick
To juggle out of sight the natural laws

22

When I rewrite 'The Adoration of the Magi' I see clearly that the message given to the old men must be a series of seemingly arbitrary commands: a year of silence, certain rules of diet, and so on. Without the arbitrary there cannot be religion – is the idea, because there cannot be the last sacrifice, that of the spirit. The recorder should refuse the care of the MS on hearing that it contains not wisdom but the supernaturally sanctioned arbitrary, the commanded pose which would make all definite. Mere wisdom would die, he knows, like any other living breath. The tree has to die before it can be made into a cross.

23

Colum has lent me his *Desert*.[1] Read for a few pages anywhere and it is remarkable enough – temperament, ideas, the matrix of genius. He has no will, he gives himself to every sensation in turn, and though he has made for himself a great opportunity by taking drifting and vagueness for his theme he does not embody his meaning. One keeps asking what has this or that to do with the subject. He is the one victim of George Russell's misunderstanding of life that I rage over. Russell, because a man of genius, needs more education than anybody else, and he has read little and taught those about him to read little. With all the fanaticism of the religious reformer, he has taught many to despise all that does not come out of their own minds and to trust to vision to do the work of intellect; and minds in which there is nothing original turn with arrogance against every talent that does not please them at the first glance. A luxurious dreaming, a kind of spiritual lubricity takes the place of logic and will. A sensitive, naturally dreaming man like Colum, even if he does not

And grow a self-sufficient man because
He that was once a flea is now a tick.
Another version
No more a parasite, he has learned the trick
To change a lively flea into a tick.

[1] Padraic Colum, *Mogu the Wanderer : or, The Desert* (Boston, 1917). Yeats has written in the margin beside this entry: 'I am not sure that I was right about *The Desert*. It clings so to the memory. 11 August 1909.'

consciously share their ideas, is lost in a world like this, a world where no technique is respected, no merely laborious attainment applauded, but where all the bad passions of the disappointed sit like crows. Nothing is respected except successes – generally small political ones – which are too far from the arts to be jealous of, and dreams for the future that perish in conversation. It is the wreckage of youthful enthusiasms that were led away from life instead of being set to build there some house for body or mind.

24

I have noticed that when these men take to any kind of action it is to some kind of extreme politics. Partly, I think, because they have never learned the discipline which enables the most ardent natures to accept obtainable things, even if a little sadly; but still more because they cannot believe in any success that is not in the remote future, and because, like the artist described by Balzac in *Unconscious Mummers*,[1] they long for popularity that they may believe in themselves. There is also the desire of the weak for strong sensation.

25

Russell endures them because he has the religious genius, and to the religious genius all souls are of equal value: the queen is not more than an apple-woman. His poetical genius does not affect his mind as a whole, and probably he puts aside as unworthy every suggestion of his poetical genius which would separate man from man. The most fundamental of all divisions is that between the intellect which can only do its work by saying continually 'thou fool', and the religious genius which makes all equal. That is why we have discovered that the mountain-top and the monastery are necessary to civiliza-

---

[1] 'Balzac, in *Les Comédiens sans le Savoir*, describes a sculptor, a follower of the Socialist Fourier, who has made an allegorical figure of Harmony, and got into his statue the doctrine of his master by giving it six breasts and by putting under its feet an enormous Savoy cabbage.' *Explorations*, p. 238; also p. 271. The sculptor is Dubourdieu.

tion. Civilization dies of all those things that feed the soul, and both die if the Remnant[1] refuse the wilderness. Jan. 25 [1909].

26

An error of the group is to continually make[2] a philosophical idea for a spiritual experience. The very preoccupation of the intellect with the soul destroys that experience, for everywhere impressions are checked by opinion. I heard one member of it, Ella Young, speak the other day with scorn of someone who could not distinguish beauty from beautiful things. I said to so distinguish it was very hard. She said she found it quite easy. An abstract opinion and a vague sentiment seemed to her one thing with the supreme perception of mystic meditation, attained but twice, if I remember rightly, by Proclus. Another of them, Norman,[3] said to Evans[4] at his Bible class that he was surprised that he had not more to say about 'Faith, Hope, and Charity', because he himself 'could go on about them for three weeks'. Evans answered, 'There would be more religion in three weeks of silence.' With them, the experience of the soul is lived out not with emotion or desire, or with facts, but with opinions; and their opinions, fed by no learning, are in the end the commonplaces of theosophical textbooks.

27

Any real life being despised is only prized when sentimentalized over, and so the soul is shut off alike from earth and Heaven.

28

Ella Young: 'We have such a wonderful cat and it is so full of dignity that if the kitten goes to take its food it leaves the dish. It will not

---

[1] Reviewing John Eglinton's *Two Essays on the Remnant* (Dublin, 1895) Yeats said the book was 'a passionate and lofty appeal to the "idealists" to come out of the modern world as the children of Egypt came out of Egypt.' *Uncollected Prose*, vol. I, p. 357.

[2] 'mistake', *Autobiographies*, p. 467.

[3] Harry F. Norman (1868–1947), Assistant Secretary of the Irish Agriculture Organization Society; editor of *The Irish Homestead* from *c*. 1899 to 1905; one of the original members of the Irish National Theatre Society.

[4] Edward Evans, a member of the Arts Club. He became a lay brother in the Anglican Franciscan Order.

struggle. If will not assert itself. And, what's more, our cat won't eat at all if there is not a perfectly clean napkin spread under the plate. I assure you it's quite true. I have often noticed it. It will not eat if there is even a spot on the napkin.'

29[1]

When Russell and I were fellow-students at the art school there was a strange mad pious student who used to come in sometimes with a daisy chain round his neck. Russell lent him a little theosophical book, *Light on the Path*. He stayed away for several days and then came one day looking very troubled. He gave the book back saying, 'You will drift into a penumbra.'

30

In Christianity what was philosophy in Eastern Asia became life – biography, drama. A play passes through the same process in being written. At first, if it has psychological depth, there is a bundle of ideas, something that can be stated in philosophical terms; my *Countess Cathleen*, for instance, was once the moral question, may a soul sacrifice itself for a good end? – but gradually philosophy is eliminated more and more until at last the only philosophy audible, if there is even that, is the mere expression of one character or another. When it is completely life it seems to the hasty reader a mere story. Was the *Bhagavad Gita* the 'scenario' from which the Gospels were made?

31

Jan. 26 [1909]. One reason for the tendency of the Russell group to extreme political opinion is that a taste fed for long on milk diet thirsts for strong flavours. In England the reaction would be vice, in Ireland it is politics.

32

Ella Young: 'O, it was not because of the pictures that I said I liked

───────────

[1] Wrongly numbered 28 in MS.

Mr Lane's gallery.[1] I like it because it has such a beautiful atmosphere, because of the muffed glass.'[2]

33

All empty souls tend to extreme opinions. It is only in those who have built up a rich world of memories and habits of thought that extreme opinions affront the sense of probability. All propositions, for instance, which set all the truth upon one side can only enter rich minds to dislocate and strain, if they can enter at all, and sooner or later the mind expels them by instinct.

34

There is a relation between discipline and the theatrical sense. If we cannot imagine ourselves as different from what we are and try to assume that second self, we cannot impose a discipline upon ourselves, though we may accept one from others. Active virtue as distinguished from the passive acceptance of a current code is therefore theatrical, consciously dramatic, the wearing of a mask. It is the condition of arduous full life. One constantly notices in very active natures a tendency to pose, or a preoccupation with the effect they are producing if the pose has become a second self. One notices this in Plutarch's heroes, and every now and then in some modern who has tried to live by classical ideas, in Oscar Wilde, for instance, and less obviously in men like Walt Whitman. Wordsworth is so often flat and heavy partly because his moral sense has no theatrical element, it is an obedience, a discipline which he has not created. This increases his popularity with the better sort of journalists, the *Spectator* writers, for instance, with all who are part of the machine and yet care for poetry.

35

All my life I have been haunted with the idea that the poet should

---

[1] Sir Hugh Lane (1875–1915), art collector: his gallery was at Clonmell House, 17 Harcourt Street, Dublin.
[2] Muff or muffle, 'to render [glass] semi-opaque by giving it a crinkled surface', *O.E.D.*

know all classes of men as one of themselves, that he should combine the greatest possible personal realization with the greatest possible knowledge of the speech and circumstance of the world. Fifteen or twenty years ago I remember longing, with this purpose, to disguise myself as a peasant and wander through the West, and then shipping as a sailor. But when one shrinks from even talking business with a stranger, and is unnatural till one knows a man for months, because one underrates or overrates all unknown people, one cannot adventure far. The artist grows more and more distinct, more and more a being in his own right as it were, but more and more loses grasp of the always more complex world. Some day setting out to find knowledge, like some pilgrim to the Holy Land, he will become the most romantic of all characters. He will play with all masks.

36

Tragedy is passion alone and, instead of character, it gets form from motives, the wandering of passion; while comedy is the clash of character. Eliminate character from comedy and you get farce. Farce is bound together by incident alone. (Eliminate passion from tragedy and you get melodrama.) In practice most works are mixed: Shakespeare being tragicomedy. Comedy is joyous because all assumption of a part, of a personal mask, whether the individualized face of comedy or the grotesque face of farce, is a display of energy, and all energy is joyous. A poet creates tragedy from his own soul, that soul which is alike in all men, and at moments it has no joy, as we understand that word, for the soul is an exile and without will. It attains to ecstasy, which is from the contemplation of things which are vaster than the individual and imperfectly seen, perhaps, by all those that still live. The masks of tragedy contain neither character nor personal energy. They are allied to decoration and to the abstract figures of Egyptian temples. Before the mind can look out of their eyes the active will perishes, hence their sorrowful calm. Joy is of the will which does things, which overcomes obstacles, which is victorious. The soul only knows changes of state. These changes of state, or this gradually enlarging consciousness, is the self-realization of modern culture. I think the motives of tragedy are connected more with these changes of state than with action. I feel this but cannot see my way clearly. But I am hunting truth too far into its thicket. It is my business to keep close to the impression of the senses, and to daily thought. Yet is not always the tragic ecstasy some realization or fulfilment of the soul in itself, some slow or sudden expansion of it like an overflowing well? Is not that what we mean by beauty?

37

Jan. 28 [1909]. The tragic mask expresses a passion or mood, a state of the soul; that only. (The mask of musician or of the dying slave.) The mask of comedy an individual. (Any modern picture.) The mask of farce an energy; in this the joyous life by its own excess has become superficial, it has driven out thought. (Any grotesque head.) Then these are connected in some way with the dominant moods of the three classes which have given the cradles, as it were, to tragedy, comedy, and farce: aristocracy, the middle class, and the people – exaltation, moral force, labour.

38

Allingham[1] and Davis are two different kinds of love of Ireland. In Allingham I find the entire emotion for the place one grew up in which I felt as a child and which I sometimes hear of from people of my own class. Davis was possessed on the other hand with ideas of Ireland, with conscious patriotism. His Ireland was artificial, an idea built up in a couple of generations by a few commonplace men. This artificial idea has done me as much harm as the other has helped me. I tried to free myself from it, and all my enemies come from my fighting it in others. The beauty of peasant thought comes partly from its naturalness, from its being unspoiled by this artificial town-made thought. One cannot sum up a nation intellectually, and when the summing up is made by half-educated men the very idea fills one with alarm. I remember when I was nine or ten years old walking along Kensington High Road[2] so full of love for the fields and roads

---

[1] William Allingham (1824–89), poet of Ballyshannon, Co. Donegal. Author of *Day and Night Songs* (1854) and *Laurence Bloomfield in Ireland* (1864). Yeats wrote of Allingham's poetry in his Introduction to *A Book of Irish Verse* (London, Methuen, 1895).

[2] 'Kensington High Street', *Autobiographies*, p. 472.

of Sligo that I longed – a strange ritual of sentiment for a child – for earth from a road there that I might kiss it. I had no politics; a couple of years before, I had read with delight a volume of Orange verses belonging to my grandmother's stable-boy, and my mother, who loved Sligo where she had been born and bred with the same passion, was, if she had any politics, Unionist. That love was instinctive and left the soul free. If I could have kept it and yet never felt the influence of Young Ireland I had given a more profound picture of Ireland in my work. Synge's purity of genius comes in part from having kept this instinct and this alone. Emotion is always justified by time, thought hardly ever. It can only bring us back to emotion.

39

Jan. 31 [1909]. I went to see Synge yesterday and found him ill: if he dies it will set me wondering whether he could have lived if he had not had his long, bitter misunderstanding with the wreckage of Young Irelandism. Even a successful performance of one of his plays seems to have made him ill. My sister reminded me of this the other day and urged me not to revive the *Playboy* while he is ill. In one thing he and Lady Gregory are the strongest souls I have ever known. He and she alike have never for even an instant spoken to me the thoughts of their inferiors as their own thoughts. I have never known them to lose the self-possession of their intellects. All the others here – even Moore for all his defiance – possess their own thoughts above the general flood only for a season, and Moore has in addition an extreme combativeness that makes even his original thought a reaction, not a creation. Both Synge and Lady Gregory isolate themselves, Synge instinctively and Lady Gregory consciously, from all contagious opinions of poorer minds: Synge so instinctively and naturally – helped certainly by the habits of an invalid – that no one is conscious of rejection. Lady Gregory's life is too energetic and complex for her rejections to be other than deliberate. I do neither one nor the other, being too talkative, too full of belief in whatever thought lays hold on me to reject people from my company, and so I only keep from these invasions of the soul, which in old days used to come upon me also, by a series of angry outbreaks which are pure folly. One must agree with the clown or be silent, for he has in him the strength and confidence of the multitudes.

40

Yesterday Henderson was abusing Molière and for weeks he has been pressing on me and rousing Miss Allgood[1] to press on me a poor sentimental play which has, or seems to have, popular qualities. I at last turned on him with, 'Henderson, I won't listen to you; I am a dramatic critic and you are not.' A piece of stupid self-assertion, for I have allowed him to talk and argue with me on terms of equality. I should have been friendly with him and polite always, but I should never have permitted discussion on any play. He is now through my own fault the chief voice, and the only effective voice in the Theatre, of the general commonness of things in Ireland. All my worst faults of self-assertion and temper come from being too indolent and careless to keep a distance between myself and men and women in all those things where they are my inferiors. One should always live with one's betters, but if one has self-control and subtlety one should find one's betters sometimes by confining friendship to a single element. We do it with our loves, why not with our friendships? All our follies are from the drowsiness of the will. A perpetual choice of the element of friendship, being a daily creation, would be a perpetual exultation, and is not all strength and faculty an exultation?

41

When we are moved to intolerance by some provincial folly or stupidity, one should look at the man or woman and think: 'From that blood may yet come some man of genius, perhaps the saviour of a race. That stupidity may be even necessary to his being.'

42

Lady Gregory is planting trees; for a year they have taken up much of her time. Her grandson will be fifty years old before they can be

[1] Sara Allgood (1883-1950), distinguished Abbey actress.

cut. We artists, do not we also plant trees and it is only after some fifty years that we are of much value? Every day I notice some new analogy between [the] long-established life of the well-born and the artist's life. We come from the permanent things and create them, and instead of old blood we have old emotions and we carry in our head that form of society which aristocracies create now and again for some brief moment at Urbino or Versailles.[1] We too despise the mob and suffer at its hands and when we are happiest we have some little post in the house of Duke Frederick where we watch the proud dreamless world with humility, knowing that our kingdom is invisible and that at the first breath of ambition our dreams vanish. If we do not see daily beautiful life at which we look as old men and women do at young children, we become theorists – thinkers as it is called – or else give ourselves to strained emotions, to some overflow of sentiment 'sighing after Jerusalem in the regions of the grave'. How can we sing without our bush of whins, our clump of heather, and does not Blake say that it takes a thousand years to create a flower?

43

Perhaps we may find in the spectacle of some beautiful woman our Ferrara, our Urbino. Perhaps that is why we have no longer any poetry but the poetry of love.

44

I begin to wonder whether I have and always have had some nervous weakness inherited from my mother. (I have noticed my own form of excitability in my sister Lolly,[2] exaggerated in her by fits of prolonged gloom. She has ♂ □ ♄ while I have ☽ ☍ ♂.)[3] In Paris I felt that if the strain were but a little more I would hit the woman who irritated me, and I often have long periods during which Irish things – it is always Irish things and people that vex, slight follies enough –

---

[1] Undated letter from Violet Martin to Edith Somerville (i.e. 'Ross' to 'Somerville'): 'Yeats is a little affected and knows it – he has a sense of humour and is a gentleman – hardly by birth, I fancy – but by genius.'
[2] Elizabeth Corbet Yeats, born at 23 Fitzroy Road, 11 March 1868.
[3] She has Mars in square with Saturn while I have Moon in opposition to Mars.

make life nearly unendurable. The feeling is always the same: a consciousness of energy, of certainty, and of transforming power stopped by a wall, by something one must either submit to or rage against helplessly. It often alarms me; is it the root of madness? So violent it is, and all the more because I seldom lose my temper in the ordinary affairs of life. I do not think I have ever scolded my housekeeper, no paragon, in eleven years, or is it twelve? Then, too, I notice that my old childish difficulty of concentration is as great as ever. I can evade it in a thousand ways; I can return to a subject again and again, but I cannot give it many minutes at a time. Yesterday after a lesson, a French conversation,[1] my head began to ache just as it did when I overworked some eight days ago, and yet I had done little for days. I am writing this that a friend[2] for whom and for myself I write may know me for good and evil, and that I may watch it and amend. One can at least see around the circumstance of irritation. I should learn to exclude this irritation from my conversation at any rate, as certainly as I have learned to exclude it from my writings and my formal speech. In one way it has helped me, for the knowledge of it has forced me to make my writings sweet-tempered and, I think, gracious. There was a time when they were threatened by it; I had to subdue a kind of Jacobin rage. I escaped from it all as a writer through my sense of style. Is not one's art made out of the struggle in one's soul? Is not beauty a victory over oneself?

45

In what toils, in what life, in what war of the Amazons did women, whose beauty is more than the promise of physical pleasure and an easy path to get it, win their beauty? For Castiglione says, speaking the high Urbino thought, that all such beauty 'is the spoil and monument of the victory of the soul'.[3]

[1] 'I am working at French and a French teacher comes every day for an hour....' Yeats to his father, 17 January 1909, *Letters* (Wade), p. 525.

[2] Probably Maud Gonne, though Yeats intended to show the Diary to Florence Farr, *Letters* (Wade), p. 526.

[3] 'Therefore, Beautie is the true monument and spoile of the victory of the soule when she with heavenly influence beareth rule over martiall and grosse nature, and with her light overcommeth the darknesse of the bodie.' *The Book of the Courtier*, tr. Sir Thomas Hoby (London, Dent, 1956 reprint), p. 311. Quoted again in *A Vision*, p. 293.

46

Feb. 3 [1909]. Blake talking to Crabb Robinson said once that he preferred to any man of intellect a happy thoughtless person, or some such phrase. It followed, I suppose, from his praise of life – 'all that lives is holy' – and from his dislike of abstract things. Balzac, though when he is praising some beautiful high-bred woman [he] makes one think he had the same preference, is yet too much taken up with his worship of the will, which cannot be thoughtless even if it can be happy, to be aware of the preference if he had it. Nietzsche had it doubtless at the moment when he imagined 'the superman' as a child. We artists suffer in our art if we do not love most of all *life* at peace with itself and doing without forethought what its humanity bids it and therefore happily. We are, as seen from life, an artifice, an emphasis, an uncompleted arc perhaps. Those whom it is our business to cherish and celebrate are complete arcs. Because the life we see is not the final end of things, the moment we attain to greatness of any kind by personal labour and will we become fragmentary, and find no task in active life which can use our highest faculties. We are compelled to think and express and not to do. Faust in the end was only able to reclaim land like some officer of the Agricultural Board.[1] It is right that Romeo should not be a man of intellect or learning, it is enough for us that there is nature in him. We see all his arc, for in literature we need completed things. Our works, our celebrations of life and passion, should be in all men's eyes, but it is not well that we should be too much talked of. Plutarch was right when he said the artist should not be too prominent in the State because no young man, born for war and love, desires to be like Phidias. Life confesses to the priest and honours him, but we confess to life and tell it all that we would do if we were young, beautiful and rich, and life answers, 'I never could have thought of all that for myself, I have so little time.' And it is our praise that it goes upon its way with shining eyes forgetting us.

[1] '... his Faust after his hundred years but reclaiming land like some Sir Charles Grandison or Voltaire in his old age.' *A Vision*, p. 298.

47

I have to speak tonight at the Arts Club and have no time for much preparation. I chose 'The Ideas of the Young' for a title, as I thought that vague enough to let me say almost anything that would be uppermost in my mind at the time. Partly for the speech's sake and partly because some talks with Colum have brought up certain thoughts, I have decided to say something of what follows. I will speak of the life of a young Irishman, his gradual absorption in some propaganda. How the very nature of youth makes this come readily. Youth is always giving itself, expending itself. It is only after years that we begin the supreme work, the adapting our energies to a chosen end, the disciplining of ourselves. A young man in Ireland meets only crude, impersonal things, things that make him like others. One cannot discuss his ideas or ideals, for he has none. He has not the beginning of aesthetic culture. He never tries to make his rooms charming, for instance. The slow perfecting of the senses which we call taste has not even begun. When he throws himself into the work of some league he succeeds just in so far as he puts aside all delicate and personal gifts. I myself have suffered from the sense of strain that comes when one speaks to ignorant or, still worse, half-ignorant men. There is a perpetual temptation not merely to over-simplification but to exaggeration, for all ignorant thought is exaggerated thought. I can only wish a young Irishman of talent and culture that he may spend his life, from eighteen to twenty-five, outside Ireland – can one prescribe duties to a developed soul? – and I suppose him to become conscious of himself in those years. If one can, I would wish him to return. I will then describe the idea of modern culture as it exists in some young Oxford man: to have perfect taste; to have felt all the finest emotions that art can give. The young Dublin man who sticks to his books becomes a pedant because he only believes in external things. I will then describe the debate at Oxford a few years ago when I felt so much pity for that young brilliant man so full of feminine sensitiveness. Surely the ideal of culture expressed by Pater can only create feminine souls. The soul becomes a mirror not a brazier. This culture is really the pursuit of self-knowledge in so far as the self is a calm, deliberating, discriminating thing, for when we have awakened our tastes and our criticism of the world as we taste it, we have come to know ourselves; ourselves, I mean, not as misers or spendthrifts, as magistrates or pleaders, but as men, as souls face to face with what is permanent in the world. Newman defines culture as wise receptivity, though I do not think he uses these words. Culture of this kind produces its most perfect flowers in a few high-bred women. It gives to its sons an exquisite delicacy. I will then compare the culture of the Renaissance, which seems to me founded not on self-knowledge but on knowledge of some other self – Christ or Caesar – not on delicate sincerity but on imitative energy.

48

I must stop writing and lie down, or go out and walk. I have the old stopping of my faculties when I ask for serious thought. I have a slight headache also, and palpitations.

49

7.30 p.m. An hour and a half or two hours ago Miss Allgood came to see me about theatre things. I left her for a few moments and when I returned she said she had seen my double, but young, some twenty years old and with a very white collar, and not so big as I am, leaning towards the bookcase as if to take out a book. I was often in this room (Nassau Hotel) eighteen years ago with Maud Gonne.

50 (On 6 and 7 of month ♂♂ ♃ p)[1]

Feb. 4 [1909]. This morning I got a letter telling me of Lady Gregory's illness. I did not recognize her son's writing at first, and my mind wandered, I suppose because I am not well. I thought my mother was ill and that my sister was asking me to come at once: then I remembered that my mother died years ago[2] and that more than kin was at stake. She has been to me mother, friend, sister and

[1] Mars conjunction Jupiter progressed.
[2] On 3 January 1900.

1. *Autobiography*, f 40, showing opening to Section VIII (VIIa), see page 34.

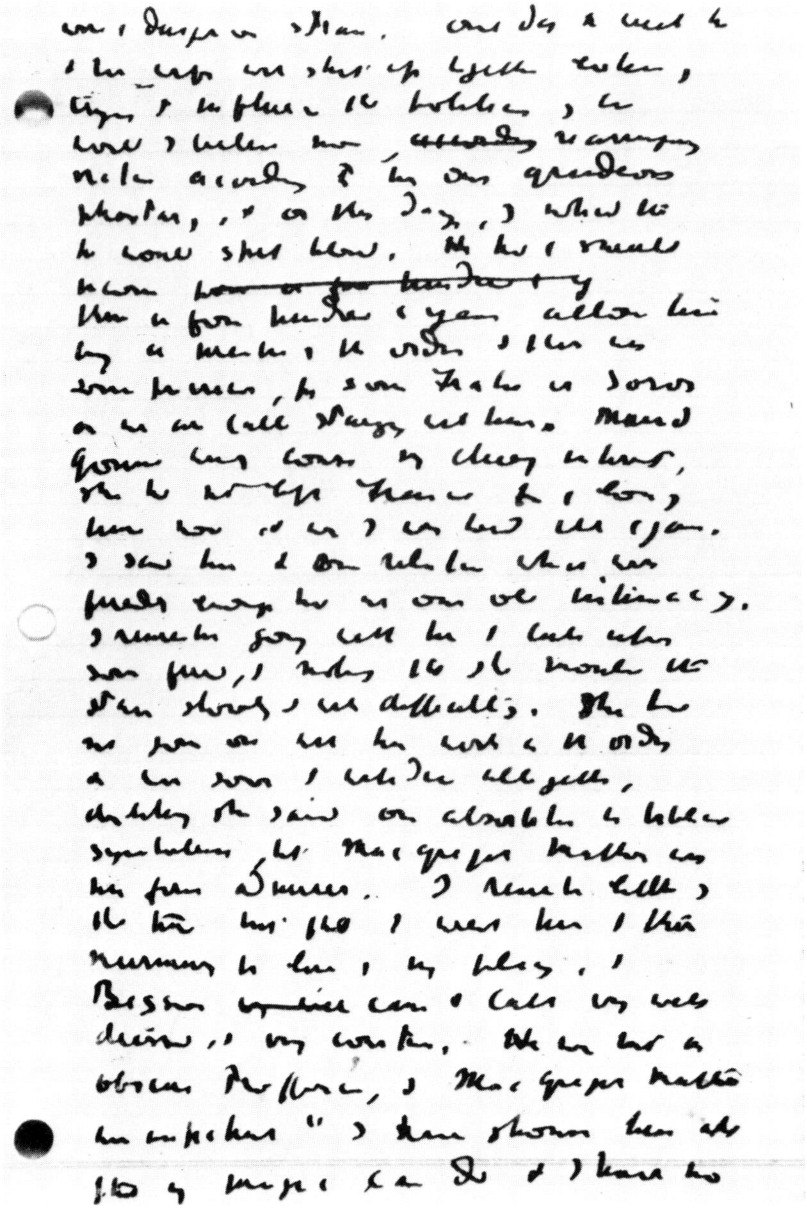

2. *Autobiography*, f 133, see page 73.

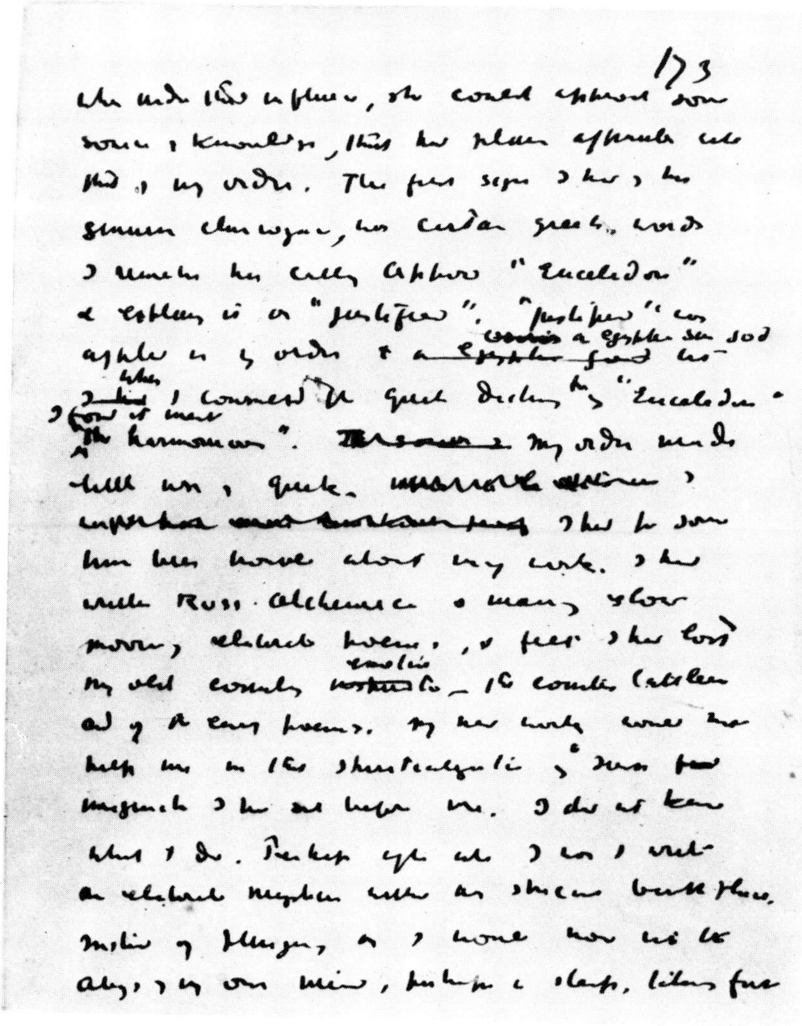

3. *Autobiography*, f 173, see pages 99–100.

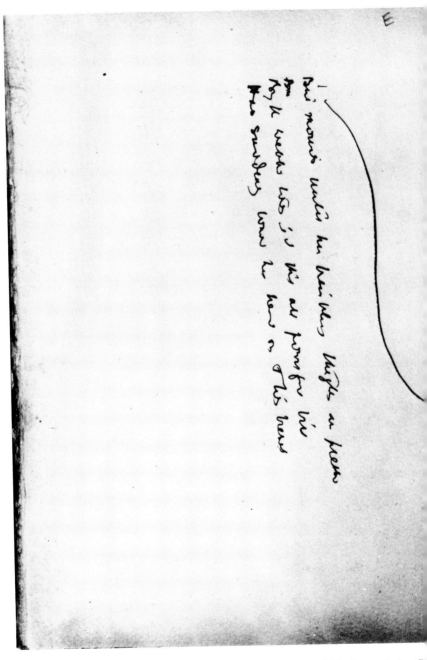

4. First version of 'Leda and the S[wan'

Annunciation

How can the swooping godhead have her will
Yet hover, though her helpless thighs are pressed
By the webbed toes; and that all powerful bill
Has suddenly loosed her face upon his breast.
How can those terrified vague fingers push
The feathered glory from her loosening thighs.
All the stretched body 's laid on the white rush
And feels the strange heart beating where it lies
A shudder in the loins engenders there
The broken wall, the burning roof and Tower
And Agamemnon dead. . . .
                              Being so caught up

Did nothing pass before her in the air?
Did she put on his knowledge with her power
Before the indifferent beak could let her drop.

                              Sept 18 1523

The swooping godhead is half hovering still,
            climbs
Yet hovers upon her trembling body pressed
By the toes; & that thigh all powerful bill
Her suddenly loosed her face upon his breast..
How can those terrified vague fingers push
The feathered glory, from her loosening thighs
all the stretched body' laid on the white rush
                        or
her feathery body there on the white rush
on her body can but lean on the white rush

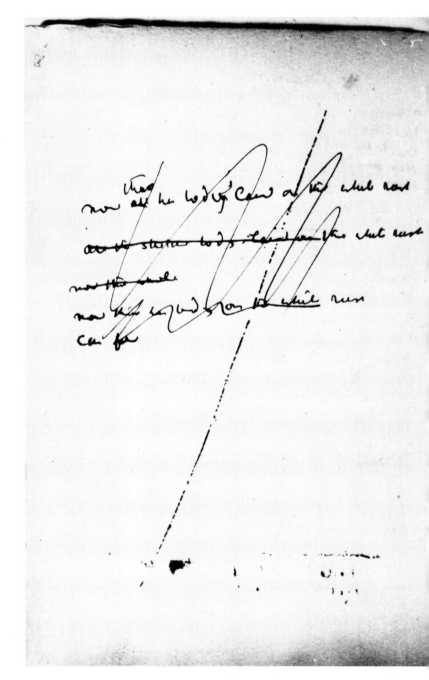

5. Second version of 'Leda and the Sw

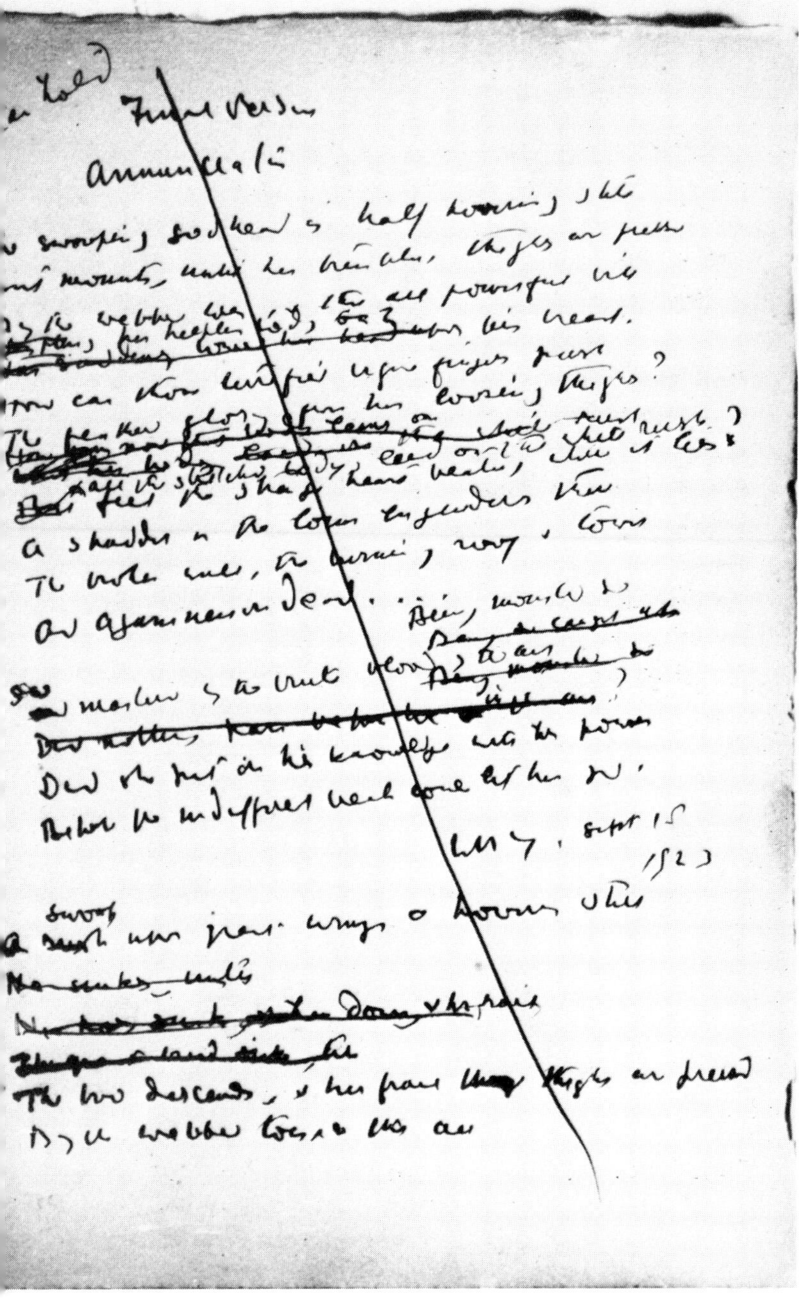

First Version

Annunciation

[heavily corrected handwritten draft, largely illegible]

...swooping... half hovering... still
...movements... her... thighs...
...webby...
...can... fingers...
...feather...

A shudder in the loins engenders there
The broken wall, the burning roof... tower
And Agamemnon dead...

...masters of the truth...

...not his knowledge...
...her...

Leda . Sept 15
1923

...swoop... wings a hovering still
...
...down...
...
The bird descends, + her... thighs are pressed
By the webby toes + his...

al, Section 248, see pages 273–4.

6. Final version of 'Leda and the Swan', Section 250, see pages 274–5.

brother. I cannot realize the world without her – she brought to my wavering thoughts steadfast nobility. All day the thought of losing her is like a conflagration in the rafters. Friendship is all the house I have.

51

Feb. 6 [1909]. Lady Gregory better but writes in pencil that she 'very nearly slipped away'. While she has been bringing herself near death with overwork to do all her household duties as few women have ever done things, keeping all in stately order while giving us enough plays, translated or original, often working much against the will, often with difficulties, our base half-men of letters, or rather half-journalists, that coterie of patriots who have never been bought because no one has ever thought them worth a price, have been whispering everywhere that she takes advantage of her position as Director to put her own plays upon the stage. When I think, too, of Synge dying at this moment of their bitterness and ignorance, as I believe, I wonder if I have been right to shape my style to sweetness and serenity. Then it is that comes into my mind that verse that Fergus spoke, 'No man seeks my help because I be not of the things I dream.'[1] Perhaps the always gracious thought was only right in old days when one had a dumb sword to carry one's ungraciousness. On the night of the *Playboy* debate[2] they were all there, silent and craven, not in the stalls for fear that they might be asked to speak and face the mob – to speak on either side; and Russell himself,[3] who had promised to take the chair, refused by a subterfuge and joined the others in the gallery. No man of all literary Dublin dared show his face but my own father, who spoke to, or rather in the presence of, that howling mob with sweetness and simplicity.[4] I fought them, he was nobler – he forgot them.

[1] In the first version of 'Fergus and the Druid' the Druid's speech which now reads, 'No woman's loved me,' etc., read: 'No woman loves me, no man seeks my help/Because I be not of the things I dream.'

[2] 4 February 1907. P. D. Kenny was in the Chair, and the speakers included W. B. Yeats, J. B. Yeats, W. J. Lawrence, Sheehy-Skeffington and Cruise O'Brien.

[3] 'the chief among them' deleted.

[4] 'My father upon the Abbey stage, before him a raging crowd:
"This Land of Saints", and then as the applause died out,
"Of plaster Saints"; his beautiful mischievous head thrown back.'
    'Beautiful Lofty Things', *Collected Poems*, p. 348.

52

Of Lady Gregory one can say what Shakespeare said of another, 'She died every day she lived.'[1]

53[2]

Sickness has taught/would teach me this
With that poor soul/scale of his
To be no way dismayed
Though flames eat up the whole
Now that I have seen it weighed
Against one soul.

Sickness showed/taught/showed me this,
With that/those poor scales of his;
Not to be dismayed
Though flames eat the whole
Now I have seen it weighed
Against one/a soul.

Sickness brought me this
Thought in that scale of his
Why should I be dismayed
Though flames burn up/had burned the whole
World, as it were a coal
Now I have seen it weighed
×   With one most lofty soul.
Against a soul.

John Butler Yeats's own version of this incident is given in his *Letters to His Son W. B. Yeats and Others* (1944). Lily Yeats told Oliver Edwards that some of the uproar on that occasion was caused by mistake, the audience thought J.B.Y. had said, 'blasted saints'.

[1] '... the queen that bore thee,/Oft'ner upon her knees than on her feet,/Died every day she lived.' Macduff to Malcolm, *Macbeth* IV iii 111.

[2] 'A Friend's Illness,' *Collected Poems*, p. 109. Of the three versions in the MSS. the second has been cancelled entire, and the third is written in the margin.

54

All Wednesday I heard Castiglione's phrase ringing in my memory, 'Never be it spoken without tears, the Duchess, too, is dead.'[1] That slight phrase, which – coming where it did among the numbering of his dead – has often moved me till my eyes dimmed, and I felt all his sorrow as though one saw the worth of life fade for ever.

55

Those that attribute base motives[2] are the great-grandchildren of those that accused Smith O'Brien[3] after his failure of being paid by government to fail. It is of such as these Goethe thought when he said, 'The Irish seem to me always like a pack of hounds dragging down some noble stag.'[4]

56

Feb. 7 [1909]. I went for a walk through the mountains with little Evans and we talked of religion. He said, 'There is no longer belief, nobody with belief ever comes to my Bible class but you yourself. If people believed they would talk of God and Christ. They think it good taste not to speak of such things, and yet people always talk of what they care for. Belief makes a mind abundant.' I thought of the perpetual desire of all lovers to talk of their love and how many

---

[1] 'But the thinge that should not be rehersed wythout teares is, that the Dutchesse she is also dead.' *The Book of the Courtier*, p. 10.

[2] 'Those who accuse Synge of some base motive . . .', *Autobiographies*, p. 483.

[3] William Smith O'Brien (1803–64) who with John Blake Dillon, Terence Bellew MacManus, and Thomas Francis Meagher led the abortive Rising of 1848.

[4] J. P. Eckermann, *Gespräche mit Goethe* . . . (Biedermann, vol. 1, p. 274), 7 April 1829: 'Die Katholiken vertragen sich unter sich nicht, aber sie halten immer zusammen, wenn es gegen einem Protestanten geht. Sie sind einer Meute Hunde gleich, die sich untereinander beissen, aber sobald sich ein Hirsch zeigt, sogleich einig sind und in Masse auf ihn losgehen.' 'The Catholics squabble among themselves but they are always prepared to make common cause against a Protestant. They are like a pack of hounds, snapping out at one another, but the moment they catch sight of a stag they herd together and attack.' (Translation by Oliver Edwards.) 'During the quarrel over Parnell's grave a quotation from Goethe ran through the papers, describing our Irish jealousy: "The Irish seem to me like a pack of hounds, always dragging down some noble stag."' *Autobiographies*, p. 316.

lovers' quarrels have come from it. I said, 'But there are Russell's following.'[1] He said fiercely, 'They are thieves. They pick up names and thoughts all over the world and these never become being in their minds, never become their own, because they have no worship.' He is not easy to understand, but I gradually drew from him these thoughts. 'They are all self, all presumption. They do not know what it is to abase themselves, before Christ, or their own gods, or anything. If one does that, one is filled with life. Christ is so full of life that it flows into us. The whole world is vivid to us. They are all self, and so they despise the foundation.' He means by the foundation, life, nature. I said, 'But what are the forms they see?' He answered, 'They can only be lesser spirits – part of what they call the astral – creatures that live on them and draw away their life.' I said, 'Must one therefore either feed or be fed?' He said, 'Yes, surely. Have you not noticed that they are all fluid, tenuous, flimsy-minded? You know Ella Young. They are all like that. It is the astral fluid. There is no life, the life has been sucked out. They despise the foundation, and that no one can do till after the resurrection. Of course there are a few chosen spirits who need not enter into life, but they are very few. Ah! if one could only see all boys and girls after nineteen married. That would do the theosophists good. They are all self and so they live on stolen goods.' He told me earlier in the day how when he was mountaineering once he would have fallen and been killed. Someone had slipped and dragged down another till he had the weight of two men hanging from the rope – but then he felt a great being descending into him and strengthening him. Even when the danger was over he felt no loss of nerve as he looked back on the danger. He had been filled with life.

57

On the way back Evans said, 'There is so little life now. Look at the modern soldier – he is nothing – the ancient soldier was something – he had to be strong and skilful, they fought man to man.' I said, 'There are some books like that – ideas as wonderful as a campaign by Moltke, but no man. The plan of campaign was not so impressive

[1] '... the Dublin Theosophists', *Autobiographies*, p. 479.

in the old books, but all was human!' He answered, 'When races cease to believe in Christ, God takes the life out of them, at last they cease to procreate.'

58

Evans himself, all muscular force and ardour, makes me think of that line written, as one believes, of Shakespeare by Ben Jonson – 'So rammed with life he can but grow in life with being.'[1] The irregular line of his thought which makes him obscure is itself a sign of this. He is as full of twists and turns as a tree.

59

Feb. 8 [1909]. The other day when I was speaking upon 'The Ideas of the Young' someone asked me what life I would recommend to young Irishmen, the thought my whole speech should if it were logical have led up to. I was glad to be able to answer, 'I do not know, though I have thought much about it.' Who does not distrust complete ideas?

60

Feb. 9 [1909]. There is an astrological sense in which a man's wife or sweetheart is always an Eve made from a rib of his body. She is drawn to him because she represents a group of stellar influences on the radical horoscope. These influences also create an element in his character and his destiny, in things apart from love or marriage. Whether this element be good or evil she is therefore its external expression. The happiest have such horoscopes as enable them to find what is good and happy in themselves in their wives, others must find what is evil, or a man may have both affinities. Sometimes a man may find the evil of his horoscope in a woman, and in rescuing her from her own self may conquer his own evil (as with Simon Magus who married a harlot). Others may find in a woman the good that conquers them and shapes them. All external events of life are

[1] Horace on Virgil's poetry in Ben Jonson's *Poetaster*, v i 136–7: 'so rammed with life/That it shall gather strength of life with being/And live hereafter more admired than now.'

of course an externalization of character in the same way, but not to the same degree as the wife, who may represent the gathering up of an entire web of influences. A friend if represented by a powerful star in the eleventh house may be the same, especially if the ☉[1] apply to that star. We are mirrors of stellar light and we cast this light outward as incidents, magnetic attractions, characterizations, desires. This casting outward of the light is that fall into the circumference the mystics talk of.

61

Feb. 12 [1909]. By implication the philosophy of Irish faery lore declares that all power is from the body, all intelligence from the spirit. Western civilization, religion and magic alike insist on power and therefore body and these three doctrines – efficient rule, the Incarnation, and thaumaturgy. Eastern asceticism answers to these with indifference to rule, scorn of the flesh, contemplation of the formless. Western minds who follow the Eastern way become weak and vapoury because they become unfit for the work forced upon them by Western life. Every symbol is an invocation which produces its equivalent expression in all worlds. The Incarnation involved modern science and modern efficiency and also modern lyric feeling which gives body to the most spiritual emotions. It produced a solidification of all things that grew from the individual will. It did not, however, produce the idea of the State; that comes from another evocation, polytheistic Greece and Rome. The historical truth of the Incarnation is indifferent, though the belief in that truth was essential to the power of the evocation. All civilization is held together by a series of suggestions made by an invisible hypnotist, artificially created illusions. The knowledge of reality is always by some means or other a secret knowledge. It is a kind of death.

62

The work of some writers, of Edgar Allan Poe for instance, suggests to the imagination a fever of the personality which keeps admiration from being ever complete. Nearly all modern writers who have

[1] 'sun' deleted.

great ecstasy, or pretend to it, leave one unsatisfied, whereas old writers, Crashaw for instance, give one a full meal. The reason is that the images of old writers are drawn from the common mind and so, no matter how dizzy their thought is, there is always an evocation of normal mankind and general law. Their images imply that they are exceptions and not for all men's copying. The landscape of the world is behind them.

63

Today Henderson told me that he thought *Kincora*[1] in its old form was better. He did not like the dialect, or rather I knew he was about to say this when I stopped him with, 'The old version pleased the half-educated because of its rhetoric; the new displeases because of its literature.' This was folly and rudeness. Anger with stupidity is the most exhausting of emotions for, knowing itself of little force with that enemy, it exhausts in a moment all the resources of emotion. The anger which does or believes it can conquer is always of a definite amount; anger with the fool is indefinite. Nothing is so hard to conquer, so far as I am concerned, nor more really ridiculous than our desire to convince where conviction is unnecessary. I often think it is the speaker in me; I want to convince instead of being satisfied to be obeyed. I would really rather be disobeyed than not convince. This makes practical work too exhausting and also less effective. It creates in our subordinates a habit of argument and therefore of resistance. As I watch people, I find myself noticing that almost all are of one of two kinds: those who are accustomed to be obeyed without question from early life, no matter how small their sphere, have a kind of dignity.[2] The desire to convince is curiously destructive, too, in general conversation, where one never has time to really convince. The division is perhaps that between executive and legislative mind.

[1] The revised version of Lady Gregory's *Kincora* was produced at the Abbey on 11 February 1909. The first version had been produced at the Abbey on 25 March 1905 and was published in that year.

[2] Yeats evidently forgot to describe the second kind.

64

Feb. 13 [1909]. There is no wisdom without indolence. Nobody running at full speed has either a head or a heart.

65

Last night Miss Allgood, who had been bad the night before, gave a good performance in *Kincora*.[1] This play gives me the greatest joy – colour, speech, all has music, and the scenes with the servants make one feel curiously intimate and friendly with those great people who otherwise would be far off – mere figures of speech. The first Act, which used to be the best, is now the worst Act; it is too external, I think. I am not, however, sure. The pleasure I get from the play makes me understand all the more how much I dislike plays like *The Man who Missed the Tide*[2] and *The Suburban Groove*,[3] this last especially, and of course works like *The Country Dressmaker*.[4] If at all possible I will now keep at the Theatre till I have produced there a mass of fine work. If we can create a taste for translated work – which we have not yet done – we can carry on the theatre without vulgarity. If not, the growth of its audience will more and more make the work vulgar, for the average town mind in Ireland today wishes the expression of its own vulgarities and will by many channels, private and public, press work of this kind upon us. The only chance is to appeal to the desire for self-improvement, which is just beginning in Ireland. If this can be roused, the theatre can be carried on as we have shaped it. If not, it must for the sake of our future influence, the influence of our example, be allowed to pass completely out of our hands, or cease. We must not be responsible for any compromise. It will not be possible, if we do not succeed with foreign work, to play our own work constantly. The Irish public, which has been excited into an active state of democratic

---

[1] In the role of Gormleith.

[2] By W. F. Casey (1884–1957). First produced at the Abbey, 13 February 1908.

[3] By W. F. Casey. First produced at the Abbey, 1 October 1908.

[4] By George Fitzmaurice. First produced at the Abbey, 3 October 1907. 'A harsh, strong, ugly comedy. . . . Even I rather dislike it, though I admire its sincerity, and yet it was received with enthusiasm.' Yeats to John Quinn, 4 October 1907, *Letters* (Wade), p. 495.

envy and jealousy, will not accept the pre-eminence of one or two
writers – of Lady Gregory, let us say. In its present phase it dislikes,
or rather the expressive part of it dislikes, all individual eminence.
It lacks generosity. As soon as it has helped to raise any man or
woman to a position of importance, it becomes jealous. O'Leary
told me of this long ago. This feeling is increased when it recognizes
in that individual the free mind, the mind that plays with life and
expresses great things lightly. It distrusts all that is not plainly
organized and determined, all that is not plainly logical work. A play
with a purpose, or a moral let us say, is as much a part of social
organization as a newspaper or a speech. It likes to see the railway
tracks of thought. It is afraid of the wilderness. It would go down a
steep place into the sea if it accepted the devilish doctrine, from which
arises the seeming frivolity of noble minds, that truth is a state of
mind and not a thought nor a remembered syllogism nor an opinion.
It dreads all liberated things and is all the time half-fascinated by
what it dreads. It loves rhetoric because rhetoric is impersonal and
predetermined, and it hates poetry whose suggestiveness cannot be
foreseen. It does not hate the freedom of the rich and the high-bred
more bitterly than the fantasy of the poor. It holds to all rules because it cannot live without them and it would turn all art and literature into a blackboard for its own instruction. Fortunately, noble
thought when it has been a long time in the world is so written
about and so obscured by common minds that it seems at last safe
reading for slaves, and almost worthy to instruct them.

66

One thought must be continually pressed upon all free souls – here
in Ireland above all – to resist ill-breeding in thought as our fathers
in their more leisurely lives – alike in country poverty, where most
of all they brooded over this one thing, or in great houses – resisted
ill-breeding in manners. These are associated, and even though we
be called the worst names, the hardest to bear, we must keep the
fountains pure. Education, newspapers, a thousand impersonalities
have filled the world with the imitation of what once was gold – an
imitation worse than the ill-manners of the parvenu, for he would

have preferred the gold had he found it. We have everywhere now counterfeit that is thought better, instead of merely more obtainable, than true metal.

67

Feb. 17 [1909]. Opinion (perhaps even philosophy is too definite if more than a protection) is the enemy of the artist because it arms his uninspired moment against his inspiration. What was once inspiration is systematized and is used by the heavier part of the mind to strengthen itself against the finer. A mechanism is created which may attack life itself. The artist has vulgarized himself the moment his systematized thought passes out of his passion as from under a fiery cloud. May it not be so with nations? Perhaps a great popular thinker, a Rousseau, a Voltaire, a Wesley is a misfortune. He is too clever, too logical, too definite. He enables the little to believe themselves great, to believe they understand, till they muddy all the fountains of truth. Only the pure artist whose truth is identical with a form of life, because it is sight and but a sight, can do no hurt. He initiates by slow degrees. He never has to say as Renan said in his *Autobiography* with so much sorrow, 'That vulgar oyster-seller is my ally.' Even God has found it necessary to be invisible.

68

Feb. 23 [1909]. Last night I read Evans a passage in Coventry Patmore in which he says we cannot teach another religious truth, we can only point out to him a way by which he may find it for himself. Evans said, 'If one could show another religious experience, which is of the whole being, one would have to give one's whole being, one would be Christ. He alone can give himself.'

69

Today, for the first time, I lost my temper with an actor. Sinclair[1] refused to play the part he was given. I made a mistake; my temper was over in one minute and the interview had to last longer. As a

[1] Arthur Sinclair (1883–1951).

result there was no climax; on the contrary, I must have seemed to have weakened. One should not lose one's temper unless one is certain of getting more and more angry to the end.

70

Headache again, brought on by very slight amount of work. I begin to think that the worry of years, trying to do too many different things, has upset my nervous system. For years now I have had the most intense desire for a life of routine in which it would be possible to live undisturbed the life of imagination. For years I have had for long periods a kind of fright, a sense of spiritual loss.

Feb. 24 [1909]. 11:15 to 1:00 – Theatre. 1:30 to 4:45 – letters and plays read for Abbey. 5:00 – Arts Club Committee.

Feb. 25 [1909]. 11:30 to 1:30 – Miss Elvery[1] about scenery and then Henderson. 2:00 to 3:30 – reading plays, etc. 3:30 to 4:50 – letters.

71

Feb. 25 [1909]. I often wonder if my talent will ever recover from the heterogeneous labour of these last few years. The younger Hallam says that vice does not destroy genius but that the heterogeneous does. I cry out vainly for liberty and have ever less and less inner life. Evil comes to us men of imagination wearing as its mask all the virtues. I have known, certainly, more men destroyed by the desire to have wife and child and to keep them in comfort than I have seen destroyed by harlots and drink. Le Gallienne[2] used at the Rhymers' Club to say that he meant to keep a butler and to say very seriously that he thought it his duty to keep up his house on that scale. Harlots in his case finished what the virtues began, but it was the virtues, not the harlots, that killed his knack of verse. I thought

[1] Miss Beatrice Elvery, later Lady Glenavy, wrote to Curtis Bradford: 'I once made a drawing for a stage set for a play by W. B. Yeats. I think it might have been The Countess Cathleen. It was a woodland scene with mountains, sea and sky, and I think a castle in the distance. I heard later that Sean Barlow the scene painter looked at it and said, "It would take Beerbohm Tree to make anything out of that lot." That was the last I heard of it. Yeats asked me to make the drawing – I wasn't paid!'

[2] Richard Le Gallienne (1866–1947). Yeats's letter to Florence Farr, July 1905, refers to the 'vulgar element' in Le Gallienne's work. *Letters* (Wade), p. 455.

myself free, loving neither vice nor virtue; but virtue has come upon me and given me a nation instead of a home. Has it left me any lyric faculty? Whatever happens I must go on that there may be a man behind the lines already written. I should have avoided the thing – but being in it!

Feb. 26 ['1909]. ♀ just passed ☌ ☽ R ♀ 21.48.[1] 11:00 to 12:00, Abbey. 12:00 to 1:30, Letters and writing mystical notes, etc. 1:30 to 2:40, Visit. 2:40 to 4:50, Letters. 5:00 to 6:00, Letters.

72

I made the following poem about six months ago, but write it here that it may not be lost:[2]

> Some may have blamed you that you took away
> The verses that they cared for on the day
> When the ears being deafened the sight of the eyes blind
> With lightning, you went from me; and I could find
> Nothing to make a song about but kings
> Helmets and swords and half-forgotten things
> That were like memories of you – but we
> Will tumble crown and helmet in the sea.

Or it might end:

but now

> ✕   That you have come again,
>   That you have come to me again I'll throw
> ✕   Crown
>   Helmet and sword and crown into a pit
>   There's not a

>   That you have come again I'll throw, I'll bury
> ✕   Helmet and sword and crown into a pit
>   Helmet and crown and sword into a pit
>   ~~For~~/As in a sudden crying laughing fit
> ✕   ~~For~~

[1] Venus just passed conjunction Moon radical (Venus 21.48).
[2] 'Reconciliation', *Collected Poems*, p. 102. Cf. no. 228.

  ×   We've so remade the world
  ×   Trample leaves now upon them
  ×   Trample the dull leaves over them
      Find all the living world you took away[1]
                            but now
  ×   That you have come again I ~~throw/~~I'll throw
  ×   Helmet and crown and sword in a pit
      That you have come again we'll out and throw
      Helmet and sword and crown into a pit
      And in a sudden crying laughing fit
      Trample them down in the slimy[2] mound,
  ×   But it let me take those awhile and hold
  ×   Them near[3]

                        But now
  ×   The world's alive again
      We'll out – for the world lives as long ago
      And in a sudden ~~laughing/~~crying laughing fit
  ×   Tumble the crowns and helmets in a pit
      ~~We'll/But/~~And tumble the crowns and helmets in ~~a/~~the pit
  ×   But dear cling close – you have been a long while gone
  ×   And barren thought has chilled me to the bone
  ×   But cling more close – you have been a long while gone
  ×   And barren thought has chilled me to the bone
      But dear cling close to me – since you were gone
  ×   A barren thought has chilled me to the bone.
               or
      My barren thoughts have chilled me to the bone.

      And while we're in this ~~crying/~~laughing weeping fit
  ×   Tumble the crowns and helmets in a pit
      Hurl helmet, crown and sword into the pit
               or
                        But now
      That you have come again we'll out and throw

---

[1] The entire passage from 'but now' to 'took away' is cancelled.
[2] Doubtful reading.
[3] Again the entire passage from 'But now' has been cancelled.

While we are in this laughing weeping fit
Helmet and sword and crown into the pit[1]

But now
We'll out – for the world lives as long ago
And while we're in our crying laughing fit
or
laughing, weeping fit
Hurl helmets, crowns and swords into

×   ~~Tumble the crowns and helmets in~~ the pit
But dear cling close to me – since you were gone
My barren thoughts have chilled me to the bone.

Feb. 27 [1909]. Bad night. Breakfast 10:45. 11:00 to 1:10, Letters and revising scripts for Theatre. 2:30 to 3:40 at Abbey. 4:00 to 7:00, Letters. Evening, Abbey.

Feb. 28 [1909]. Letters. Tired out. 11:15 to 1:15, Letters. 2:30 to 3:30, Letters.

73

Tonight as I sat in idleness, my eyes too tired to read or write, I saw plainly how I could not only change the constitution of the United Arts Club so as to make the Club more vigorous – all the arguments, all the details – but how to get that command over wavering opinion, even over now hostile opinion, which would give the power to me to shape the Club afterwards in other ways. A first step – to avoid giving a victory to either of two warring parties – was to get a certain man[2] to go on the committee. I was triumphant; I saw before me victory over all those who can least understand the manhood of mere art. Then I remembered that the renunciation of the artist is those things which in others are virtues, and I did not go to find the man I would have had to persuade. Why have I these faculties which I cannot use? I know I have them and I know they are the chief temptation of life. It is easy to give up all thoughts of wealth and of

---

[1] The last four lines, following 'or', have been cancelled.
[2] Probably Harry F. Norman, whose nomination to the Committee of the Arts Club for 1909–10 was proposed by Crawforth Smith and seconded by Elizabeth Yeats.

domestic life even, but it is hard to give up those generalizations through which the will flings itself upon the world, those gleams of future victory that come to one as though one cried aloud, all that makes one for a moment of the race of the eagles. It is hard to become a mere hand and ear. Did the first of us all hate the blindness that kept him from the oblivion of activity?[1]

74

March 2 [1909]. Two hours' idleness – because I have no excuse but to begin creative work, an intolerable toil. Little Sarojini[2] of Hyderabad told me that in her father's garden one met an opium-eater who made poems in his dreams and wrote the title-pages when he awoke but forgot the rest. He was the only happy poet. 11:15 to 1:00, Idleness. 1:00 to 1:45, *Player Queen*. 2:30 to 5:00, reading plays and writing letters.

75

March 3 [1909]. A couple of days ago I went to see Dr Hyde. He spoke of the attacks on both him and myself in *Sinn Féin* and of their untruthfulness. He said, 'I congratulated Martyn some time ago on being leader of an important political party,[3] and he answered, "I don't want to be, I want to do my own work." Says I, "I want to do my own work also", and then says he, "The worst of it is that those fellows would not leave either of us there for five minutes if they thought we liked it."' Mrs Hyde joined in then with, 'I tell Douglas that whatever happens he must never take anything from them.'

---

[1] Yeats has written across this entry: 'Was not able to resist. Did transform it after all.'

[2] Sarojini Naidu, poetess and Nationalist, was a frequent guest at Yeats's 'Monday Evenings'.

[3] Edward Martyn was President of Sinn Féin from November 1905 until the summer of 1909. Yeats wrote to his father on 17 July? 1909: 'I think the only Galway news is that I dined with Edward Martyn the other day and that he told me he has left the Sinn Féin organization, retired from politics altogether. He did not say, but I suspect the collecting of shares for a proposed Sinn Féin daily paper had something to do with it. Some time ago, ardent Sinn Féiners were called upon to refuse to pay Income Tax. He, poor man, and one other being the only members of the party who paid any.' *Letters* (Wade), p. 532.

76

The root of it all is that the political class in Ireland – the lower-middle class from whom the patriotic associations have drawn their journalists and their leaders for the last ten years – have suffered through the cultivation of hatred as the one energy of their movement, a deprivation which is the intellectual equivalent to the removal of the genitals. Hence the shrillness of their voices. They contemplate all creative power as the eunuchs contemplate Don Juan as he passes through Hell on the white horse.[1]

77

Two hours' idleness as before. Astrology, the foregoing notes, sitting staring in fire, then about an hour at *Player Queen*.

March 4 [1909]. Idleness, vacillating work, a few good sentences. A bad day.

78

Tonight Henderson said to me that he has always thought the bad luck of Ireland comes from hatred being the foundation of our politics. It is possible that emotion is an evocation and in ways beyond the senses alters events – creating good or evil luck. Certain individuals who hate much seem to be followed by violent events outside their control. Maud Gonne has been so followed always. It is possible to explain it by saying that hatred brings certain associates and causes a tendency to violent action. But there are times when there seems to be more than this – an actual stream of ill-luck. Certainly evocation with symbol has taught me that much that we think of as limited to certain obvious effects influences the whole being. A meditation on sunlight, for instance, affects the nature throughout, producing all that follows from the symbolical nature of the sun. Hate must, in the same way, make sterile,

---

[1] Yeats wrote to Lady Gregory, 8 March 1909: 'I wrote a note a couple of days ago in which I compared Griffith and his like to the Eunuchs in Ricketts's picture watching Don Juan riding through Hell.' *Letters* (Wade), p. 525. This note was turned into the verse of 'On Those that Hated *The Playboy of the Western World*', *Collected Poems*, p. 124. Also cf. no. 211.

producing many effects which would follow from the meditation on a symbol capable of giving hate. Such symbol would produce not merely hate but associated effects. At least so I think. An emotion produces a symbol – sensual emotion dreams of water, for instance – just as a symbol produces emotion. The symbol is, however, perhaps more powerful than an emotion without symbol. Hatred as a basis of imagination, in ways which one could explain even without magic, helps to dry up the nature and makes the sexual abstinence, so common among young men and women in Ireland, possible. This abstinence reacts in its turn on the imagination, so that we get at last that strange eunuch-like tone and temper. For the last ten or twenty years there has been a perpetual drying of the Irish mind, with the resultant dust-cloud.

79

March 5 [1909]. I saw Synge today and asked him how much of his *Deirdre* was done. He said the third Act was right, that he had put an extra character in [the] second Act and intended to weave him into Act One.[1] He was to come in with Conchubar, carrying some of his belongings, and afterwards at end of Act to return for forgotten knife – just enough to make it possible to use him in Act Two. He spoke of his work this winter doubtfully, thought it not very good, seemed only certain of his third Act. I did not like to ask more questions for fear he would understand that I wished to know if another could complete his work if he died. He is certainly too ill to work himself, and will be for a long time.

80

March 6 [1909]. Met MacDonagh[2] yesterday – a man with some literary faculty which will probably come to nothing through lack

[1] The extra character is Owen. Cf. Synge, *Collected Works*, vol. IV, *Plays*, book II, ed. Ann Saddlemyer (London, Oxford University Press, 1968), Appendix C, pp. 382–93.
[2] Thomas MacDonagh (1878–1916), poet, executed for his part in the Easter Rising. The *Leader* essay is probably 'The Gaelic League and Politics', first of a series of essays, signed 'Lee', which appeared on 3, 10, 17 April and 1 May 1909. The school was St Enda's, near Rathfarnham.

of culture and encouragement. He had just written an article for the *Leader*, and spoke much as I do myself of the destructiveness of journalism here in Ireland, and was apologetic about his article. He was very low-spirited about Ireland. He is managing a school on Irish and Gaelic League principles but says he is losing faith in the League. Its writers are infecting Irish not only with English idiom but with the habits of thought of current Irish journalism, a most un-Celtic thing. 'The League', he said, 'is killing Celtic civilization.' I told him that Synge about ten years ago foretold this in an article in the *Academy*.[1] He thought the national movement practically dead, that the language would be revived but without all that he loved it for. In England this man would have become remarkable in some way, here he is being crushed by the mechanical logic and commonplace eloquence which gives the most power to the most empty mind because, being 'something other than human life'[2] it has no use for distinguished feeling or individual thought. I mean that within his own mind this mechanical thought is crushing as with an iron roller all that is organic.

81

The soul of Ireland has become a vapour and her body a stone.

82

Ne se vend

March 7 [1909]. In spite of myself my mind dwells more and more on ideas of class. Ireland has grown sterile, because power has passed to men who lack the training which requires a certain amount of wealth to ensure continuity from generation to generation, and to free the mind in part from other tasks. A gentleman is for one thing a man whose principal ideas are not connected with his personal needs and his personal success. In old days he was a clerk or a noble, that is to say, he had freedom because of inherited wealth

---

[1] 'The Old and New in Ireland', *The Academy and Literature*, 6 September 1902; reprinted in *Collected Works*, vol. II, *Prose*, ed. Alan Price (London, Oxford University Press, 1966), pp. 383–6.

[2] 'Houses of Commons & Houses of Lords appear to me to be fools; they seem to me to be something Else besides Human Life.' Blake, *Complete Writings*, p. 600. Cf. no. 108, p. 192.

and position, or because of a personal renunciation. The names are different today, and I would put the artist and the scholar in the category of the clerk, yet personal renunciation is not now sufficient or the *hysterica passio*[1] of Ireland would be inspiration, or perhaps it is sufficient but is impossible without inherited culture. For without culture or holiness, which is always the gift of a very few, a man may renounce wealth or any other external thing but he cannot renounce hatred, envy, jealousy, revenge. Culture is the sanctity of the intellect.[2]

83

March 9 [1909]. I have been talking of the literary element in painting with Miss Elvery and turning over the leaves of Binyon's book on Eastern painting,[3] in which he shows how traditional, how literary it is. The revolt against the literary element in painting was accompanied by a similar revolt in poetry. The doctrine of what he called the Aesthetic School was put by the younger Hallam in his essay on Tennyson,[4] and when I was a boy the unimportance of subject was a canon. A French poet had written of girls taking lice out of a child's hair. Henley was supposed to have founded a new modern art in his 'Hospital Poems', though he would not have claimed so. Hallam argued that poetry was the impression on the senses of certain very sensitive men. It was such with the pure artists, Keats and Shelley, but not so with the impure artists who, like Wordsworth, mixed up popular morality with their work. I now see that the literary element in painting, the moral element in poetry are the means whereby the two arts are accepted into the social order and become a part of life, and not things of the study and the exhibition. Supreme art is a traditional statement of certain heroic and religious

---

[1] 'But popular rage,
Hysterica passio dragged this quarry down.'
'Parnell's Funeral', *Collected Poems*, pp. 319–20.

[2] 'However my discontents enlarge my diary. I have written a number of notes lately. I wound up my notes this morning with the sentence, "culture is the sanctity of the intellect". I was thinking of men like Griffith and how they can renounce external things without it but not envy, revenge, jealousy and so on.' Yeats to Lady Gregory, 8 March 1909. *Letters* (Wade), p. 525.

[3] Laurence Binyon, *Painting in the Far East* (London, 1908).

[4] Arthur Henry Hallam, 'On Some of the Characteristics of Modern Poetry', *The Englishman's Magazine*, August 1831.

truths passed on from age to age, modified by individual genius but never abandoned. The revolt of individualism came because the tradition had become degraded, or rather because a spurious copy had been accepted in its stead. Classical morality – not quite natural in Christianized Europe – had become a powerful element of this tradition at the Renaissance, and had passed on from Milton to Wordsworth and to Arnold, always growing more formal and empty until it became ignoble in our own time – just as classical forms passed on from Raphael to the Academies. Anarchic revolt is now coming to an end, and the arts are about to restate the traditional morality. A great work of art, the 'Ode to a Nightingale' not less than the 'Ode to Duty', is rooted in the past, as the Mass which goes back to savage folk-lore. In what temple-garden did the nightingale first sing?

84

No art can conquer the people alone – the people are conquered by an ideal of life upheld by authority. As this ideal is rediscovered, the arts, music and poetry, painting and literature, will draw close together.

85

The Abbey Theatre will fail to do its full work because there is no accepted authority to explain why the more difficult pleasure is the nobler pleasure. The fascination of the national movement for me in my youth was, I think, that it seemed to be an image of a social ideal which could give fine life and fine art authority. One cannot love a nation struggling to realize itself without an idea of the nation as a whole being present in one's mind. One could always appeal to it in the mind of others. National spirit is, for the present, dying, because the influence of the *Nation* newspaper, which had this synthetic thought, has passed away. The result is that plays like *Kincora* (which should have certain poems and traditions to help it, and at its first production caused so much excitement), rouse a slight interest, while Casey's[1] plays grow more and more popular. Casey alone requires nothing but his own thought.

[1] W. F. Casey.

86

A mind without traditional culture, moral or literary, is only powerful in hate. A clever man unhelped by a synthetic social ideal, or the remnant of it which lives on as culture in certain social regions, becomes an executioner. Ricketts[1] said this to me a year ago: 'Artists begin to hesitate to accept public tasks because the almost certain attack may ruin their reputation.' In Ireland, where the cultivated remnant has no power on public opinion, what is a little true of all modern states becomes a portent, a prophecy of what is to come.

87

I cry out continually against my life. I have sleepless nights, thinking of the time that I must take from my poetry, from the harvest of the Lord – last night I could not sleep – and yet perhaps I must do all these things that I may set myself into a life of action, so as to express not the traditional poet but that forgotten thing, the normal active man.

88

We require a new statement of the moral doctrine, which shall be accepted by the average man, but which will at the same time be plainly beyond his power in practice. Classical morality in its decay became an instrument in the hands of commonplace energy to overthrow distinguished men. A true system of morals is obviously from the first a weapon in the hands of the most distinguished. The Catholic Church created a system only possible for saints – hence its prolonged power. Its definition of the good was narrow, but it did not set out to make shopkeepers. A lofty morality should be tolerant, for none declare its laws but those worn out with its warfare, and they must pity sinners. Besides, it will have taken a personal form in their minds and they will have the timidity of discoverers, as well perhaps as the courtesy of soldiers.

[1] Charles Ricketts (1866-1931), painter and stage-designer. Several meetings with Yeats are described in *Self-Portrait taken from the Letters and Journals of Charles Ricketts*, compiled by T. Sturge Moore, edited by Cecil Lewis (London, Peter Davies, 1939).

89

The preference for certain subjects in any art is a sign of a compact between the artist and society.

90

On George Moore.

> Moore once had visits from the Muse
> But fearing that she would refuse
> An ancient lecher took to geese
> He now get novels at his ease.

Made long ago but written now because it comes up into memory, and it may amuse me in some moment of exasperation with that artless man.

91

March 10 [1909]. Yesterday a childish sensation suddenly came back to me. I was looking at a great red flag with a Union Jack in the corner, hanging in the rain over a shop. I remembered suddenly a long-forgotten delightful sensation: the sensation of holding between my fingers when a child of six or seven the red bunting of a small flag of the same kind somebody had given me. It was bright sunlight and I seemed to smell a bit of tarred cord, which I suppose was fastened to the flag.

92

I notice some slackness in Miss Allgood's rehearsals.[1] I noticed the same in Fay's. All these young people are the first generation in their families to do intellectual work, and though with strong, fresh and simple imagination and unspoiled taste, prolonged application is difficult to them. They have no acquired faculties. Most of them are naturally sweet-tempered, but they have no control over their tempers once they are aroused. Miss Allgood, for instance, cannot distinguish between necessary reproof to some actor and anger

---

[1] Sara Allgood served as a producer at the Abbey for a short time after W. G. Fay's resignation.

against him; this injures her authority. The reverse is of course true; one should find fault as little as possible when angry.

93

March 12 [1909]. Last night my sister Lily told me that a week or so ago one of her work-girls dreamed that she saw my sister Lolly being married. There were tables and wedding cake and broken wine-glasses. She woke, and then slept and dreamed again. This time she saw my sister Lolly in bed in a brightly lit room. Someone was holding a child, and there was a doctor in the room and there were broken medicine bottles. Ruth Pollexfen spoke of the dream to a woman who is wise in dreams, and she said, 'It means a marriage broken off by a deceitful woman, but it comes on again.' A few days ago Lolly herself dreamed she saw what seemed to be three dead bodies on a bed. One had its face to the wall, one had a mask, a pink mask like a child's toy mask, and before she could look at the third somebody put a mask on it too. While she was looking at them the body with its face to the wall suddenly moved. The same night Ruth dreamed that she saw three very long funerals and also that she saw what she thought was a dead body on [a] bed. She thought it was the body of a brother of hers who died lately. She lay down on the bed by it, and it suddenly moved. The same night Lily dreamed that she had received three telegrams. I shall show this account to my sister and I leave a blank for her corrections if I have made a mistake.

My sister says the above is quite correct. WBY. 26 March [1909].

94

March 12 [1909]. There is a sinking away of national feeling which is very simple in its origin. You cannot keep the idea of a nation alive where there are no national institutions to reverence, no national success to admire, without a model of it in the mind of the people. You can call it 'Kathleen-ni-Houlihan' or the 'Shan Van Vocht' in a mood of simple feeling, and love that image, but for the general purposes of life you must have a complex mass of images, making up a model like an architect's model. The Young Ireland poets created this with certain images rather simple in their conception that filled the mind of the young – Wolfe Tone, King Brian, Emmet, Owen Roe, Sarsfield, the Fisherman of Kinsale. It answered the traditional slanders on Irish character too, and started an apologetic habit, but its most powerful work was this creation of sensible images for the affections, vivid enough to follow men on to the scaffold. As was necessary, the ethical ideas involved were very simple, needing neither study nor unusual gifts for the understanding of them. Our own movement began by trying to do the same thing in a more profound and enduring way. When I was twenty-five or twenty-six I dreamed of writing a sort of *Légende des Siècles* of Ireland, setting out with my *Wanderings of Oisin* and having something of every age. Johnson's work and, later, Lady Gregory's work carried on the dream in a different form; and it was only when Synge began to write that I saw that our movement would have to give up the deliberate creation of a kind of Holy City in the imagination, a Holy Sepulchre, as it were, or Holy Grail for the Irish mind, and saw that we must be content to express the individual. The Irish people were not educated enough to accept as an image of Ireland anything more profound, more true of human nature as a whole, than the schoolboy thought of Young Ireland. When the attack began on Lady Gregory's style, because of the peasant elements, I was confirmed in this. You can only create a model of a race which will inspire the action of the race as a whole, as apart from exceptional individuals, if you share with it some simple moral understanding of life. Milton and Shakespeare inspire the active life of England, but they do it through exceptional individuals whose influence on the rest is indirect. We must not try to create a school. We have no understanding of life we can teach to others. If we could create a conception of the race as noble as Aeschylus and Sophocles had of Greece, it would be attacked on some trivial ground and the crowd would follow either some mind which copied the rhetoric of Young Ireland, or the obvious sentiments of popular English literature with a few Irish thoughts and feelings added for conscience' sake.

Meanwhile the need of a model of the nation, of some moral

diagram, is as great as in the early nineteenth century when national feeling was losing itself in a religious feud over tithes and emancipation. Neither the grammars of the Gaelic League nor the industrialism of the *Leader*, nor the attacks on the Irish Party in *Sinn Féin* give any sensible image for the affections. Yet from Lady Gregory almost always, from parts of Synge, from Katharine Tynan and Lionel Johnson, from O'Grady, from my work, could be taken material that would enable a school of journalists with very simple moral ideas to build up an historical and literary nationalism as powerful as the old and nobler. They could then bid the people love and not hate.

95

I told my sister that I have offered, if the Dublin branch of the Psychical Research Society would arrange it, to spend the night in the Baggot Street haunted house. She said, 'Oh, I know about that house. I saw a furniture-van there one day and furniture going in, and ten days after the house was empty again; and one day somebody I know was passing by in the early morning and she saw an old woman on a window-sill, clinging to the sash. She was the caretaker. The ghost had driven her out and there was a policeman trying to get her down. But the pious Protestants say that there is no ghost or anything but the young novices in the Convent opposite screaming in the night-time.'

96

To put the matter of my note on the page before this clearly. In our age it is impossible to create, as I had dreamed, an heroic and passionate conception of life worthy of the study of men elsewhere and at other times, and to make that conception the special dream of the Irish people. The Irish people till they are better educated must dream impermanent dreams, and if they do not find them they will be ruined by the half-sirs with their squalid hates and envies. There was a time when I thought of a noble body for all eyes, a soul for subtle understandings, and, to unite these two, Eleusinian rites. Instead, the people cry out for stones and vapour, pedantry and hysteria, rhetoric and sentiment.

97

Why does the struggle to come at truth take away our pity and the struggle to overcome our passions restore it again?

98

March 14 [1909]. The national feeling which is, I believe, dying could be roused into all its old intensity if some man with good education – and, if a Catholic, he should have been educated outside Ireland – gathering about him a few men like himself, were to found a new *Nation*, forbidding to it all personal attacks and all arguments that assume a base motive in opponents,[1] and choosing for its national policy not what seems to be most desirable in the abstract but such policy as might stir the imagination while getting the support of the greatest possible number of educated men. Ireland is ruined by abstraction, and should for a session learn to prefer what may seem a worse policy if it brings her better men. So long as all is ordered for attack, and that alone, leaders will instinctively increase the number of enemies that they may give their followers something to do, and Irish enemies rather than English because they are the more easily injured, and because the greater the enemy the greater the hatred and therefore the greater the power. They would give a nation the frenzy of a sect. The sign that this policy, very powerful in the time of Parnell, is over is that the national parties are more and more drifting into the hands of feebler or more ignorant men. Able men do not join, as a rule, what seem hopeless causes. The success of the Saturday *Daily Express* under Gill[2] proved that the ideas of cultivated life could at this moment be made most powerful

---

[1] 'They must to keep their certainty accuse
All that are different of a base intent.'
                'The Leaders of the Crowd', *Collected Poems*, p. 207.
   [2] 'Horace Plunkett had bought the *Daily Express*. Under T. P. Gill, an ex-Parnellite Member and London journalist, it expounded Plunkett's agricultural policy, avoiding all that might excite passion. Gill had spent his life manipulating incompatibles; at the Parnellite split he took neither side.' *Autobiographies*, p. 420. Thomas Patrick Gill (1858–1931) was editor of the Dublin *Daily Express* from July 1898 to December 1899. During that time he published, in the Saturday numbers, essays by Yeats, Lady Gregory, AE, John Eglinton, Synge and other writers.

in Ireland. Half-a-dozen men with a little money and, a thing much harder to get, knowledge, united to a passion like that of the ignorant, could change the future of Ireland.

99

The education given by the Catholic schools seems to me to be in all matters of general culture a substituting of pedantry for taste. Men learn the dates of writers, the external facts of masterpieces, and not sense of style and feeling for life. I have never met a young man from an Irish Catholic school who did not seem to me injured by the literature and the literary history he had learned at it. The arts have nothing to give but that joy of theirs which is perhaps the other side of sorrow. They are always an exhausting contemplation, and we are very ready in our youth, before habits have been formed, to turn from it to pedantry, which offers to the mind a kind of sensual ease. The young men and women who have not been through the Secondary Schools seem to me upon the other hand much more imaginative than Protestant boys and girls and to have better taste. My sisters have the same experience. Catholic education seems to destroy the qualities which they get from their religion. Provincialism destroys the nobility of the Middle Ages.

100

March 17 [1909]. Coole. As I go to and from my room, I pass a wall covered with Augustus John etchings.[1] He is the extreme revolt from academic form. I notice, for they are most before my eyes, a

[1] 'Augustus John has just left and I have time for letters. He has done numberless portraits of me to work up into an etching – all powerful ugly gypsy things.' Yeats, writing from Coole, to Florence Farr, 25 September 1907, *Letters* (Wade), pp. 492–3. John wrote to Alexandra Schepeler from Coole, letter undated but postmarked 17 September 1907: 'Painting Yeats is becoming quite a habit. He has a natural and sentimental prejudice in favour of the W. B. Yeats he and other people have been accustomed to see and imagine for so many years. He is now 44 and a robust virile and humorous personality (while still the poet of course). I cannot see in him any definite resemblance to the youthful Shelley in a lace collar. To my mind he is far more interesting as he is, as maturity is more interesting than immaturity. But my unprejudiced vision must seem brutal and unsympathetic to those in whom direct vision is supplanted by a vague and sentimental memory.' Huntington Library, HM 28292.

woman with a back showing the shoulder-blades strongly and a half-turned face with a big nose, and an *Epithalamium*. In the *Epithalamium* a boy, ill-grown and ungainly, holds out his arms to a tall woman with thin shoulders [and] a large stomach. Near, there is another study of a woman with the same large stomach and thin shoulders. Through all these fifty or sixty etchings there is not one that does not break with violence the canons of measurement which we derive from the Renaissance. These bodies are the bodies of clerks and seamstresses and students, of all upon whom the burden of sedentary life weighs heavily, or of those broken by some kind of labour. A gymnast set to train the body would find in all these some defect to overcome, and when he had overcome them he would have brought them in every case nearer to that ancient canon which comes down to us from the gymnasium of Greece, and which when it is present marks, like any other literary element, a compact between the artist and society, a purpose held in common with his time to create emotions or forms which Nature also desires. John is interested not in the social need, in the perpetual thirst for ever more health and physical serviceableness, for bodies fitted for the labour of life, but in character, in the revolt of the individual from all that makes it like others. The old art, if it [had] gone to its logical conclusion, would have led to the creation of one single type of man, and one single type of woman, in whom would have been concentrated, however, by a kind of deification, the capacity for all energy and all passion, a Krishna, a Christ, a Dionysus, or a drawing of all into a single mind as at the end of the cycles; and at all times a poetical painter, a Botticelli, a da Vinci, a Watts, a Rossetti, creates as his supreme achievement one type of face, known afterwards by his name. The new art creates innumerable types, but in each of these types the capacity for passion has almost disappeared before some habit of body or mind. That woman with the bad shoulders, for instance, a nature too keen, too clever, with the cleverness of people who cannot rest for any passion; and that young lad with his arms out will, one is certain, sink back into disillusionment from physical exhaustion after the brief pleasure of a passion that is in part mere curiosity. Everywhere some limiting environment or idiosyncrasy is suggested; everywhere it is the fact that is studied, and not that energy which seems measureless and hates all that is not itself. It is a powerful but prosaic art, celebrating the fall into division not the resurrection into unity.[1] Did not even Balzac, who looked at the world so often with similar eyes, find it necessary to deny character to his great ladies and young lovers that he might give them much passion? What beautiful woman delights us by her look of character? That shows itself when beauty is gone, being the creation of habit; it's the stalk that remains after the flowers of spring have withered. Beauty consumes character with what Patmore calls 'the integrity of fire'.

101

[2]It is this absence of the capacity for passion, compensated by an intellectual interest that pleases men, which makes women dislike all the schools of characterization, and makes the modern artist despise woman's judgment. Women for the same reason dislike pure comedy. How few women like Molière!

102

My room[3] is hung with Arundel prints, a very large number from Botticelli, Benozzo Gozzoli, Giorgione, Girolamo dai Libri, Melozzo da Forli, Mantegna, the Van Eycks. Here everywhere is the expression of desire, though in the Van Eycks the new interest has begun. All these people have such bodies and are so arrayed as to make happy an amorous woman or a great king. The martyrs and saints even must show the capacity for all they have renounced.

103

♂♂ M.c.p.[4] Miss Allgood accepted an invitation to sing at a concert got up by Lady Lyttelton,[5] without consulting me. She now writes

---

[1] 'Daughter of Beulah, Sing
His fall into Division & his Resurrection to Unity.'
Blake, *Vala or the Four Zoas*, Night the First, lines 20–1, *Complete Writings*, p. 264.
[2] 'March 18' deleted.
[3] 'Here at Coole my room is hung . . .', *Autobiographies*, p. 502.
[4] Mars conjunction mid-heaven progressed.
[5] Wife of the Commander-in-Chief of the British Army in Ireland.

saying that it will injure her; I have told her to get out of it, alleging 'indisposition' as her reason for withdrawal. An avowed objection to 'God Save the King' would drive away from the Abbey some of our most constant supporters and we cannot make it pay on pit alone. I have written to Lady Lyttelton a letter with the following statement on the matter generally: 'This absurd question embitters life in Ireland constantly, and prevents the two parties uniting outside politics. The responsibility is mainly with the party which has most education and official power. It insists on pressing the thing, where no principle is involved, knowing that it at once raises what Nationalists look upon as a fundamental principle, and that when it carries its point it generally does so by lowering an opponent in his own eyes. Much of the passion which Nationalists throw into the question comes from the fact that there is so often some material advantage to be gained by the individual if he gives way. The pressing of the matter is from the Unionist point of view pure folly, for it forces expression of disloyalty upon Nationalists, and in this country drove a Deputy Lieutenant into anti-English politics.'

104

I was talking of Patmore's Odes with Lady Gregory the other night and saying that I thought his mood nobler than Tennyson's. She said, 'Tennyson had the British Empire for God, and Queen Victoria for Virgin Mary.'

105

March 18 [1909]. I dare say that these notes, if some chance eye light on them, may seem morbid; but they help me to understand myself, and I remember hearing a man of science once argue that all progress is at the outset 'pathological'. I know that I have already made moral gains.

The pain others give us passes away in their later kindness; the pain of one's own blunders, especially when they hurt one's vanity, never passes away. One's own acts are isolated and one act does not buy absolution for another. They are always present before a strangely abstract judgment. One is never a unity, a personality: to oneself,

small acts of years ago are so painful in the memory that often one
starts at the presence a little below 'the threshold of consciousness'
of a thought that remains unknown. It sheds a vague light like that
of the moon before it rises, or after its setting. Vanity is so intimately
associated with one's spiritual identity that the errors or what hurt
it, above all if they came from it, are more painful in the memory
than serious sins, and yet I do not think this means that one is very
vain. The harm one does to others is lost in changing events and
passes away, and so is healed by time, unless it was very great.
Looking back, I find only one offence which is as painful to me as a
hurt to vanity. It was done to a man who died shortly after.[1] Because
of his death it has not been touched by the transforming hand –
tolerant Nature has not rescued it from Justice.

106

Made another attempt to work at play[2] and failed. I think it may be
partly health, as I have that slight headache I used to have at the
time of my breakdown. The mood of creation is very fragile.

107

I think all happiness depends on having the energy to assume the
mask of some other self, that all joyous or creative life is a rebirth
as something not oneself, something created in a moment and perpetually renewed in playing a game like that of a child where one
loses the infinite pain of self-realization, a grotesque or solemn
painted face put on that one may hide from the terrors of judgment,
an imaginative Saturnalia that makes one forget reality. Perhaps all
the sins and energies of the world are but the world's flight from an
infinite blinding beam.

108

March 20 [1909]. Maud Gonne writes that she is learning Gaelic.
I would sooner see her work at Gaelic propaganda than any other

[1] Section VII of 'First Draft', pp. 33–4.
[2] *The Player Queen.*

Irish movement I can think of, except some movement of decorative art. I fear for her any renewed devotion to an opinion. Women, because the main event of their lives has been a giving of themselves, give themselves to an opinion as if [it] were some terrible stone doll. We take up an opinion lightly and are easily false to it, and when faithful keep the habit of many interests. We still see the world, if we are strong of mind and body, with steady and careful eyes, but opinions become as their children or their sweethearts, and the greater their emotional nature the more do they forget all other things. They grow cruel, as if [in] defence of lover or child, and all this is done for something other than human life. At last the opinion becomes so much a part of them that it is as though a part of their flesh becomes, as it were, stone, and much of their being passes out of life. It was part of her power in the past that, though she made this surrender with her mind, she kept the sweetness of her voice and much humour, yet I cannot but fear for her.[1] Women should have their play with dolls finished in childish happiness, for if they play with them again it is amid hatred and malice.

109

Women should find in the mask enough joy to forget the doll without regret. There is always a living face behind the mask.

110

The Turn of the Road.[2] Performance of the 'Theatre of Ireland' tonight. A good honest performance, and a great contrast to the

---

[1] In 'A Prayer for My Daughter' (1919) Yeats wrote:

'An intellectual hatred is the worst,
So let her think opinions are accursed.
Have I not seen the loveliest woman born
Out of the mouth of Plenty's horn,
Because of her opinionated mind
Barter that horn and every good
By quiet natures understood
For an old bellows full of angry wind?'
Collected Poems, p. 213.

[2] By Rutherford Mayne. The play began its run at the Rotunda on 19 March 1909.

performance of *Maeve*[1] some months ago. Nesbitt[2] good, very quiet and yet with enough of emotion. The author himself quiet and experienced. The man who played the father of the two sons restless and indistinct, but the making of a good actor. The brother of the hero good. The whole a real study of Northern life. Mrs Fitzpatrick[3] the popular success of the piece, but I am not quite certain that I do not see under her Northern peasant the *mannequin d'osier* of a traditional stage cockney; I am not sure, however. The audience carried me back to our own first audiences in St Theresa's Hall.[4] It laughed at everything, but not more at a good line than when a hat fell on the head of an actor from a rack. It was certainly quite unused to plays, and would be useless for delicate work. But where did it come from? It was a large audience, but more I should think called out by a desire to serve its country than by desire of entertainment. It was certainly, taken as a whole, not an Abbey audience, though it was a little like our 'paper'.[5] Must find out where they come from. It was Saturday, but even on Saturday we do not get this kind of untrained audience. Was our audience made from like stuff?

The play is loose in structure. The first Act is 'a completed action', and so like a separate play, and the 'Epilogue' could have followed on the second Act without a break. The author made the break because he had not skill to make the transition by dialogue. The first Act should not have ended with the burning of the fiddle, which suggests an ended action. I think the fiddle should be destroyed before the curtain goes up. The broken fragments might be there. This would make the wandering fiddler and his fiddle more important. If it closed with the call of the music outside, that would have cast the imagination forward, or with this call conquered by the proposed marriage. As it is, the play has dialogue and character, but nothing else.

The authorities of the Rotunda, I notice, supply – though their

---

[1] By Edward Martyn. In 1906 he was elected first President of the Theatre of Ireland.
[2] George Nesbitt played the part of Robbie John.
[3] Nora Fitzpatrick, who played the part of Mrs Granahan.
[4] St Theresa's Total Abstinence Hall, Clarendon Street, Dublin, where Yeats's *Cathleen Ni Houlihan* was first performed on 3 April 1902.
[5] Shopkeepers who were given free passes to the Theatre in return for exhibiting Abbey posters in their shop windows.

costumes are Irish and most of the plays Gaelic League plays or the like – the picturesque cottage of the English stage, except that the beams in the wall are not placed as one has ever seen them. I have little doubt that the scene painter is Irish and, like the amateur actors and playwrights and the managers of the Rotunda, has never seen a cottage with beams in the wall. He agrees with them to honour tradition. At the Abbey there is a drawing-room scene which we never use, but which Miss Horniman[1] has been told was essential for amateurs who hire the Abbey. It is the usual elaborately wainscoted room, French in style, which everyone knows at amateur entertainments. It is the most difficult form of room to make look real, for there is much woodwork in relief. All the shadows by which this relief is shown necessarily contradict the real lighting of the stage. The scene has probably come down, reflected from scene painter to scene painter from the eighteenth century, perhaps from French theatres, for it was, I think, the type of drawing-room in France when scenery was still a new thing in England.

Returning to the 'Theatre of Ireland' performance, one actor, Seaghan MacMurchadha,[2] who played William John Granahan, showed real acting capacity but required much sterner teaching. He was inaudible at the start, and later on repeated one good effect, a curious sly upward turn of the eyes when he looked towards the audience as if to commune with himself, till he got on my nerves. He showed a slight tendency to clown the part, or else was so little at ease that he gave that impression through over-anxiety. The general performance was rough, but with this doubtful exception perfectly honest and sincere, and throughout a real reflection of life. There was nothing like the acting of the part of Jane Graeme by one of the Ulster players,[3] a wonderful display of a half-sensual but wholly self-sacrificing love, an unforgettable thing, but the principal men were as good. The hostile accounts of this play, except in so far as they referred to the players not knowing their parts at the first production (and of this I cannot judge), which were sent to me last autumn, were certainly unjust. George Moore, I understand, con-

[1] Annie E. F. Horniman bought and restored the Abbey Theatre, then gave the Irish National Theatre Society free use of it, with a subsidy, from 1904 to 1910.
[2] Jack Morrow.
[3] Una Walker, Máire Nic Shiubhlaigh's sister.

demns this performance which I have just seen, but I think he is blind
and deaf to all that comes from folk life; both he and Bernard Shaw,
as one could foretell from their work, dislike all crooked illogical
things.[1] All their buildings are made by science in an architect's
office, and erected by joyless hands. I did not see the first play, but
hear it was bad.

111

March 21 [1909]. I have been reading Taylor's *Owen Roe O'Neill*, an
able historical book, very interesting to me because I think I find in
Owen Roe[2] that directness and simplicity of mind which is today
Protestant and Ascendancy, and in his now opponents, now allies, of
the Kilkenny Council that slackness and vagueness which is today
Catholic. He was in Irish affairs a last representative of Celtic
Catholic aristocracy, and simple because of the habit of personal
energy and of an aim accepted by associates not too far below him.
But even more interesting to me than Owen Roe is Taylor. In all
this able book there is not one sentence of universal meaning, not
one phrase because of wisdom or beauty detachable from its context;
everything is argued from a premise, and wisdom and style and
noble life come from the self-evident things, from the things that
only require statement. I realize for the first time the reason of my
own hostility to a man I always admired. He had the pedantry of
Irish Catholic education, inspired by an almost mad energy which
made his mind like some noisy and powerful machine. This pedantry
comes from intellectual timidity, from the dread of leaving the mind
alone among impressions where all seems heretical, and from the
habit of political and religious apologetics. This pedantry destroys
religion as it destroys poetry, for it destroys all direct knowledge.
We taste and feel and see the truth. We do not reason ourselves into

[1] '. . . I listened to *Arms and the Man* with admiration and hatred. It seemed to me
inorganic, logical straightness and not the crooked road of life . . .', *Autobiographies*,
p. 283.
[2] After the Confederation of Kilkenny in October 1642 O'Neill was the leader of the
Old Irish Catholics. Victor at Benburb in June 1646, he was the only commander who
might have faced Oliver Cromwell with any hope of success, when Cromwell landed in
Dublin on 15 August 1649. O'Neill's death on 6 November 1649 made the defeat of the
Catholics inevitable. The book to which Yeats refers is John F. Taylor, *Owen Roe O'Neill*
(London, Unwin, 1896).

it. He on his side because of those very things that give me, I hope,
a little wisdom, a little poetry, probably thought me effeminate. A
stone is always stronger, more masculine than a living thing. He
was a great orator because the passion of his voice was a portion of
self-evident truth. He became when he spoke like a great actor in a
poor play. His passion, the nobility of his will, had universal significance, was a part of wisdom, though his logic was but a temporary
thing, the apologetics of a moment, a mere woven thing as the web of
a spider, instead of being, like living thought, an intricacy of leaf and
twig.

112

Duncan[1] has been looking up my coat of arms for the purpose of a
bookplate. I gave him the crest, a goat's head in a coronet. He found
that a Mary Yeats of Lifford, who died in 1675, had the following:

The gates are not, he thinks, correctly drawn as he had to do the
whole from description and has never seen gates on a coat of arms.
Being a woman, there was no crest, but the English 'Yates' had the
goat's head. Description of coat of arms, Per fess embattled argent
and sable. Three gates countercharged. Can my sister get back to
'Mary Yeats'? Mary is an old family name, and we had relations,
not very far from Lifford, in north Sligo. Some of the English family
had on the fess three goats' heads.

113[2]

  ×   To lie no more
  ×   To give up falsehood is to be undone
      Who lies no longer is undone:

---

[1] James Duncan, who took a leading part in founding the Arts Club.
[2] 'The Coming of Wisdom with Time', published as 'Youth and Age' in *McClure's
Magazine*, December 1910, *Collected Poems*, p. 105.

× All through the days of my lying youth
    Through all the lying days of youth

× I plucked the flower and blossom in the sun
    I swayed my blossoms in the sun

Now I may wither into truth.

Though leaves are many, the root ~~but~~ is one
               or
To give up falsehood is to be undone
(in which case read 'Blossom' for 'flower' and take out
   'my' in line 2)
Through all the lying days of my youth
I swayed my leaves and flowers in the sun
Now I may wither into the truth.

114

Last night at 'The Theatre of Ireland' I talked with the man next me. He liked the performance but complained of not hearing its lines. He then said, 'I have been to your theatre too. I like your popular plays, *The Suburban Groove* and those plays by that Frenchman, I do not remember his name,[1] but I don't like your mysteries.' I thought he meant something of mine as the word 'mystery' is the popular reproach invented since *The Shadowy Waters*, but found he meant *Kincora*. I said, 'Why do you find that mysterious?' He said, 'O, I know nothing about all that history.' I replied, 'When I was young every Irish Nationalist young man knew as much about Brian Boru as about St Patrick.' He thought I was talking of the peasants and began to tell how he was afraid that sort of knowledge was dying out among them. He evidently thought it their business alone, like the rath and the blessed well.

115

March 23 [1909]. I heard last night that Lane has little chance of getting the Irish party to help the Corporation to carry out their

[1] '... evidently Molière', *Autobiographies*, p. 505.

promise to pay for the gallery.[1] Boland[2] says, 'We all feel that the one thing wanted is commercial education.' I urged a public deputation to Redmond, asking for a Bill, and the temporary closing of the gallery if necessary. One should insist on all important decisions of this kind being public. If the thought of Ireland is to be educated for commerce alone, the decision should be recorded for future use. After our present industrialism will come reaction, and the more decisive the industrialism can be forced to be, the sooner will come reaction. Besides, I doubt Nationalists liking to acknowledge in public that they accepted a gallery they could not or would not support. If Redmond refused or said he could do nothing, some man like Iveagh[3] might come forward, if only to score off his political opponents. The deed of gift to the Corporation has never been signed.

116

March 23 [1909]. MacDonagh in today. Very sad about Ireland. Says that he finds a barrier between himself and the Irish-speaking peasants, who are 'cold, dark and reticent' and 'too polite'. He watches the Irish-speaking boys at his school. When nobody is looking at them and they are alone or with the Irish-speaking gardener,[4] they are merry, clever and talkative; when they meet an English-speaker or one who has learned Gaelic, they are 'stupid'. They are a different world. I read him my note on Taylor and he said, 'I wonder, was he a Catholic? I do not know any Catholics except a few priests. All nearly conform, but they are unbelievers. It cannot last long. Even some priests do not believe. They "form their conscience", that is the phrase. I was nine years in a monastery, but I had to give it up.' I asked about monastic life and he said, 'Everybody is very simple and happy enough. There is a little jealousy sometimes. If one brother goes into the town with the Superior, another brother will be jealous, and they drink sometimes more than

[1] In 1907 Sir Hugh Lane founded the Municipal Gallery in Dublin, to exhibit the work of modern and contemporary artists. He lent thirty-nine pictures, and promised to give them when a proper Gallery was built to receive them. Meanwhile the Dublin Corporation housed the pictures in Harcourt Street.

[2] John P. Boland, Vice-President of the Industrial Development Association 1907–18.

[3] Edward Cecil Guinness, then Viscount, later Earl of Iveagh (1847–1927).

[4] Micheál MacRuairi, at St Enda's.

is good for them.' He then told me that the Bishop of Raphoe has forbidden anybody in his See to contribute to the Gaelic League because its Secretary has 'blasphemed against the holy Saint Adamnan'. The Secretary had said, 'The Bishop is an enemy, like the founder of his See, Saint Adamnan, who tried to injure the Gaelic language by writing in Latin.' MacDonagh says, 'Two old countrymen fell out and one said, "I have a brother who will make you behave", meaning the Bishop of Raphoe, and the other said, "I have a son who will put sense into you", meaning Cardinal Logue.'

117

Molly Allgood[1] came today to ask where I should be tomorrow, as Synge wished to send for me if he is strong enough. He wants 'to make arrangements'. He is dying. They have ceased to give him food. Whether to close the Abbey or to keep it open while he still lives? Poor Molly is going through her work as always; perhaps that is best for her. I feel Synge's coming death less now than when he first became ill. I am used to the thought of it and I do not find I pity him. I pity her. He is fading out of life. I felt the same when I saw Symons in the madhouse – I pitied his wife. He seemed already dead. One does not feel that death is evil when one meets it – evil, I mean, for the one who dies. One's daimon is silent as was that of Socrates before his own death. The wildest sorrow that comes at the thought of death is to think, 'Ages will come and no one in the world ever again look at that nobleness and that beauty.' What is this but to pity unborn multitudes of the living and to praise the dead?

118

March 24 [1909]. Synge is dead. In the early morning he said to the nurse, 'It is no use fighting death any longer', and he turned over and died. I called at the Hospital this afternoon and asked the assistant matron if he knew he was dying. She answered, 'He may have known it for weeks, but he would not have said so to anyone. He would

[1] The actress Máire O'Neill, Sara Allgood's sister: she was engaged to marry Synge.

have no fuss. He was like that.' She added, with emotion in her voice, 'We were devoted to him.'

119

March 28 [1909]. Mr Stephens, Synge's brother-in-law,[1] says he suffered no pain, only great weakness. On Sunday he questioned the doctor and convinced himself that he was dying. He told his brother-in-law next day and was quite cheerful, even making jokes. In the evening he saw Molly and told her to be brave and sent her to me that I might arrange about his writings. On the morning when I heard of his death a heavy storm was blowing and I doubt not when he died that it had well begun. That morning Lady Gregory felt a very great depression and was certain that some evil was coming, but feared for her grandchild, feared it was going to be ill. On the other hand, my sister Lolly said to my other sister at breakfast, 'I think it will be all right with Synge, for last night I saw a galley struggling with a storm and then it shot into calm and bright sunlight and I heard the keel grate on the shore.' One remembers the voyages to Tír na nÓg, certainly voyages of the soul after death to its place of peace.

120

I have been looking through his poems and have read once more that one on page 21, 'I asked if I got sick and died'. Certainly they were there,[2] his 'idiot' enemies. Lawrence[3] who against all regulations rushed up to the dressing-rooms after the *Playboy* to tell the actors they should not have played in so 'disgraceful a play'; Holloway[4] who has always used his considerable influence with the company as well as speaking in public against Synge; there, too, were the feeble friends who pretended to believe but gave no help. And there was

---

[1] Harry Stephens, husband of Synge's sister Annie.

[2] '. . . at the funeral', *Autobiographies*, p. 508. Synge's poem 'A Question' refers to 'living idiots'.

[3] W. J. Lawrence (1862–1940), historian of the theatre. In the debate on the *Playboy*, 4 February 1907, he rebuked Yeats for staging the play at all and said that it should have been taken off at once 'in deference to public opinion' (*Irish Times*, 5 February 1907).

[4] Joseph Holloway (1861–1944), architect, playgoer, diarist. 'Poor Synge, he was a gentle and lovable man personally and not at all like his works.' Holloway, *Diary*, 24 March 1909, National Library of Ireland MSS. 1807 (ii).

O'Donoghue[1] whose obituary notice speaks of Synge's work as only important in promise, of the 'exaggeration' of those who praise it, and then claims that its writer knew Synge so well in Paris (getting the date wrong by two years, however) that he spent many hours a day with him, with Synge who, proud and lonely, almost as proud of his old blood as of his genius, had but few friends. There was Connolly,[2] the Secretary of the Society – it had sent a wreath – whose animosity had much to do with the attacks in *Sinn Féin*. It was, to quote Henderson, a funeral 'small but select'.[3] Someone has quoted to me:

> How shall the ritual then be said
> The requiem then be sung
> By you, by yours the evil eyed
> By yours the slanderous tongue
> That did to death the innocence
> That died, and died so young?

Yet these men came, though but in remorse; they saw his plays, though but to dislike; they spoke his name, though but in slander. Well-to-do Ireland never saw his plays nor spoke his name. Was he ever asked to any country house but Coole? Did anyone ever ask him to a dinner party? Often I have wished for him that he might live long enough to enjoy that communion with idle, charming and cultivated women which Balzac in one of his dedications calls the chief consolation of genius.

121

He knew how to hate, as witness this:

'To a Sister of an Enemy of the Author's, who disapproved of *The Playboy*.'

[1] D. J. O'Donoghue (1866–1917), editor of the *Irish Book-Lover*. The obituary notice is 'John M. Synge: A Personal Appreciation', *Irish Independent*, 26 March 1909.

[2] Séamus O Conghaile (Seamus O'Connolly, not the Labour leader James Connolly) was one of the first members of Sinn Féin: a Belfastman, he worked as a Civil Servant in the Law Courts in Dublin, and wrote many of the articles in *Sinn Féin*. 'While prayers were being read in rather unsympathetic way by the officiating clergyman in the Church, James Connolly and others joined us.' Holloway, *Diary*, 26 March 1909.

[3] 'Miss O'Brennan said . . . she thought the funeral would have been larger, but I mentioned that he would want to have been a publican or a butcher to command a big gathering.' Holloway, *Diary*, 26 March 1909.

Lord, confound this surly sister,
Blight her brow with blotch and blister,
Cramp her larynx, lung, and liver,
In her guts a galling give her.
Let her live to earn her dinners
In Mountjoy with seedy sinners:
Lord, this judgment quickly bring,
And I'm your servant, – J. M. Synge.

When he showed me this, he said with mirthful eyes that since he had written it her husband had got drunk, gone with a harlot, got syphilis, and given it to his wife. Lady Gregory has given me this [poem]. Fearing that his family might destroy the poem, she had copied it. I do not know how he learned the facts about the husband and wife, but he was very truthful and ever matter-of-fact, being in every way very simple.

122

In Paris Synge once said to me, 'We should unite stoicism, asceticism and ecstasy. Two of them have often come together, but the three never.'

123

I believe that something I said to him may have suggested to him the poem, 'I asked if I got sick and died'. Maurice Joy[1] had frequently attacked his work while admitting him to be a man of genius. He attacked it because, I have no doubt, he wanted to be on good terms with the people about him. When Synge was in hospital to be operated on, Joy was there too, and I told Synge how whenever I spoke of his illness to any man that man said, 'And it is so sad about Maurice Joy,' until I could stand it no longer and burst with, 'I hope he'll die,' and now I was being abused, as someone said to me, 'all over the town as without heart'. People were constantly inquiring how Joy was, I found out, but hardly anyone called to ask for Synge. Two or three weeks later Synge wrote this poem. I have no doubt my

---

[1] A minor poet and literary journalist, a member of the Arts Club. In later years he emigrated to the U.S.A. and died there in 1951.

words had set his mind running on the thought of the way the fool flourishes, more especially as I had prophesied that Joy would flourish. He saw my rage on that subject. To be operated on at the same time as Synge struck one as sheer insolence. Joy's illness did indeed win him so much sympathy that he was made private secretary to Horace Plunkett, and now when he is playing golf he will say sometimes, with the English accent he has acquired of late, to some player who has a favour to beg of some great man, 'I know him well, I will say a word for you in that quarter.'[1]

124

I said to Stephens, 'In the Theatre there is no doubt that his bad health began with the *Playboy* trouble. Even a successful performance of one of his plays made him ill.' Stephens answered, 'Oh, no, the Synges are a very strong race.' He thought, however, that Synge's end was hastened by his mother's death a few weeks ago, and certainly in men like Synge all affections supported by habit are very strong.

There are two types of men of genius. The men who, like Byron, like Goethe, like Shelley have finished personalities, active wills and all their faculties at the service of the will; and men like Goldsmith, like Wordsworth, like Keats who have little personality, little personal will, but fiery and brooding imagination. The last kind have the advantage that all they write is a part of character, but they are often powerless before events. They drift through life and have often only one visible strength, the strength to reject from life and thought all that would distract them from their work, and only this so long as it is a passive act. Synge, had he married young, would, I have little doubt, never have written or thought of writing. I doubt if he would even have helped a movement like ours. On the other hand it was easy for him to refuse any distraction alien to self-expression. I believe that in early days his family tried in vain to make him take a profession. He was a drifting, silent man, full of hidden passion, and his physical weakness increased this impression.

[1] Across this entry Yeats has written: 'Maurice Joy has since absconded leaving many debts. WBY. January 1912.'

I think he loved wild islands because wild people seemed an embodiment of his hidden dreams. His strength was moral and imaginative, and not under control of his will. He was terribly shaken by the *Playboy* riot, on the first night of it confused and excited, knowing not what to do, but it made no difference in his work. When it was over he neither exaggerated out of defiance nor softened out of timidity. He went on with his plans as if nothing had happened, altering the *Tinker* in a more unpopular form, but writing a beautiful, peaceful *Deirdre*. His strength was in character, not in will, and misfortune shook his physical nature while it left his intellect and moral nature untroubled. For the same reason, while hardly aware of the existence of other writers – neither Lady Gregory nor I know what he thought of our work[1] – he had the most perfect modesty and simplicity in daily intercourse. With him, self-assertion of any kind was impossible. The external self, the mask, the persona, was a shadow; character was all.

125

On the night of the *Playboy* trouble he said to me, 'So-and-so,' naming a friend of his, a young doctor, 'says, "It is all I can do to keep myself from jumping up on a seat and pointing out among the howling men in the pit those whom I am treating for venereal diseases."'

126

The Irish weekly papers notice Synge's death with short and for the most part grudging notices. There was an obscure Gaelic League singer who was one of the leaders of the demonstration against the *Playboy*. He died on the same day. The *Sinn Féin* notices both deaths in the same article and gives three-fourths of it to the rioter.[2] For Synge they have but grudging words, as was to be expected.

[1] Synge's estimate of Yeats's work is given in 'Le Mouvement Intellectuel Irlandais', *L'Européen*, 31 May 1902: his review of Lady Gregory's *Cuchulain of Muirthemne* appeared in the *Speaker*, 7 July 1902. Both items are reprinted in *Collected Works*, vol. II, edited by Alan Price (London, Oxford University Press, 1966).

[2] *Sinn Féin*, vol. III, no. 152, 3 April 1909, has an obituary essay, 'The Dead', on J. M. Synge and John Lawless: 'Ireland loses a national musician in Mr Lawless. . . . Five years hence, the one thing remembered about J. M. Synge will be that he wrote *Riders to the Sea*.' John Lawless was conductor of the Emmet Choir.

127

Molly tells me that Synge went to see Stephen MacKenna[1] and his wife before going into Elpis[2] and said good-bye saying, 'You will never see me again.' The poems were some of them written long ago but revised lately.

128

Celebrations

i

He was one of those unmoving souls in whom there is a perpetual 'Last Day', a perpetual trumpeting and coming to judgment.

ii

He did not speak to men and women, asking judgment of them as lesser writers do; but, knowing himself a part of judgment, he was silent.

iii

We pity the living and not such dead as he. He has gone upward out of his ailing body into the heroical fountains. We are parched by time.

iv

He had no need of our sympathies and so kept hid from all but all the knowledge of his soon-coming death, and was cheerful to the very end, even joking a little some few hours before he died. It was as though we and the things about us died away from him and not he from us.

129

Detractions

April 2 [1909].

He had that egotism of the man of genius which Nietzsche compares to the egotism of a woman with child. Neither I nor Lady Gregory had even a compliment from him or, I think, thanks for

---

[1] Stephen MacKenna (1872–1934), friend of Synge and Yeats; classical scholar, translator of Plotinus.
[2] The private hospital in which Synge died.

working for him. After *Hyacinth*[1] Lady Gregory went home the
moment the play was over, not waiting for the congratulation of
friends, to get supper for him (for he was almost always ailing and
weakly). All he said of the triumphant *Hyacinth* was, 'I expected to
like it better.' He had under charming and modest manners, in
almost all things of life, a complete absorption in his own dream. I
have never heard him praise any writer, living or dead, but some old
French farce-writer. For him nothing existed but his thought. He
claimed nothing for it aloud, he never said any of those confident
things I say too often when angry, but one knew that he valued
nothing else. He was too confident for self-assertion. I once said to
George Moore, 'Synge has always the better of you, for you have
brief but ghastly moments during which you admit the existence of
other writers. Synge never has.' I do not think he disliked other
writers – they did not exist. One did not think him an egotist – he
was too sympathetic in the ordinary affairs of life and too simple. In
the arts he knew no language but his own.

130

I have often envied him his absorption as I have envied Verlaine
his vice. Can a man of genius ever make that complete renunciation
of the world necessary to the full expression of himself without some
vice or some lack? You were happy or at least blessed, blind old man
of Scio, 'rocky isle'.[2]

131

Two plays last night, *Time*, a fantasy, a little noble, a little profound,
and full of suggestion, and *Cross-roads*,[3] a logical work without

---

[1] *Hyacinth Halvey*, first produced at the Abbey on 19 February 1906.

[2] This sentence appears in *Autobiographies*, p. 512 as: 'You were happy or at least
blessed, "blind old man of Scio's rocky isle".' The source is Byron, *The Bride of Abydos*,
II ii 26–7: 'All – save immortal dreams that could beguile/The blind old man of Scio's
rocky isle!' Yeats associated the passage with another, from the Homeric Hymn to
Apollo, which he quotes, *Autobiographies*, p. 151: 'A blind man; he dwells upon rocky
Chios; his songs shall be the most beautiful for ever.' Chios was supposedly Homer's
birthplace. The Delian part of the Hymn is ascribed to Cynaethus of Chios.

[3] *Time*, by Norreys Connell (Conal O'Riordan), and *The Cross-roads*, by Lennox
Robinson (Esmé Stuart), were produced at the Abbey on 1 April 1909.

suggestion or nobility. I accepted this last play because of its central idea, which, though seemingly sheer superstition, is original and seemed the outset of a point of view towards life. In the four morning papers *Time* is cursed or ignored and *The Cross-roads* given great praise, more than any of our plays has had for a year at least. Yet not one of the morning papers mentions or, as it seems, understands the central idea of the play. Two of them state that the failure of the heroine was her husband's fault and the others imply it. They prefer mere logic, even when they do not understand it, to suggestion, which alone is the foundation of literature. State a logical proposition and the most commonplace mind can complete it. Suggestion is richest to the richest and so art grows unpopular in a democracy like this. They have misunderstood Robinson's proposition, fortunately for his popularity, and completed the misunderstanding till all is commonplace. In another sense the reception is typical of the lower-middle-class mind in Ireland. They allow their minds to dwell on the logic while quietly accepting (though ignoring in practice) what they would consider, if they thought of it, an utter superstition. This is how they combine religious ideas with their journalism.

A thought that stirs me in *Time* is that 'only women and great artists love time' for his own sake, others sell him for money or the like. But what is Blake's 'naked beauty displayed', visible, audible wisdom, to the shopkeeping logicians? How can they love time or anything but the day's end?

132

It is right to be gone when Henderson is the grasshopper in the hedge, and a daily burden.[1]

133

I am by nature suspicious, and I suspect Stephens. He said to me yesterday week when I asked if Synge had made his will, 'He said he was too weak, but I said I knew his wishes perfectly, and so I wrote

[1] 'And the grasshopper shall be a burden, and the caper-berry shall fail'. *Ecclesiastes* XII 5.

out a will and brought two witnesses, and he signed it.'[1] I now know that a year ago Synge made another will leaving Molly all his money. The new will, however, may only refer to what may have come to him the other day at his mother's death, but Stephens has never mentioned the nature of the will to me, nor has Robert Synge,[2] I find, to Molly. She is quite easy in her mind, however, or perhaps too indifferent of anything but her loss to care about it. She said today, 'I will spend it all, if necessary, on his work.' They may assume that she knows and that I know, and so keep silent. They are a strange people.

134

Today Molly told me that he often spoke of his coming death, indeed constantly for a year past, and tried hard to finish *Deirdre*. Sometimes he would get very despondent, thinking he could not finish it, and then she would act it for him in his room and he would write a little more, and then he would despond again, and then the acting would begin again.

135

Molly has given me the dates of the poems. 'Queens' when at York Road,[3] 1908. 'A Wish', 1908. 'On an Anniversary' is quite old. 'The Oaks of Glencree' in 1907. 'A Question', 1908. 'In Glencullen' is old. 'Epitaph' is old. 'Prelude', old. 'In May', recent. 'On a Birthday', old. 'Winter', 1908. 'Epitaph after reading Ronsard', 1908 (written in Germany). The translations were made just after Miss Tobin[4] came to Ireland.

136

Last night Sara Allgood dreamed that she was paid her salary and found with the other coins a large silver piece, a ten-shilling piece

---

[1] 13 February 1909. In the will Synge left a lifetime annuity of £80 to Molly Allgood, the amount to be reduced to £52 in the event of her marriage. He left the rest of his property to his nephews Edward M. Stephens and Edward H. Synge. Entry no. 159 refers to this matter.

[2] J. M. Synge's brother.

[3] On 2 February 1908, Synge moved to a flat at 47 York Road, Rathmines, Dublin.

[4] Agnes Tobin, poet, translator, patron of the arts; friend of Symons, Yeats, Conrad, Synge. She came to Dublin in September 1906.

she thought, and when she turned it over there was a lion on it, very bright and in high relief. I remember her old dream of lions after *Golden Helmet*. I think this dream should bring luck.

137

My sister Lily says that Lolly's ship[1] was not like a real ship but like the *Shadowy Waters* ship, a sort of allegorical thing. She knew in her dream it concerned Synge, perhaps he was in it. There was also a girl in a bright dress, but she seemed to vanish as the boat ran ashore. All about the girl was a little confused, all indeed a little confused until the ship ran ashore in bright sunlight. April 3 [1909].

138

I see that between *Time*, suggestion, and *Cross-roads*, logic, lies a difference of civilization as well as of art. The literature of suggestion, richest to the richest, does not belong to a social order founded upon argument, but to an age when life conquered by being itself and the most living was the most powerful. What was leisure, wealth, privilege but a soil for the most living? The literature of logic, most powerful in the emptiest, subduing life, conquering all in the service of one metallic premise, is the art of democracy, of generations that have only just begun to read. They fill their minds with deductions just as they fill their empty houses, where there is nothing of the past, with machine-made furniture. I used to think that the French and Irish democracies follow, as John O'Leary used to say, a logical deduction to its end, no matter what suffering it caused, because they were Celtic. I now believe that they do this because they have lost by some break with the past the self-evident truths, 'naked beauty displayed'. The English logicians are as ignorant perhaps, but more timid, yet they have Shaw and those arid translations of Ibsen, both barricades.

Robinson[2] should become a celebrated dramatist if this Theatre

---

[1] Entry no. 119, p. 200.

[2] Lennox Robinson (1886–1958), author of several plays including *The Whiteheaded Boy*, *Drama at Inish*, and *The Far-Off Hills*. From 1910 to 1914 and again from 1919 to 1923 he was manager and producer at the Abbey.

lasts long enough. He does not argue like Shaw, though his expression of life is essentially logical, hence his grasp on passion. Passion is logical when bent on action. And in suggestive drama there must either be enough loosening and slackening for meditation and the seemingly irrelevant, or a chorus, and neither is possible without rich leisurely minds in the audience, lovers of Father Time, men who understand Faust's last cry to the passing moment.

139

'Man clothes himself to descend, unclothes himself to ascend.'

140

A visionary woman once said to me, 'If we could only say to ourselves, with sincerity, "This passing moment is as good as any I shall ever know", we would perish instantly or become united to God.' I suppose because desire would be at an end. Is not logic the feet of desire?

141

April 5 [1909]. Walked home from Gurteen Dhas[1] with Magee.[2] Spoke of Dunsany.[3] Was fool enough to tell how I had taken two of Dunsany's ideas and made a scenario for his play.[4] Thought I had cured myself of this kind of boasting. Why should I want Magee's good opinion? Do I doubt myself, or was it only a desire to prove Russell, of whom we were talking, sterile? A not very amiable desire. Came home cross – had been in Egypt's brick kilns.[5] Magee states

[1] The Yeats home in Church Road, Churchtown, Dundrum, Co. Dublin.
[2] 'John Eglinton' was the pseudonym of W. K. Magee, for many years an Assistant Librarian in the National Library of Ireland. His writings include *Anglo-Irish Essays* (1917), *Irish Literary Portraits* (1935) and *Memoir of AE* (1937).
[3] Edward J. M. D. Plunkett, 18th Baron Dunsany (1878–1957), dramatist, novelist and poet.
[4] *The Glittering Gate*, produced at the Abbey on 29 April 1909.
[5] *2 Samuel* XII 31: 'And he brought forth the people that were therein, and put them under saws and under harrows of iron, and under axes of iron, and made them pass through the brick kiln: and thus did he unto all the cities of the children of Ammon.' Also Blake, *Jerusalem*, Plate 89, 15–18: 'Egypt on the Gihon, many tongued/And many mouth'd, Ethiopia, Lybia, the Sea of Rephaim./Minute Particulars in slavery I behold among the brick-kilns/Disorganiz'd.' *Complete Writings*, pp. 734–5.

everything in a slightly argumentative form. This means that the soul is starved by the absence of self-evident truth. Good conversation unrolls itself like the spring or like the dawn, while all effective argument, all merely logical statement, must found itself on the set of facts and experiences common to two or more people. Each hides what is new and rich.

142

In a very ungracious obituary notice of Synge in *Sinn Féin*[1] it is said he wrote all his plays except *Riders to the Sea* in ill health. The editor, I have not the least doubt, deliberately invented this in order to excuse his own attacks. *Riders to the Sea* was written immediately after *Shadow of the Glen* which Griffith attacked so violently and untruthfully, denying his own words and suppressing the essential part of Synge's reply, the folk story the play was founded on.[2]

143

The element which in men of action corresponds to style in literature is the moral element. Books live almost entirely because of their style, and the men of action whose influence inspires movements after they are dead are those whose hold upon abstract law and high emotion lifts them above immediate circumstance. Mitchel wrote better prose than Davis, Ferguson and Mangan better poetry, D'Arcy McGee better popular verse, Fintan Lalor saw deeper into political events, O'Connell had more power, Meagher[3] had more eloquence, but Davis alone has influenced generations of young men, though Mitchel's narrower and more faulty nature has now and again competed with him. Davis showed this moral radiance not in

[1] 3 April 1909.
[2] This refers to a controversy in the *United Irishman* which began with an editorial comment (7 January 1905) that the play 'has no more title to be called Irish than a Chinaman would have if he printed "Patrick O'Brien" on his visiting card'. In the issue of 28 January 1905, the editor described the play as 'a foul echo from degenerate Greece'. The controversy continued in the issues of 4 and 11 February; in the latter the editor published Synge's letter but not the Aran story which accompanied it.
[3] John Mitchel (1815–75), Sir Samuel Ferguson (1810–86), James Clarence Mangan (1803–49), Thomas D'Arcy McGee (1825–68), James Fintan Lalor (1807–49), Daniel O'Connell (1775–1847), Thomas Francis Meagher (1823–67).

his verse merely – I doubt if that could have much effect alone – but in his action, in his defence, for instance, of the rights of his political opponents of the Royal Irish Academy. His verses were but an illustration of principles shown by him in action. Men are dominated by self-conquest, and thought that is a little obvious, a little platitudinous if merely written, becomes persuasive, immortal even, when it has been held to amid the hurry of events. The self-conquest of the writer who is not a man of action is style.

Mitchel's influence is mainly, though not altogether, that of a writer, the influence of style, another form of power, an energy of life. It is curious that Mitchel's martyred life, supported by style, has had less force than the quiet radiance of a man who was never in the hulks, and did not write very well, and achieved no change of law.

144

The act of appreciation of any great thing is always an act of self-conquest. This is one reason why we distrust the serene moralist who has not approved his principles in some crisis. He would be troubled, a little broken even, if he had made that conquest. The man who has proved himself in a crisis may be serene in words, for his battle was not in contemplation where words are combatants.

145

Last night my sister told me that this book of Synge's[1] was the only book they ever began to print on a Friday. They tried to avoid this but could not, and that it is not well printed. Do all they could, it would not come right.

146

The lack of the moral element in Irish public life today comes largely from the badness of Catholic education, and the small number of Catholic families with traditions. The sense of form, whether that

---

[1] *Poems and Translations by John M. Synge* (Cuala Press, 1909): the printing was completed on 8 April, and the book was published on 5 July.

of Parnell or Grattan[1] or Davis, of form in active life, has always been Protestant in Ireland. O'Connell, the one great Catholic figure, was formless. The power of self-conquest, of elevation has been Protestant, and more or less a thing of class. All the tragedians were Protestant – O'Connell was a comedian.[2] He had the gifts of the market place, of the clown at the fair.

147

Molly has just told me of three pre-visions. Some years ago, when the company were in England on that six weeks' tour,[3] she, Synge and Arthur Darley[4] were sitting in a tea shop. She was looking at Synge and suddenly the flesh seemed to fall from his face and she saw but a skull. She told him this and it gave him a great shock, and since then she had not allowed images to form before her eyes of themselves, as they often used to do. Synge was well at the time. Again last year, but before the operation and at a time when she had no fear, she dreamed that she saw him in a coffin being lowered into a grave, and 'a strange sort of cross' was laid over the coffin. (The company sent a cross of flowers to his funeral. It was laid on the grave.) She told this also to Synge and he was a good deal troubled over it. Then some time after the operation she dreamed that she saw him in a boat. She was on the shore and he waved his hand to her and the boat went away. She longed to get to him but could not.

148

She said one day when she was walking with him in the country an old woman said, 'God bless you,' and he said, 'And may God bless you.' She asked him if he believed in God and he said, 'No.' She

[1] Henry Grattan (1746–1820), Irish statesman, leader of the movement for legislative independence which was temporarily embodied in 'Grattan's Parliament', 1782–1800.

[2] The association of O'Connell as comedian and Parnell as tragedian is made again in 'Parnell's Funeral', *Collected Poems*, pp. 319–20, and in a commentary on that poem in *The King of the Great Clock Tower* (1934).

[3] May–June 1906, when the players went to Edinburgh, Aberdeen, Glasgow, Newcastle-on-Tyne, Hull and Cardiff.

[4] Dublin violinist who played for Abbey productions.

said, 'But someone must have made all these pretty things,' meaning the gorse and the birds.

149

Then we spoke of a dream he had in Aran. He had told her of this dream as he had told me. He dreamed that he was in one of the stone forts and dancing to strange music. He could not stop dancing and woke very tired. It seemed to me when he told it me that he believed, or half-believed, that his soul had been out of his body that night.

150

April 11 [1909]. Stratford-on-Avon.[1] Some weeks ago Miss Tobin wrote to me that the phase through which Symons's madness was passing was to believe himself in heaven. All the great poets were there, of other times. He was helping to prepare the reception of Swinburne. The angels were to stand in groups of three. Now Swinburne is dead.[2] Miss Lister (Bullen and the other Miss Lister say) also for some months has had the feeling that he was about to die.

151

The day before yesterday I met a young poet called Lewis[3] who is an admirer of Augustus John. He mourned over John's present state, that of much portrait painting for money, and thought his work was falling off. He says that John's mistress has taken another admirer, a very clever young painter who does not admire John's work, and this influences her, and so she does not give John the old 'submissive admiration', and this is bad for John, and she has done it all for vengeance because John will not marry her. Lewis is very

[1] On 6 April 1909 Yeats set off on a brief trip to London and Stratford-on-Avon. A. H. Bullen, assisted by Miss E. M. Lister, conducted the Shakespeare Head Press at Stratford and had recently issued, in eight volumes, Yeats's collected works.

[2] 10 April 1909. Joseph Hone, writing of the *Collected Works* (1908), said: 'On the whole, the English press gave the edition a good reception, and meeting his sister in the street on the morrow of Swinburne's death (April 1909), Yeats stopped her to say: "I am the King of the Cats." ' Hone, *W. B. Yeats, 1865-1939* (London, Macmillan, second edition 1962), p. 230.

[3] Percy Wyndham Lewis (1884-1957), novelist, painter and poet.

angry and thinks John should leave her. 'What does he owe to her or her children?'

152

Dined with Ricketts and Shannon.[1] Ricketts spoke of the grief Synge's death gave him – 'the ending of all that work'.[2] We talked of John and of the disordered or broken lives of modern men of genius and the so different lives of the Italian painters. He said in those days 'men of genius were cared for', that now the strain of life was too heavy, that no one thought of them till some misfortune came – madness or death. He then spoke, as he often does, of the lack of any necessary place for the arts in modern life and said, as he often says, 'After all, the ceiling of the Sistine Chapel was the Pope's new ceiling.'

153

One difficulty in all our public arts – architecture, plays, large decorations – is that there are too many different tastes to please. Some taste is sure to dislike and to speak its dislike everywhere; and then because of the silence of the rest – half apathy, half dislike of controversy, half the difficulty of the defence as compared with the ease of the attack – creates timidity of public taste. All creation requires one mind to make and one mind for enjoyment; the theatre can at rare moments create this one mind for an hour or so, but this grows always more difficult. Once created it is like the mind of an individual in solitude, immeasurably bold – all is possible to it. The only building received with enthusiasm during my time has been the Catholic Cathedral of Westminster; religion created this one mind, I suppose. Of Webb's new buildings in Oxford Street and Regent Street one heard nothing but the complaints of the shopkeepers at the smallness of the space for glass windows in the shops.

---

[1] Charles Hazlewood Shannon (1863–1937), painter and lithographer.

[2] An entry in Ricketts's journal (23 April 1904) reads: '[Yeats] brought Synge, whom I liked greatly. He has a kindly, plain, yet attractive face, with human eyes and coarse hair. Synge's face reminds me of Gorki with a touch of Nietzsche. Later in life he may develop a resemblance to Balzac.' *Self-Portrait*, p. 104.

154

Ricketts said,[1] 'Everybody who is doing anything for the world is very disagreeable, the agreeable people are those for whom the world is doing something.'

155

'War is the father of all and the king of all, and some he has made gods and some men, some bound and some free.' Heraclitus.

'The immortals are mortal, the mortals immortal, each living in the others' death and dying in the others' life.' Heraclitus.[2]

156

April 15 [1909]. (April 14 and 15 ♂♂ asc.[3]) I asked Miss O'Neill if any words of hers made Synge write 'A Question', and she said, 'He used often to joke about death with me. One day he said, "Will you go to my funeral?" and I said, "No, for I could not bear to see you dead and others living on."'

157

I asked Stephens to see me yesterday or today, and I have heard nothing. I have probably made him suspicious as he has made me. Why is it that I always fail when I attempt to negotiate with an individual, for I have a power over a committee that is very strange to me? Do I say too much? Am I too zealous? I know that my error comes in some way from the absence of the feeling for form, which I get from the rules at any kind of meeting, but why have I this lack? I have tried to cure myself so often in vain that I should refuse all

---

[1] '. . . in comment upon some irascible act of Hugh Lane's . . .', *Autobiographies*, p. 518.

[2] Fragments 25 and 66: 'War is both father and king of all; some he has shown forth as gods and others as men, some he has made slaves and others free'; and 'Immortals become mortals, mortals become immortals; they live in each other's death and die in each other's life.' *Heraclitus*, translated by Philip Wheelwright (Princeton, Princeton University Press, 1959, reissued by Atheneum Press, New York, 1964), pp. 29, 68. Yeats quoted Fragment 66 in *The Resurrection* (*Collected Plays*, p. 594), *A Vision* (p. 275) and *On the Boiler* (*Explorations*, p. 430).

[3] Mars conjunction Ascendant.

negotiation no matter what the urgency. I should have written to Lady Gregory to come up and see Stephens. Stephens himself talks too much and it is very possible that is why I suspect him. I think one reason of my failures is that I always like or dislike when I am with an individual, whereas a committee is a thing. One possesses one's own mind, without reactive sensations, among things. Another is perhaps that my speculation comes quicker than politic thought, whereas at a meeting the longer speeches give me time. My sense of form is always my helper in life and art, for I have Jupiter as the most elevated of my planets, but why does it not help me with the individual until I have got to really know him well? Even my friendships have a dangerous middle sea between first impressions and intimacy. Does it come from ♂ in VII (house of partners, etc.), ☍ ☽ in I? The sense of form protects the ☽ ♃ * ☽ [r].[1]

158

On the other hand yesterday I got my resolution completely transforming the Arts Club and including resignation of the committee accepted by a unanimous vote of the committee.[2]

159

April 17 [1909]. Lady Gregory and afterwards Miss O'Neill have just seen Stephens. I was partly right in my suspicions. In the will written out by him, his son, and another young man, so far as one can understand, inherit the copyright, and Stephens is now reading *The Tinker's Wedding* to see if Tree is to be allowed to play it.[3] He

[1] Does it come from Mars in VII (house of partners, etc.), opposition Moon in I? The sense of form protects the Moon/Jupiter sextile Moon [radical].

[2] The resolution proposed handing over the administration of the Club to a committee of 22 members including the Hon. Secretary and the Hon. Treasurer *ex officio*; the committee would be elected annually, but outgoing members would be eligible for re-election. So that this arrangement could be put into effect at once, the existing committee resigned: the members, with the exception of Sir John Barton, the Hon. Fred Lawless and W. G. Strickland, offered themselves for re-election. Yeats's resolution was formally put and passed at the Annual General Meeting on 3 May 1909, but he had already persuaded the members of the committee to adopt it.

[3] *The Tinker's Wedding* was first produced by the Afternoon Theatre Company at His Majesty's Theatre, London (where Beerbohm Tree was Manager), on 11 November

objects to the publication of 'A Question', but cannot stop it, and it
is yet uncertain as to whether we are to be allowed to produce
Playboy. I am not to be allowed to edit the books or see the papers.
The family object to theatres of any kind and to me probably for the
same reason. Stephens the day after Synge's death said to me, 'I
know he wanted to see you about his writings, and we are anxious to
merely carry out his wishes,' and he spoke of this to Lady Gregory.
There has been a change of plan. Miss O'Neill said to him, 'If you
forbid us to play *Deirdre* and *Playboy*, you ruin my life. They were
written for me, and their performance in London is my only chance
of making out a career.' She spoke of Synge's sending for me, and
Stephens 'was very surprised, as if he never heard of it before'. Lady
Gregory tells me on Stephens's authority that Synge wanted to send
for Stephens at twelve o'clock the night he died, but gave up the
idea on being told he would live till morning. We have been promised *Deirdre* today; Miss O'Neill is to go through MSS. Miss
O'Neill inherits about £80 a year.

160

Miss O'Neill says that for the last year Synge would sometimes say
he was dying and then after talk with her cheer up and think himself
all right. When he said goodbye to Mrs MacKenna[1] (not MacKenna
too as I thought) it was before going to hospital for the first time, a
year ago. He began the conversation by talking of his marriage, and
then when he was going away said he had a feeling he would never
see Mrs MacKenna again. On Tuesday, a few hours before he died
and after he had told Stephens he was dying, he spoke to Molly
(why, she does not know, perhaps to reassure her, she thinks) of
going to lodgings and getting one of the nurses to look after him
there, and said, 'You can then see much more of me,' and also, 'I
may live to nurse you some day.' This accounts for her saying to me

---

1909. Yeats found the performance 'disgraceful' and left after the first Act. 'I have just
written to Mrs Campbell refusing to consider Tree in writing my play [*The Player
Queen*]. I have described his ideal of beauty as thrice vomited flesh.' *Letters* (Wade),
pp. 538–9, Letter of 26 November 1909.
[1] Stephen MacKenna's wife, Marie.

that day, after telling how they had ceased to give him food, 'Perhaps he will live.'

161

Later in day. It now appears it is not the family, but Stephens's hurt vanity. 'The directors want to do everything, and I will be top dog.' He evidently took my suggestions for an attempt to oust him in some way, and so is reading Synge, seemingly for the first time. He read *Tinker's Wedding* to see if he would let Tree play it, and seems to have found nothing to object to. He seems to be enjoying an unexpected form of power. No, I must never negotiate with anything less than three men, one of them in the chair.

162

April 17 [1909]. Lady Gregory who, unlike me (I always endow a stranger with much virtue) assumes that the man she has to deal with is more or less of a goose, within an hour got the will shown to Miss O'Neill and *Deirdre* promised. She has no doubt that a goose can be driven, whereas I am abashed before a symbol of humanity which seems to require all religion and philosophy before it can stir. I am interrupted before I can exhaust these subjects.

163

April 19 [1909]. Yesterday lunched with Lady Lyttelton and quoted to General Lyttelton Nevinson's opinion about modern armies. He said, 'As against that, think of the fighting of educated men in the war of North and South in America; but I doubt if we will ever again see fighting like that of the Peninsular War.' He then went on to divide soldiers into three classes: 1. The reckless. If men, these are stupid; if officers (and there are more men than officers in this class), lunatics. These are those who are never happy unless under fire. 2. The officers and men who do not like fighting and are glad when it is over, but go through with it bravely. 3. Those who won't fight at all if there is much danger. This kind is seven times commoner among the men than among the officers.

164

He said also that he had never known a pre-vision of death in battle that was not fulfilled.

165

April 22 [1909]. That old feeling in my head, and for some days past. I have a deep desire for the open air and quiet. I am kept here by Stephens from whom the promised *Deirdre* has not yet come.

166

Miss Dickinson[1] told me last night that a number of members of the Arts Club wished to protest against invitation to Lady Lieutenant, as it made club political. I have already had my protest put on minutes. Advised a private protest to committee, as a public one would be as objectionable from the point of view of the club as the invitation itself. It would be misunderstood and seem to commit the club to a political party.

167

The volatile Stephens said to Roberts[2] yesterday, 'I find it very hard to get into touch with those Abbey people.' He promises *Deirdre* between three and four.

168

Yesterday Dr Gogarty[3] told me that he had it from the doctor (he was in the same hospital with Synge and at the same time) that it was cancer. I said, 'They said it was not, to the family.' He said, 'They do that because people would fear it was hereditary.' He had cancer in two places; his liver was attacked. Some accident must have taken place or he could have lived five months longer. He was full of hope till the last two days. Gogarty added, 'But when one knows one has to die, precious little one cares about it' – meaning, I suppose, one is indifferent from weakness. The earlier swelling in Synge's neck

[1] Mabel Dickinson, sister of P. L. Dickinson, the author of *The Dublin of Yesterday*.
[2] George Roberts, minor poet, was manager of the publishing house, Maunsel & Co., which started in 1905: it published *The Works of John M. Synge* (1910).
[3] Oliver St John Gogarty (1878–1957), doctor, wit, Senator and poet.

came, Gogarty had heard, from bad teeth (one of the common signs
of poverty).

169

April 23 [1909]. *Deirdre* arrived last night, but full of mistakes and
confusion. Tuesday morning Lady Gregory telephoned that she
and I (who were waiting in Dublin to do this work) could not go on
with revision without seeing the originals. He replied later in day
that he would be in his office at 3.30 on Monday. She has now written
asking to see the MSS. tomorrow morning. He is certainly a fool, and
insolent. His letter to Lady Gregory with MSS. contained no apologies for all these delays. *Deirdre* was promised for the week after
Synge's death, then again for a little later, then for last Monday,
then for three or four yesterday – and notes and first version were
promised and only this last version delivered, ill-copied and useless,
late last night (Thursday), and though he knows he is causing us
great inconvenience he wants to put us off till Monday.

170

To AE, who wants me [to] praise some of his poets, imitators of my
own.[1]

> You tell me that I often have given tongue
> To praise what other men have said or sung
> That it would/~~I could~~ get me friends if I praised these,
> But tell me do the wolf dogs praise their fleas.
>   or
> You tell me that I've often given tongue
> In praise of what another's said or sung
> That it would get me friends if I praised these:
> But tell me do the wolf dogs praise their fleas.
>
> You say as I have often given tongue
> In praise of what another's said or sung

---

[1] 'To a Poet, Who Would Have Me Praise Certain Bad Poets, Imitators of His and
Mine', *Collected Poems*, p. 105. AE told Oliver Edwards that Yeats had in mind James
Stephens and Padraic Colum. In fact, Yeats later came to a much higher opinion of both.

'Twere politic to do the like for these:
I'll do it
But where's the wolf dog that has praised his fleas.[1]

171

April 27 [1909]. Dunsany Castle.[2] Stephens did not answer Lady Gregory's letter at all, though she said in it that she was staying in Dublin at great inconvenience to herself and others. We have now decided (advised by Norreys Connell, who has just read play) that there is no longer time to get *Deirdre* up for London, and have written this to Stephens. It is a great loss. Miss O'Neill thinks that Stephens is behaving in this way because he thinks we want Synge's work to make money out of it. I probably roused his suspicions by offering my services as editor, etc., to the family for nothing. I did this the first day I saw Stephens. But even this does not justify him in being insolent. The man has, as it were, turned a friend into an enemy.

172

Lady Gregory, in order to go through the MSS. – she was still expecting to hear from Stephens – let her grandchild go to Galway without her, and on Monday she got a telegram about the child that made her anxious, and was ill from anxiety and worry at not being with the child. Strange that Synge for whom she did so much and, as he knew, suffered so much, should have submitted her to the delays and insults of this attorney. Synge was always too self-absorbed to think much of others.

173

Went to Russell's Sunday night – everybody either too tall or too short, or crooked or lop-sided. One woman had that terrible thing in a woman, an excited voice, and an intellect without self-possession.

---

[1] This third version is in pencil. Allan Wade inserted a loose leaf in the journal at this point, with the following note in pencil: 'W.B.Y. recited this to me at lunch in the Queen's Restaurant, Sloane Square, I think in the summer of 1909. The last line then ran: "But tell me – does the wild dog praise his fleas."'
[2] Co. Meath.

There was a bad poet with a swollen neck.[1] There was a man with the look of a wood-kern, who kept bringing the conversation back and back to Synge's wrongdoing in having made a girl in the *Playboy* admire a man who had hamstrung 'mountain ewes'.[2] He saw nothing else to object to but the one thing. He declared what kept Englishmen from giving Home Rule was that they thought 'Ireland cruel' because of the hurt to animals during agrarian agitation. No Irishman should write a sentence to help them.[3] There arose before my mind a vision of this man, he had been in India, I think, arguing for years and years on this one subject with an endless procession of second-rate men. At last I said, 'When a country produces a man of genius he never is what it wants or believes it wants, he is always unlike its idea of itself. In the eighteenth century Scotland believed itself very religious and very moral and very gloomy, and its national poet Burns came not to speak of these things but to speak of lust and drink and drunken gaiety. Ireland since the Young Irelanders has given itself up to apologetics. Every impression of life or impulse of imagination has been examined to see if it helped or hurt the glory of Ireland or the political claim of Ireland. Gradually sincere impressions of life became impossible; all was artificial apologetics. There was no longer an impartial imagination delighting in things because they were naturally exciting. Synge was the rushing up of the buried fire, an explosion of all that had been denied and refused, a furious impartiality, an indifferent turbulent sorrow. Like Burns, his work was to say all that people did not want to have said. He was able to do this because nature had made him incapable of a political idea.' The wood-kern made no answer, he did not understand me, I dare say, but for the rest of the evening he kept saying over and over the same thing. He objected to nothing but that passage about the 'mountain ewes'.

[1] At the bottom of the page Yeats wrote: 'No, an excellent poet; I did not know his good work then.'

[2] Pegeen to Shawn Keogh in the first Act of the *Playboy*: 'Where now will you meet the like of Daneen Sullivan knocked the eye from a peeler, or Marcus Quin, God rest him, got six months for maiming ewes.'

[3] '. . . no Irishman should write a sentence to make them [Englishmen] go on thinking that', *Autobiographies*, p. 520.

174

When I told Lady Gregory yesterday that I was coming here,[1] she said, 'I am very glad, for you need a few days among normal and simple well-bred people. One always wants that from time to time as a rest to one's mind. They need not be clever. It is one of the reasons why I am going to Lady Layard's.'[2] (She goes to Venice in a few days.)

175

Lord Dunsany has just described to me his way of work. When he wrote his first book, he dictated it because he could not write fast enough, and the ideas would have vanished before they were written down. He would start with a very slight idea and the rest would come as he wrote. All vision, obviously, but now he writes. (I am tired. I am not yet fit for much work, very plainly.)[3]

176

April 29 [1909]. I do not listen enough. I meant to write down much of Dunsany's thought, and though he has said much I have not got it in my thoughts. It is not merely that I talk, for if I am silent in a room I still do not really listen. A word suggests something and I follow that. I am always like a child playing with bricks in the corner.

177

Today I am to give a reading at the Arts Club on 'Contemporary Lyric Poetry'. I shall read from the books of the Rhymers' Club – Plarr,[4] Johnson, Dowson – and then from Sturge Moore and explain how, coming after the abundance of the Swinburne–Rossetti–Morris movement, we sought not abundance or energy, but precise-

[1] Dunsany Castle.
[2] Enid Layard, wife of Sir Henry Layard.
[3] In a letter to Florence Farr (? March 1909) Yeats refers to a recent nervous breakdown. *Letters* (Wade), p. 526.
[4] Victor Plarr (1863–1929), Librarian at the Royal College of Surgeons. He is the 'Monsieur Verog' of Ezra Pound's 'Siena Mi Fe' in *Hugh Selwyn Mauberley*. Author of a life of Dowson (1914) and of poems, *In the Dorian Mood* (1896).

ness of form. We were the second wave of the movement and had more passion because more confidence than the first – that of Bridges, Dobson, Lang. We sought for new subject matter, and many of us were men of passionate living, expressing our lives. Our forerunners [had] been more contemplative, more calm. The movement of the present is not lyric.

178

July 8 [1909]. I dreamed this thought two nights ago: Why should we complain if men ill-treat our Muses, when all that they gave to Helen while she still lived was a song and a jest?

179[1]

August 7 [1909]. Have made no notes for a long time. Have feared to give my mind a critical bias at a time when I must create.[2]

180

August 7 [1909]. Subject for poem. 'A Shaken House'. How should the world gain if this house[3] failed, even though a hundred little houses were the better for it, for here power [has] gone forth or lingered, giving energy, precision; it gave to a far people beneficent rule,[4] and still under its roof living intellect is sweetened by old memories of its descent from far off? How should the world be better if the wren's nest flourish and the eagle's house is scattered?[5]

181

August 7 [1909].

How should the world be better/luckier if this house

---

[1] Yeats stopped numbering the entries at this point.
[2] He was working on *The Player Queen*.
[3] Coole Park, where Yeats was spending the summer.
[4] Sir William Gregory (1817–92), Lady Gregory's husband, had been Governor of Ceylon
[5] This entry and the next refer to the poem, 'Upon a House Shaken by the Land Agitation', *Collected Poems*, pp. 106–7.

Where passion and precision have been one
Time out of mind ~~should~~ ~~grow~~/~~become~~/became too ruinous
To breed the lidless eye that loves the sun
And the sweet laughing eagle thoughts that grow
Where wings have memory of wings and all
That comes ~~where~~/of the best knit ~~with~~/to the best; for
         ~~though~~/although
Mean rooftrees were the ~~luckier~~/stronger for its fall
      were the sturdier for its fall
       ~~wealthier~~/? sturdier at its fall
How ~~could~~/should their luck ~~leap~~/run high enough to reach
The gifts that govern men and after them
 ×   For crowning gift of gradual time a speech
 ×   Made simple by heroic reveries
      ~~For~~/To gradual time's last gift a written speech
 ×   Where high will plays with lovely reveries.
      Wrought of high laughter, loveliness and ease.

I wrote this on hearing the results of reductions of rent made by the courts.[1]

One feels always that where all must make their living they will live not for life's sake but the work's, and all be the poorer. My work is very near to life itself, and my father's very near to life itself, but I am always feeling a lack of life's own values behind my thought. They should have been there before the strain began, before it became necessary to let the work create its values. This house has enriched my soul out of measure, because here life moves[2] without restraint through spacious forms. Here there has been no compelled labour, no poverty-thwarted impulse.

[1] Fifteen tenants of the Gregory estate at Coole Park applied to the Land Court to have their rents reduced. The Land Commissioner, the Hon. Gerald Fitzgerald, granted their application, reducing the rents by approximately twenty per cent. Judgment was given on 30 July 1909. At the same time the Land Purchase Act of 1909 and certain provisions of the Finance Bill of 1909 imposed new burdens of taxation upon Irish landowners; notably the Increment Value Duty and the Reversion Duty. John Redmond defended these taxes as just: 'if any portion of the £2,500,000 a year given for old age pensions has to be met by a tax on any class in Ireland, the best and justest class to put it on were the great landlords of cities and towns'. Quoted in the *Irish Times*, 5 July 1909.

[2] 'creates' deleted.

182

August 11 [1909]. Yesterday a most evil day – ♂ ☍ ☽ p.[1] Trouble at
Theatre, and letter from M[aud] G[onne] saying that Quinn is
offended at something I said or am said to have said to or about
some friend of Quinn's.[2] I do not think I can have said the things he
complains of, whatever they are, but I know myself to be utterly
indiscreet. Now it is that strange, intoxicating thing, the sense of
intimacy; now it is an unrestrained sense of comedy that lays hold
of me; and in either case I forget all discretion. This and my indolence are the most humiliating faults I have; for indolence I
have disciplines which may gradually conquer it, but for the other,
nothing. I cannot say to anyone, 'Tell me all, for I need the discipline
of a great secret because of my indiscretion, and the old secrets are
no longer new enough to stir the imagination.' When they are new
they have all their dangerous time, my own through sympathy and
those of others through my sense of comedy. I think the passion for
expression weakens greatly the power of keeping silent, and it is
precisely what one should be silent about that makes up the most
living part of the comedy of actual life. What one says may be
innocent enough, except for its indiscretion: and the malice of
another may pervert it, as when my telling Lane that Russell would
not do for a selector of pictures, because when he liked a man he
over-rated his talent out of measure, came to Russell in the form that
I accused him of jobs.[3]

183

August 17 [1909]. Have been to Dublin – saw Quinn and had whole
thing out. Various incautious sayings of mine to a friend of his in

---

[1] Mars in opposition to the progressed Moon.

[2] In *The Man from New York: John Quinn and His Friends* (New York, Oxford
University Press, 1968), p. 74, B. L. Reid writes of Quinn's holiday in Ireland in the
summer of 1909: 'On the whole it had been a fine vacation, though the matter of the
portrait rankled rather sorely and a grievous quarrel with W. B. Yeats more sorely still.
Quinn and Yeats had come to bitter words and a loud parting over Dorothy Coates.
Quinn thought Yeats had been gossiping loosely and injuriously about his relationship
with her, and he charged Yeats with trying to take over his mistress for himself.' Quinn
(1870–1924), American lawyer and art collector.

[3] i.e. jobbery.

Paris have been made the foundation for an architecture of lies. As usual (through being ☽ influenced by ♂ ☽ in first house and in a ♄ sign[1] and giving self-doubt), I accepted the worst case possible against myself and did years' work of repentance in ten minutes. Quirin is between a bad woman and a good one and the bad can control nothing in her nature, least of all her imagination and her speech.

Note. Must look up pre-natal transits to see what caused Monday, Saturday and Friday to be so full of ♂.* August 11 had its post-natal transit. ☽ ⚼ ♂ primary, as well as the coming violent ♂ aspects, but this influence exploded at a particular moment for some reason. Of course the fixed stars may have the secret and keep it; we know little of them. Row with Castle looks like the devil dancing of ☉ and ♂ and ☽ for next October's disturbance. There are aspects of the Revolutionary figure which should make the next few days disturbed also, but at present I don't believe in the Revolutionary figure – it seems to me even more fantastic than the Progress given with it by Lilly.

* No need to look for further explanation. ♂, post-natal, is practically stationary ☍☽p the entire month.[2]

184

August 27 [1909]. To write something in *Samhain* on the union of love of ideas with love of country. Easy to have one without the other, easy to hate one in service of the other, but if they are com-

[1] Through Moon being influenced by Mars (Moon in first house and in a Saturn sign).
[2] 'Must look up pre-natal transits to see what caused Monday, Saturday and Friday to be so full of Mars. August 11 had its post-natal transit. Moon quincunx Mars primary, as well as the coming violent Mars aspects. . . . Row with Castle looks like the devil dancing of Sun and Mars and Moon for next October's disturbance. . . . No need to look for further explanation. Mars, post-natal, is practically stationary in opposition to progressed Moon the entire month.' ('Row with Castle' refers to the dispute Yeats and Lady Gregory were having with Dublin Castle, centre of British government in Ireland, over the Abbey production of Shaw's *The Shewing-Up of Blanco Posnet*, eventually produced on 25 August 1909. October's disturbance was astrological: Yeats's map showed a quarrelsome set of positions, transitting Moon and Mercury going over his progressed Mars. William Lilly was the author of *Christian Astrology, Modestly Treated of in Three Books* (London, second edition 1659). Yeats should have written 'Revolution figure' and 'Progression'.)

bined one gets a great epoch. *Samhain* also should give extracts from patent and show that Shaw's play came within it.[1] It should also insist on freedom from censor and quote basis in Lawrence's article on censorship in Ireland.[2] Quite apropos of ideas, perhaps article in *Sinn Féin* on Friday, August 27. 'London monstrosity' is its description of Shaw's play.[3]

185

September [1909]. Subject: To complain of the fascination of what's difficult. It spoils spontaneity and pleasure and it wastes time. Repeat the line ending 'difficult' three times, and rhyme on bolt, exult, colt, jolt. One could use the thought of the wild-winged and unbroken colt must drag a cart of stones out of pride because it's difficult, and end by denouncing drama, accounts, public contests – all that's merely difficult.[4]

186

September 8 [1909]. A bad morning for work. Letter of Horniman used up my emotional power and the result is that the little good work I could do has made my head queer. Sensation of last Spring.

187

September 16 [1909]. Head not very good. Two days ago Lady

---

[1] There was no issue of *Samhain* in 1909. A statement by Yeats and Lady Gregory on Shaw's play was published in the *Arrow*, no. 5, 25 August 1909. One of the categories of plays to be produced by the Abbey, according to the patent of 1905, was 'plays written by Irish authors or on Irish subjects'.

[2] W. J. Lawrence, 'Irish Censorship: An Account of its History', *Freeman's Journal*, 24 August 1909. Lawrence's review of Shaw's play appeared in the *Stage*, 2 September 1909.

[3] *Sinn Féin* (daily edition) of 26 August 1909 praised Shaw's play ('a moral play') and its performance at the Abbey, but the issue of 27 August has a long column, 'The Shaw Play', giving the views of 'Fear gan Ainm' (i.e. Anon.), including the following: 'One outstanding fact remains clear to me. We don't want this sort of play in Ireland just at present. We are not ready for it, and I can quite imagine it would be a happy condition of affairs if we were never ready for it. Let Mr Shaw keep on juggling to English audiences who have no such inconvenient thing as conviction. Mr Yeats has created a sensation in putting this play on at the Abbey Theatre. But he has done nothing whatsoever thereby for the movement towards a National drama that is slowly growing in this country. He has given us a taste of London monstrosities. That is all.'

[4] 'The Fascination of What's Difficult', *Collected Poems*, p. 104. See also entry 209, pp. 242–3.

Gregory said, when they spoke of her grandchild's[1] going to Harrow in 1921, 'Where will his grandmother be then?' I thought of this house, slowly perfecting itself and the life within it in ever-increasing intensity of labour, and then of its probably sinking away through courteous incompetence, or rather sheer weakness of will, for ability has not failed in young Gregory. And I said to myself, 'Why is life a perpetual preparation for something that never happens?'[2] Even an Odysseus only seems a preparation; and think of ruins[3] reverenced.[4] Is it not always the tragedy of the great and the strong that they see before the end the small and the weak, in friendship or in enmity, pushing them from their place and marring what they have built, and doing one or the other in mere lightness of mind?[5]

188

September 16 [1909].

A Birrell

He thinks he is a master of the laws
That made his soul mere parasite/him but an empty
                                        soul because
He's grown to be a master of the trick
That turns a lively flea into a tick.

Attempt to turn into rhyme a joke of Robert Gregory's at dinner last night, but too savage to be much good. I had described an old conversation with Birrell.[6]

On a certain ~~cabinet minister~~/middle-aged office-holder

                              or

On a ~~middle-aged~~/prosperous mimic of other's thoughts

×   He thinks that in the teeth of natural laws

---

[1] Robert Gregory's son Richard.

[2] '... all life weighed in the scales of my own life seems to me a preparation for something that never happens', *Autobiographies*, p. 106. Cf. also entry 193 and the following passage from Stephen MacKenna, *Journal and Letters*, ed. E. R. Dodds (London, Constable, 1936), p. 112: 'Never, I think, was man born to be, more than myself, a Waiter: I am like the Princes of Greece round Penelope, a ten years' Wooer: I am always in my mind waiting for some bell to ring that never rings, for some wonderful thing to happen that never happens.'

[3] 'barely' deleted; but the reading is doubtful.   [4] A doubtful reading.

[5] Yeats added here in pencil: 'Rhymes for poem: preparation, generation, station.' No such poem has survived.   [6] Cf. entries 20, 21, pp. 145-6.

✕ He is a self-sufficing man because
He thinks to set his world aright/to have set all things
                                                                     right
   And be no longer parasite
   ~~Because~~/Now that he's master of the trick
   That turns a flea into a tick.

Not worth giving by itself, would seem mere party politics, but
might come at end of old note of conversation at Bailey's,[1] names
left out. 'Cabinet minister who had been a lively chatterbox in his
youth' would be enough of a description.

189

Corrected version of poem[2] written a year ago:

   I swayed upon the gaudy stern
   The butt-end of a steering oar
   And everywhere that I could turn
   Men ran upon the shore

   And though I would have hushed the crowd
   There was no mother's son but said
   'What is the figure in a shroud
   Upon a gaudy bed.'

   And fishes bubbling to the brim
   Cried out upon that thing beneath
   It had such dignity of limb
   By the sweet name of Death.

[1] William F. Bailey (1857–1917), Irish Land Commissioner, traveller, and *bon viveur.*
His flat at 3 Earlsfort Terrace, Dublin, was a meeting-place for artists and politicians.
[2] 'His Dream', first published in *The Nation*, 11 July 1908, with the following note:
'A few days ago I dreamed that I was steering a very gay and elaborate ship upon some
narrow water with many people upon its banks, and that there was a figure upon a bed in
the middle of the ship. The people were pointing to the figure and questioning, and in
my dream I sang verses which faded as I awoke, all but this fragmentary thought, "We
call it, it has such dignity of limb, by the sweet name of Death." I have made my poem
out of my dream and the sentiment of my dream, and can almost say, as Blake did, "The
Authors are in Eternity." ' *Collected Poems*, p. 99.

Though I'd my finger on my lip
What could I but take up the song?
And fish and crowd and gaudy ship
Cried out the whole night long;

Crying amid the glittering sea
Naming it with ecstatic breath
Because it had such dignity
By the sweet name of Death.

190

September 20 [1909].

Thought for *Player Queen* Act III

That the heroism of love is to feel, shudder and yet withstand; to do what one knows is necessary, even to the seeming cold, to seeming an enemy, and all the while to be on fire. Or, it is easy for the light lovers to be wise in love. They wear their mask without suffering; they have not to cut themselves in two. This would seem but an empty subtlety to the jealous Player Queen. She would have the right to talk so, not hero.

A half-line: 'Kinship that fierce feathery thing.'

191

September 20 [1909]. An idle man has no thought. A man's work thinks through him; on the other hand, a woman gets her thought[1] through the influence[2] of a man. Man is a woman to his work, and it begets his thought.

192

The old playwrights took old subjects, and did not even try to arrange the fable in any very new way. They were absorbed in expression, that is to say in what is most near and delicate. The new playwrights invent their subjects and dislike anything customary in

---

[1] 'which may yet be original' deleted.   [2] 'will' deleted.

the arrangement of the fable, but their expression is as common as the newspapers where they first learned to write.

193

September 22 [1909]. Could I not get in opening of Act III, where will come that symbolic drinking of the wine, the thought that life, apart from ecstasy, is perpetual preparation for what never happens?[1]

194

October [1909]. Saw *Hamlet* on Saturday night, except for the chief 'Ophelia' scenes; missed these, as I had to be away for a while at the Abbey, without regret.[2] I know not why, but their pathos, as it [is] played, always leaves me cold. I came back for Hamlet at the grave, where my delight begins again. I feel in *Hamlet*, as always in Shakespeare, that I am in the presence of a soul lingering on the storm-beaten threshold of sanctity. Has not that threshold always been terrible, even crime-haunted? Surely Shakespeare, in those last seeming idle years, was no quiet country gentleman, enjoying, as men like Dowden[3] think, the temporal reward of an unvalued toil. Perhaps he sought for wisdom in itself at last, and not in its passionate shadows. Maybe he had passed the threshold, and none the less for Jonson's drinking bout. Certainly one finds here and there in his work – is it not at the end of *Henry VI*, for instance – praise of country leisure sweetened by wisdom.

Am I perhaps going against nature in my constant attempt to fill my life with work? Is my mind as rich as in idle days? Is not perhaps the poet's labour a mere rejection? If he seeks purity – the ridding

---

[1] Cf. entry 187, p. 230.
[2] The Martin-Harvey production of *Hamlet* at the Theatre Royal in Dublin on Saturday, 23 October 1909.
[3] Edward Dowden (1843-1913), Professor of English Literature at Trinity College, Dublin; author of *Shakespeare, His Mind and Art* and other studies. John Quinn's copy of *Ideas of Good and Evil* is inscribed by Yeats as follows: 'I think the best of these Essays is that on Shakespeare. It is a family exasperation with the Dowden point of view, which rather filled Dublin in my youth. There is a good deal of my father in it, though nothing is just as he would have put it.'

of his life of all but poetry – will not inspiration come? Can one reach God by toil? He gives himself to the pure in heart. He asks nothing but attention.[1]

195

October 27 [1909]. I have been looking at some Venetian costumes of [the] sixteenth century as pictured in *The Mask*[2] – all fantastic; bodily form hidden or disguised; the women with long bodices, the men with stuffed doublets. Life had become so leisured and courtly that men and women dressed with no thought of bodily activity. They no longer toiled much. One feels that, if they still fought and hunted, their imagination was not with these things. Does not the same happen to our passions when we grow contemplative and so liberate them from use? They also become fantastic and create the strange lives of poets and artists.

196

Saturday, October 30 [1909]. Last night I proposed asking Leonard Sweete, when his school ends, to take charge at the Abbey for a time.[3] Lady Gregory wanted an Irishman. When I got home I made this poem in bed:

> ~~Patriots~~/Irishmen if they prefer
> ~~The native~~/Irishman to ~~the~~ foreigner

---

[1] Cf. p. 36.

[2] Gordon Graig's magazine. Beginning with vol. I, no. 12, February 1909, *The Mask* published, under the title 'Venetian Costume', extracts from *The Book of Cesare Vecellio* (1590), translated by D. Nevile Lees. The extracts were continued in vol. II, nos. 4–6, October 1909, vol. II, nos. 7–9, January 1910, and vol. II, nos. 10–12, April 1910. The illustrations to which Yeats refers are in vol. I, no. 12, pp. 226, 229, 230.

[3] Lady Gregory quotes, in *Our Irish Theatre* (New York, Putnam, 1913), p. 93, part of a letter from Yeats on this matter. Like Synge, Lady Gregory was opposed to the appointment of any English stage-manager at the Abbey. Yeats wrote to her: 'I think we should take Vedrenne's recommendation unless we have some strong reason to the contrary. If the man is not Irish we cannot help it. If the choice is between filling our country's stomach or enlarging its brains by importing precise knowledge, I am for scorning its stomach for the present. . . . I should have said that I told Vedrenne that good temper is essential, and he said the man he has recommended is a vegetarian and that Bernard Shaw says that vegetables are wonderful for the temper.' J. E. Vedrenne (1868–1930) was manager, with Harley Granville Barker, at the Savoy Theatre, London, 1907–8, and thereafter at the Theatre Royal, Haymarket. Leonard Sweete was not appointed. In 1910 Lennox Robinson was appointed manager and producer.

Where that foreigner ~~have~~/has just
The sleight of ~~hand~~/mind they need the most
Magnify for all their pains
Ireland's stomach not her brains
or
× The stomach and not the brains

197

November 9 [1909].

1. An ideal of love: To love with all desire and yet to be as kind as an old man past desire.

2. The other day Kerrigan[1] said to me that when he spoke the lines in *Deirdre* which begin, 'Stood the ever-living there, old Lir and Aengus', etc., he feels they are too long or too meditative for the character. He wants 'Stood the ever-living there to warn us hence.' I must change scene where Naisi speaks to messenger, make it more poetical. I can re-write the challenge thus:

Where none can come between us but our swords
For I have found no truth on any tongue
That's not of iron.
Messenger
I am Conchubar's man
× And I will take no message but at his bidding.
And take no message but he bids me to it.[2]

198

Last night, walking home late, I felt as I passed the canal bridge a desire to throw a ring which I value more than anything I possess, because of her that gave it, into the canal. It passed off in a moment or two, but it was almost as strong as the desire I felt when at San

[1] J. M. Kerrigan played Conchubar in the first production of Yeats's *Deirdre* at the Abbey, 24 November 1906. The lines quoted, first assigned to Naisi, appear in 'A Different Version of Deirdre's Entrance', Appendix II in the second volume of *The Collected Works in Verse and Prose of William Butler Yeats* (1908), a revision made for the Abbey production of 9 November 1908. In that production Kerrigan played Naisi, and Mrs Patrick Campbell played Deirdre.

[2] These lines first appear, with very slight changes, in the 1911 printing of the play (Stratford-upon-Avon, Shakespeare Head Press). Cf. Variorum *Plays*, pp. 370-1.

Marino[1] to throw myself from the cliff. Once when I was walking in a wood with a dear friend, holding an axe in my hand, the impulse had for a moment a homicidal form, which passed off the moment I held the axe by the head instead of the handle. My father says that when he is on the top of an omnibus and another passes he wants to jump from one to the other. Is there violent madness at the root of every mind, waiting for some breaking of the leash?

199

November 9 [1909]. I want to re-write 'The Arrow', this second stanza:

> Tall and noble but with face and bosom
> Delicate in colour as apple blossom[2]

200

December 7, 1909.

> Would it were anything but merely ~~noise~~/voice
> The no-king thought who after that was king
> Because he had not heard of anything
> That balanced with a word was more than noise
> And yet/Yet old Romance being kind let him prevail
> Somewhere and somehow that I have forgot
> Though he'd but cannon. Whereas we that had thought
> To have lit upon as clean and sweet a tale
> Have been defeated by that pledge you gave
> In momentary anger long ago
> And I that have not your faith how shall I know
> That in the blinding light beyond the grave
> We'll find so good a thing as that we have lost –
> The hourly kindness, the day's common speech
> The habitual content of each with each
> When neither soul nor body has been crossed.[3]

---

[1] Spring 1907.
[2] First published in *In the Seven Woods* (Dun Emer Press, 1903), *Collected Poems*, p. 85.
[3] 'King and No King', *Collected Poems*, pp. 102–3. The poem is related to the Beaumont and Fletcher play of the same title, in which King Arbaces falls in love with his

201

January 6, 1910. Ill with bad cold for some days and dreamed much. Awoke Monday having dreamed in early morning that I was in Dublin[1] and wanted to go to England, but in a trireme. I proposed the trireme to an assembly of people, members of the company at Abbey, and some fashionable young men who stood at other end of table. I saw the fashionable men whisper to one another and smiling. They used no argument that I could hear, but put the project away. I thought they were misrepresenting my motives to one another. The project had to be given up, and I surprised myself by doing this without regret, but said, 'One has a thousand ideas and one or two are carried out, and yet I am right; one cannot understand the *Odyssey* if one has not sailed in a trireme.' Was it all a symbol of the Abbey's need of capital?[2]

On Tuesday morning I dreamed that I was awake in bed and someone or something told me that I was to help two people, and I knew the names – women's names. I was to pray to be able to help, and I knelt in bed to do so – helped up by an invisible hand. When I had prayed I saw the forms of two persons, one a grown woman, but that vanished, and then that [of] a child. Then I dreamed that I went asleep, and in my sleep my soul or shade went to some far-off village where it stood or I stood among many village children. The child I was to help was crying, and I knew I was to teach it to pray. The child saw me and the others but I did not seem strange to them. When I began to teach it a prayer, I knew by the comments of the children that the prayer was unusual to them in form. I stopped, for I thought, 'if I teach the child an unusual prayer it will be persecuted'. I allowed myself to be corrected word by word, as if I were hesitating or slow of speech. I found that the people of that village, some Eastern

---

sister Panthea. In Act IV Scene IV he protests that he is overthrown by the words 'brother' and 'sister'. In a conceit of the forces against him, he rages: 'Let 'em be anything but merely voice.' Romance was kind: Arbaces was found to be an adopted child and no king, so he was able to marry Panthea and become King. 'That pledge you gave' may refer to the episode in the 'First Draft', p. 134. 'Your faith': Maud Gonne became a Catholic in 1897.

[1] Yeats was at Woburn Buildings on Monday, 3 January.

[2] Yeats to his father, 10 October 1909: 'We are trying to get enough capital to buy out Miss Horniman and go on after 1910.' *Letters* (Wade), p. 535.

place, I think, prayed to Elihu or Elijah. After I had taught the prayer, I wandered away with the child into a garden, comforting it, but presently I knew by its ecstatic face that it knew now I was not a person of flesh like itself. I understood that I was fading. It said, 'Will you not come again?' I said, 'If you are in great need, you may call for me, but I may not be able to come. Your words will not reach me unless I am asleep at the time.' Then seeing that she did not understand, I said, 'I am a ghost, and I am only sometimes allowed to come,' and she understood. Presently I saw a man running along the garden path. He was coming for the child. I stepped forward and lifted my arm with a last effort, for I was fading, making myself visible. I saw him stop in terror and then run away. A moment later I woke.

On either Sunday or Monday night I dreamed I saw PIAL's tomb stone, but old and moss-covered. I could not read the date or age. I think there was a 3, and before it a 6 or 4, I think, but when I tried to read, I was waking. (Note about this time aspect of ☽ p to R ♆.)[1]

202

December 10.[2] Another strange dream. A slow-moving barge, a steam barge, and a bus were going side by side. The barge was manned by a handsome young man and girl. The bus driver was accusing them of stealing two out of four amethysts. They were pleading passionately. 'It was terrible; it was utter ruin,' and so on. The driver persisted. Presently I saw the two young people, who were, I knew, lovers, alone in a sort of desert. They were lamenting their fate in a wild Irish sort of way, praising their life and their relation. At one time I thought they were raised up on two crosses. The woman's words I remember best. After much wild lamentation she complained that the young man had not so good right as she to lament, or that because of this he did not lament enough, I forget which. 'Never had any such relation as she had, never would any have such a death, so great a shipwreck.' (I do not think their death and shipwreck were immediate. They seemed rather to lament that this

[1] Aspect of progressed Moon to Neptune radical.
[2] Evidently a mistake for 10 January 1910.

accusation would break them from their love and the life they cared for – the noble, beautiful life as it seemed to me.) I asked them where they came from, and they said, 'Pomerania,' I think; some vague, barbarous place. The dream was so vivid that after I woke for a time I blamed myself for not having offered money to help them to make restitution, and kept going over my affairs in my mind to find what I could have afforded. As I lay awake some association between them and the thieves on the Cross was in my mind.

203

December 15.[1] *Deirdre of the Sorrows*.[2] I was anxious about this play and on Thursday both Lady Gregory and I felt the strain of our doubts and fears. Would it seem mere disjoined monotony? Would the second Act be intelligible? The audience seemed to like it, and in the last Act certain passages moved me very greatly. I thought the quarrel on the graveside with its last phrase, 'It is a pity that we should miss the safety of the grave, and we trampling its edge,' and Deirdre's saying to the quarrelling kings, 'Move a little further off with the quarrelling of fools' as noble and profound drama as any man has written. On the first night the thought that this was Synge's reverie over death, his own death, made all poignant. 'The filth of the grave,' 'an untidy thing death is, though it is a queen that dies,' and the like, brought him dying before me. I remembered his extreme gentleness in the last weeks, that air of being done with rivalry and ambition. Last night the audience was small – just under £10 – and less alive than the first night. No one spoke to me of the great things. Someone thought the quarrel at the last too harsh, others picked out those rough peasant words that give salt to his speech as 'of course adding nothing to the dialogue, and very ugly'. Others objected to the little things in the costumes of the play which were intended to echo these words, to vary the heroic convention with something homely or of the fields, or to make one believe that these persons were really hunters. No one had understood anything. Then

---

[1] A mistake for 15 January 1910. *Deirdre of the Sorrows* was first performed at the Abbey on 13 January 1910.
[2] '(first performances)', *Autobiographies*, p. 523.

as I watched the acting I saw that Donovan[1] and Miss O'Neill were as passionless as the rest. Miss O'Neill had personal charm, pathos, distinction even, fancy, beauty, but never passion – never intensity; nothing came out of a brooding mind. All was but observation, curiosity, desire to please. Her foot never touched the unchanging rock, the secret place beyond life; her talent showed itself, like that of all the others, social, modern, a faculty of comedy. Pathos she has, the nearest to tragedy the comedian can come as a rule, for that is conscious of our presence and would have our pity. Passion she has not, for that looks beyond mankind and asks no pity, not even of God. It realizes, substantiates, attains, scorns, governs, and is most mighty when it passes from our sight.

204

December 16.[2] Last night Miss O'Neill had so much improved her performance that I begin to think she may have some real tragic power. The lack of power, the uncertain wavering inspiration which I still find amid great charm and distinction comes perhaps more from lack of construction, through lack of reflection and experience, than from lack of the emotion itself. There are passages where she does nothing, or where she allows herself little external comedy impulses, more, I now think, because these are habitual than because she could not create emotion out of herself. The chief failure is at the end. She does not show immediately after the death of Naisi enough sense of what has happened, enough normal despair to show a gradual development into the wild unearthly feeling of the last speeches, though these last speeches are in themselves exquisitely spoken. The little external movements where one wanted alarm, indignation, or some other tragic mood were chiefly in the scene with Owen in Act II. My unfavourable impression on Friday may have come partly from the audience, which was heavy and, I thought, bored. Yesterday the audience – the pit entirely full – was enthusiastic and moved, raising once again to the utmost height my hope for the theatre and the movement.

[1] Fred O'Donovan, who played Naisi.
[2] Evidently 16 January 1910. Máire O'Neill played Deirdre.

205

December 16.[1] I should have noted that I had ♂ ☍ ♄ r[2] on 12th and 13th and felt a good deal of gloomy anger over some troubles in Theatre. S. Allgood late without apology, Lady Gregory worn out with her work at play, Sally[3] chief trouble. I should also note that Deirdre's gold dress in Act I makes her look thin and pale. If she wears it next time, she should have a more ruddy make-up.

206

January 7 [1910].[4] A couple of nights ago I got a new poetical thought in half dream or wholly dream. I would write a poem I had long thought of about the man who left Aoibhinn of Craiglea[5] to die at Clontarf and put in it all the bitter feeling one has sometimes about Ireland. The life of faery would be my lyric life. I thought of doing Cuchulain and Fand in the same way, of making some pre-vision by Maeve cause the need of waking him from his magic sleep.

January 11 or day before or after will bring some trouble, a quarrel of some kind. (♂ ☌ Mcp.)[6] A bad day for *Helmet* and *Playboy*,[7] but may be something else. Won't be very bad. (No, nothing to notice; very busy, but no quarrel.)

In the poem as my dream planned it, Aoibhinn was to mourn for the dance[8] deserted on the mountain. This was to occur like a burden, a couple of times at least.

207

March 7 [1910]. Re-writing of

> O that none ever loved but you and I
> For there the stag and the stag's lady cry

[1] 16 January 1910. [2] Mars in opposition to Saturn radical.
[3] Sara Allgood. [4] In this entry 'January' should read 'February'.
[5] Dubhlaing Ua hArtacáin, despite the entreaties of Aoibhinn of Craig Liath, goes to fight and die beside Murcadh at the Battle of Clontarf: one of many Irish traditions associated with that battle.
[6] Mars conjunct mid-heaven progressed.
[7] *The Green Helmet* was first produced at the Abbey on 10 February 1910, as a curtain-raiser for the *Playboy*.
[8] A doubtful reading.

  ✗ O hurry to the wood for there O there
  ✗ I'll hollo all these lovers out and cry
      O hurry where by water among trees
      The delicate stepping stag and his lady sigh
      When they have but looked upon their images
      Would none had ever loved but you and I
      O hurry to the ragged wood for there
      I'll hollo all those lovers out and cry.[1]

208

March 13 [1910]. Congreve's definition of 'humour': a singular and unavoidable manner of doing anything, peculiar to one man only, by which his speech and actions are distinguished from all other men. 'Passions are too powerful in the sex to let humour have its course.'[2] Traces abundant British humour to gross feeding and liberty. Distinguishes humour from 'habit' and 'affectation' which are impressed from without, the last being an imitation. Wit is different from humour, being part of its expression.

209

March [1910].

      The fascination of what's difficult
      Has dried the sap out of my veins and rent
      Spontaneous joy and natural content
      Out of my heart. ~~What is it/~~There is something ails our colt
      That must, as if it had not holy blood
      Nor on Olympus leaped from cloud to cloud
      ~~Endure/~~Shiver at the lash, and strain and sweat and jolt

---

[1] The first version of 'The Ragged Wood' had appeared, without title, in *Stories of Red Hanrahan* (Dun Emer Press, 1904). *Collected Poems*, p. 92.

[2] This is clearer in Congreve. Humour is 'a singular and unavoidable manner of doing, or saying any thing, peculiar and natural to one man only; by which his speech and actions are distinguished from those of other men. . . . But I must confess I have never made any observation of what I apprehend to be true humour in women. Perhaps passions are too powerful in that sex to let humour have its course. . . .' *Complete Works*, ed. Montague Summers (London, Nonesuch Press, 1923), vol. III, pp. 165–6.

As though it dragged road metal. My curse on plays
That have to be set up in fifty ways
On the day's war with every ~~fool~~/knave and dolt
On the day's letters/Theatre business/On correspondence,
management of men.
I swear before the dawn comes round again
I'll find the stable and pull out the bolt.[1]

Life is memory of what has never happened and hope for what
never will happen.

-----

     on[2]
× On the day's war with every fool and dolt
× Content to
× Arranging this/and that
× Arranging this
× On plans
    Arranging this/that, to call the tune
    I swear this night, if but there is no moon
    To find etc.
              or
    Arranging that, and setting this ~~thing~~/to right
× I'll swear I'll
    I swear ~~it that if~~/if but there is no moon tonight
    ~~I'll~~/To find the stable and pull out the bolt.
× On ~~settling~~/planning, or setting that thing straight

210

When Adam named the beasts, there was one beast that he forgot
to name, or else, taking it for some common horse, named wrongly;
and so as time went on men came to have much knowledge of what
lives and moves, but of the creature whose name they did not know
they had no knowledge, for they could not call it and, having looked

[1] Cf. entry 185, p. 229.
[2] The rest of this entry is written on the opposite page.

at it, speak to one another. That creature permits us to call it
Pegasus,[1] but it does not answer to that or any name.

211

April 5 [1910].   On the attack on the *Playboy*.

> Once, when midnight smote the air
> Eunuchs ran through Hell and met
> Round about Hell's gate to stare
> At great Juan riding by
> And like these to rail and sweat
> Maddened at his sinewy thigh.[2]

Alteration in 'Adam's Curse'.

>   for whose mild sake
> Many a man shall find out all heartbreak
> In finding out that it can murmur so.
>   or
> Many a man shall light upon heartbreak
> In finding out that it can murmur so.[3]

In my 'To My Heart Bidding It Have No Fear' change 'proud' to
'lonely'.[4]

212

April 18 [1910].

> If any man drew near
> When I was young
> I shook with hate and fear   I thought 'He holds her dear'
> Because he held her dear   And shook with hate and fear
> But O 'twas bitter wrong
> If he ~~should~~/could pass her by
> With an indifferent eye

---

[1] Cf. entry no. 232, p. 261.
[2] 'On Those that Hated *The Playboy of the Western World*', *Collected Poems*, p. 124.
Cf. entry 76, p. 176.
[3] *Collected Poems*, pp. 88–90.   [4] Ibid. p. 71.

2

~~Since then~~/Whereon I wrote and wrought
And now being grey
×   I dream that I have brought I ~~boast~~/dream that I have
                                              brought
×   To such a pitch my thought To such a pitch my thought
×   That I at last can say,   That coming time ~~shall~~/can say
×   I have shadowed in ~~this~~/a glass ~~I have~~/He has shadowed in
                                       a glass
×   That thing her body was.   ~~That~~/What thing her body was

3

For she had fiery blood
When I was young;
And trod so sweetly proud
As 'twere upon a cloud
~~The queen by Homer Sung~~/(A woman Homer sung)
That life and letters seem
But an heroic dream.[1]

213

May [1910]. Colleville, Calvados.[2]

    Ah that time ~~should~~/could touch a form
    That could show what Homer's age
    ~~Fashioned for the~~/Bred to be a hero's wage
    'Was not all her ~~youth~~/life but storm
    ~~Painters could but~~/Would not painters paint a form
    ~~With~~/Of such noble lines?' I said
    Such a delicate high head
    So much sternness and such charm
×   That they'd change us to like strength
    Till they~~'d changed~~/had roused us to ~~like~~/that strength?
×   Ah that peace should come at length
×   But when Time has ~~touched~~/changed that form
×   Now that

[1] 'A Woman Homer Sung', *Collected Poems*, p. 100.
[2] Les Mouettes, Colleville, Maud Gonne's house near Calvados in Normandy

Ah but peace that came/comes at length
Came when Time had touched that/her form[1]

Subject for a poem. Any young man to any woman.

You say that you're nothing to me
That there is no love in my heart
Is it so little thing this, that your bright eyes
Your laughing lips, your mouth full of wit, have smoothed
away the violent heartache of youth?

214

May 11 [1910].

O heart be at peace because
Nor knave nor dolt can break
What's not for their applause
But/Being for a woman's sake
Enough if the work has seemed
So did she your strength renew
A dream that a lion had dreamed
Till the wilderness cried aloud
A secret between you two
Between the proud and the proud
If you'd still have/What, you'd still have their praise?
                              (What, still you would have
                                      their praise?)
Then choose/But here's a haughtier text
The labyrinth of her days
By/That her own strangeness perplext
How all that her dreaming gave (And how what her dreaming
                                                    gave)

Earned slander and ingratitude
× Aye and worse wrong than these
From self same dolt and knave
Aye and worse wrong than these
Yet she, singing where/on her round
Half lion, half child is at peace.[2]

[1] 'Peace', *Collected Poems*, p. 103.
[2] 'Against Unworthy Praise', *Collected Poems*, pp. 103-4.

215

May [1910]. Les Mouettes, Colleville, Normandy. Yesterday afternoon, there being much wind and rain, we all stayed indoors –
Mrs Clay,[1] Iseult, Maud Gonne; and Maud Gonne and I got into
the old argument about *Sinn Féin* and its attack on Synge, and the
general circumstances that surrounded the first split in the Theatre.
I notice that this old quarrel is the one difference about which she
feels strongly. I for this very reason let myself get drawn into it
again and again, thinking to convince her at last that apart from wrongs
and rights impossible to settle so long after, it was fundamental. I
could not have done otherwise. My whole movement, my integrity
as a man of letters, were alike involved. Thinking of her, as I do, as
in a sense Ireland, a summing up in one mind of what is best in the
romantic political Ireland of my youth and of the youth of others
for some years yet, I must see to it that I close the Synge essay[2] with
a statement of national literature as I would re-create it, and of its
purpose. It is useless to attack if one does not create.

I must touch on these things. All literature created out of a conscious political aim in the long [run] creates weakness by creating a
habit of unthinking obedience and a habit of distrust of spontaneous
impulse. It makes a nation of slaves in the name of liberty. Literature
created for its own sake or for some eternal spiritual need can be
used by politicians – Dante is said to have unified Italy – but it
seldom can be used at once. (In the time she and [I] dispute about
I did not know this.) Practical movements are created out of emotions
expressed long enough ago to have become general, but literature
discovers; it can never repeat. It is the attempt to repeat an emotion
because it has been found effective which has made all provincially
political literature – the ballad movement of Germany, for instance –
so superficial. Literature is inspired by the vision also of the naked
truth, but she clothes herself before she walks out onto the roads.

---

[1] A cousin of Maud Gonne: they shared the Colleville house.

[2] Yeats was writing an essay designed as Preface to the Maunsel edition of Synge's
works (1910). He withdrew it, however, after a quarrel with the managing editor, George
Roberts, cf. p. 263. Yeats maintained that the fourth volume included some items which
stood in need of revision and ought not to be entered in a definitive edition. The essay
was published separately as *Synge and the Ireland of His Time* (Cuala Press, 1911).

This clothing of truth is [a] necessary illusion of practice, such as Davis's 'The troops live not that could withstand the headlong charge of Tipperary.' Had this been true it would not have been necessary to write it.

But all this is still mere attack. I must describe the effect, on the energies of a people, of the habit of entirely spontaneous emotion and of that headlong plunge into the future, that rage to create that comes [from] delight in emotional discovery. How this in drama such as Synge's means a general sense of power in the persons represented, for all dramatic characters in emotional or poetical work are creators. Contrast with this the weakness of the idealized peasantry of the Irish novelists. The representation of active evil has always been delighted in, in periods of strength; such evil, a defiance of human and divine law, is a form of strength. Everyone learns obedience by its means before obedience can be lifted into wisdom by passion and become a part of intellect.

I should then go on to explain that the fruit of Robert Burns and Scott with their lack of ideas, their external and picturesque view of life, has been to create not a nation but a province with a sense of the picturesque. A nation can only be created in the deepest thought of its deepest minds – the literature that makes it (and this making takes a long time) – who have first made themselves fundamental and profound and then realized themselves in art. In this way they rouse into national action the governing minds of their [time] – few at any one time – by an awakening of their desire towards a certain mood and thought which is unconscious to these governing minds themselves. They create national character. Goethe, Shakespeare, Dante, Homer have so created, and many others in less degree. The external and picturesque or political writer leaves the strongest intellects of their countries empty (and in the case of Scotland, England has crowded into this emptiness), and is content to fill with kilts and bagpipes, newspapers and guidebooks, the days of the least creative.

The more unconscious the creation, the more powerful. A great statesman, let us say, should keep his conscious purpose for practical things. But he should have grown into and find about him always, most perhaps in the minds of women, the nobleness of emotion created and associated with his country by its great poets. If a man is not born into this, he cannot acquire it if he is to do anything else, for it will fill all his life. This is the golden cradle which in my *King's Threshold* Seanchan would prepare for his future children. It is this culture that makes the birth of heroes possible but it is always most powerful when forgotten, when a vague presence in the mind of soldier or orator in some supreme crisis. All popular art, on the other hand, aims at being remembered by this alone, and checks the creative energy, which requires all, by the will.

A cause for the beauty of the popular writing in old times was that the more subtle emotions of the people were organized by religion. They were not left empty. They were there in the depths and in relation with the popular art. Probably when a new culture has spread from the printed book, and a new religious feeling from philosophy and science, popular art will be good again. It will then be, as it were, but part of a great work of art which is the whole art of the nation. Modern popular poetry is isolated, the art of Longfellow, for instance, and generally it is a condescension, a wilful simplification. It should be the work of a man of the people expressing himself to the full.

216

May 16 [1910]. Yesterday I asked Maud Gonne – we had been at many churches and were at Mont-Saint-Michel – finding she prayed to God while in each church, what she was praying for. She said, 'I pray a great deal for the new university.'[1] She had also offered a candle to St Michael.

Two days before, we were crossing a little stream here at Colleville when she told me that six months before her son[2] was born she had had a picnic there. One day, passing the place with him for the first time – he was   [3] years old – he said, 'That is where we lit the fire.' He could not have known the fact in any ordinary way. Iseult corroborates the story. She too heard the words. Both also tell how one day in a place they have never been before he said, 'There's a stream up there,' and it was true, though it was too far off

[1] The National University of Ireland, established in 1908.
[2] Seán MacBride, born on 26 January 1904.
[3] Yeats's blank.

for him to have heard the sound of water. They say he has now lost these faculties.

217

In Synge essay explain melancholy – morbidity – of genius by the fact that a man of genius sees the world as Adam did, as it were for the first time. He's face to face with death and change, breaks away use and routines that hide them. The fact that he reflects the world in a strange mirror – not strange to him, perhaps – makes us also see them for a moment as if we were Adam. He has therefore his double effect; his sincerity that makes us share his feeling, his strangeness that makes us share his vision. He shows us a picture, as a painter might, reversed in a looking-glass, that we may see it as it is. But this strangeness wears off and leaves only his sincerity. Strangeness is, however, more often than not the cause of the first successes of writers as well as of their first failures. Every writer has, however, his mirror, which is the creation of his sincerity. He is different.

218

Yet at Mont-Saint-Michel I have been seeing a different art, a marvellous powerful living thing created by a community working for hundreds of years and allowing only a very little place for the individual. Are there not groups which obtain, through powerful emotion, organic vitality? How do they differ from the mob of casual men who are the enemies of all that has fineness? Why is it that the general thought is our enemy in the towns of Ireland, and would be our friend in the country places if we had the same symbols? I cannot see clearly, but think the difference is like that between a monastery and a modern town. I would have said there must be a discipline of thought and body, but the country people have only this in a very vague sense in their folklore. One thing I do see. The unifying principle must come from and perpetually appeal to what is deepest, and it must enclose the entire lives of all within its circle. Without that, it will be a convention in the colloquial sense of the word, a mere formalism or a mob tyranny; the soul will be in perpetual revolt. Young Irelandism, because a condescension, a conscious simplification, could only perish or create a tyranny. No sacrifice for a cause necessarily ennobles the soul unless the soul is a part of the cause. One cannot have a national art in the Young Ireland sense, that is to say an art recognized at once by all as national because obviously an expression of what all believe and feel, though one can have an imitation, because no modern nation is an organism like a monastery by rule and discipline, by a definite table of values understood by all, or even, as the Western peasants are, by habit of feeling and thought. Am I not right; is there not an organism of habit – a race held together by folk tradition, let us say? And this is now impossible because thought old enough to be a habit cannot face modern life and shape educated men, and an organism of discipline has hitherto proved impossible in the modern world because no nation can seclude itself. When I try to create a national literature, for all that, do I not really mean an attempt to create this impossible thing after all, for the very reason that I always rouse myself to work by imagining an Ireland as much a unity in thought and feeling as ancient Greece and Rome and Egypt; and hate the mob of casual men who are only one in moments [of] hysterical feeling, in its service, not in the service of the individual? Am I not therefore un-national in any sense the common man can understand? He means by national a mob held together not by what is interior, delicate and haughty, but by law and force which they obey because they must. I must therefore be content to be but artist, one [of] a group, Synge, Lady Gregory – no, there is no other than these[1] – who express something which has no direct relation to action. We three have conceived an Ireland that will remain imaginary more powerfully than we have conceived ourselves. The individual victory was but a separation from casual men as a necessary thing before we could become naturalized in that imaginary land which is, as it were, the tradition-bound people of the West made independent from America or from London, and living under its own princes.

---

[1] 'We three alone in modern times had brought
Everything down to that sole test again,
Dream of the noble and the beggar-man.'
'The Municipal Gallery Revisited', *Collected Poems*, p. 369.

219 [1]

August [1910].

I

My dear Robert:[2] I want you to understand that I have no instincts in personal[3] life. I have reasoned them all away, and reason acts very slowly and with difficulty and has to exhaust every side of the subject. Above all, I have destroyed in myself, by analysis, instinctive indignation. When I was twenty or a little more, I was shocked by the conversation at Henley's. One day I resolved if the conversation was as bad again, I would walk out. I did not do so, and next day I reasoned over the thing and persuaded myself that I had thought of walking out from vanity and did not do so from fear. As I look back, I see occasion after occasion on which I have been prevented from doing what was a natural and sometimes the right thing either because analysis of the emotion or action of another, or self-distrustful analysis of my own emotion destroyed impulse. I cannot conceive the impulse, unless it was so sudden that I had to act at once, that could urge me into action at all if it affected personal life. All last week the moment that my impulse told me I should demand with indignation an apology from Gosse, my analysis said, 'You think that from vanity. You want to do a passionate thing because it stirs your pride.'

I was once told by a relation that my father had done some disgraceful thing – of course it was absurd and untrue – and I found with amused horror that I was coldly arguing over the probabilities and explaining (to myself, I am glad to say) why it could not be true. In impersonal and public things, because there this distrust of myself does not come in, I have impulse. I would have explained it by saying that it is the world I have been brought up in – you have always lived among defined social relations and I only among defined ideas – but then my family seemed to me to have more than enough of the usual impulses. I even do my writing by self-distrusting reasons. I thought to write this note in the same way as I write the

---

[1] Several of the following entries arise from an occasion on which Sir Edmund Gosse sent Lady Gregory an insulting letter. The question was the proposed Civil List pension for Yeats. Lady Gregory and her son Robert felt that Yeats should have demanded a full apology from Gosse. Some details of the episode are given in Appendix E, pp. 289–91.

[2] Robert Gregory (1881–1918).   [3] 'practical' deleted.

others. And then I said, 'I am really explaining myself to Robert Gregory. I am afraid to write to him directly or speak to him directly, and so I am writing this note thinking that some chance may show it to him. So I will write it as if to him.' Since then, while writing it, I have thought this an insincerity, for I have understood that I am trying to put myself right with myself even more than with you.

I want you to understand that once one makes a thing subject to reason as distinguished from impulse, one plays with it even if it is a very serious thing. I am more ashamed because of the things I have played with in life than of any other thing.

All my moral endeavour[1] for many years has been an attempt to re-create practical instinct in myself. I can only conceive of it as of a kind of acting.

II

One thing I want you to understand, and that is that I was never influenced by any fear of a quarrel with Gosse. There were moments when, thinking over that letter which I believed to have been posted, I thought that Gosse would probably prevent my getting that pension. I never hesitated on that ground; I can say that with sincerity. I was simply thinking the matter out in an impersonal way and talking of it that I might think the better, and trying to remember kind acts by Gosse while weighing my letter.

But, after all, nothing that I have written will interest you. You will merely say, 'He is thinking of himself, and not of my mother, who has been insulted by Gosse.' Yes, and you will be right. That is just the trouble. Only the self I have been thinking of is not self-interest.

August 2, 1910

220

I

[2]No, there is no use tracing, as I was going to do, the steps by which I reasoned myself into writing the three letters I did write. All, as I

---

[1] 'philosophy' deleted.
[2] 'My mind works like this. When I was younger and more natural my first impulse would have been indignation, but now it was only surprise. I said, why has Gosse done this ridiculous thing. Has he fits of madness? I went over it and over it trying to see what caused it. I gave up that problem.' deleted.

still think, proper letters, except that they should have been done without thinking, at once and without any discussion which showed my attitude of mind and distressed everybody. Private individuals should not need a council of the church before they act.

II

I see always this one thing, that in practical life the mask is more than the face. I believe that I am speaking with more self-condemnation than self-defence when I say, 'There are moments of life when one must say, "Such-and-such an act proves such-and-such a man to be cad or fool" and not "Such-and-such a man has shown himself by this or that good action to be neither cad nor fool, so why did he do this?" That one must say, "Such-and-such a person could never have done such-and-such a thing," even though one's imagination suggests an endless array of circumstances in which anyone might be moved to do anything. That one must continually write and speak what one's reason denies.' What is more, that one must continually feel and believe what one's reason denies. I am so unfortunate that I can only conceive of this as a kind of play-acting. I feel no emotion enough to act upon it but faint lyrical emotion which only affects life indirectly. Then there is this difficulty, that words are with me a means of investigation, rather than a means of action.

221

Oh masters of life, give me confidence in something, even if it be but in my own reason. I can never believe in anything else now, for I have accused the impulses of too many sins. I know that reason is almost a blasphemous thing, a claim to an infinity of being while we are limited social creatures, half artificial. Twenty, no, a hundred times if I had acted upon impulse and against reason I should have created a finer world* of rights and wrongs, a more personal and passionate life than impersonal reason could give. Reason is the stopping of the pendulum, a kind of death. Life is a perpetual injustice.

* Yes, but I should have gone from my world. The passionate man must believe he obeys his reason.

222

I remember saying to myself at Burren[1] an hour or two after I saw Gosse's letter, I want to write a long letter to Gosse, pointing out to him that he had done a disgraceful thing, but to do this without indignation, because I remembered some kindness to myself and his very great and patient kindness to Arthur Symons. I wanted to ask if there was some misunderstanding. Then I came to see that he was not himself, and so it was no use thinking he would answer sensibly, and that Lady Gregory was naturally very indignant, so that it was necessary for me to write as if I judged Gosse by this one act. Punchinello must speak his mind to Punchinello, or be no gentleman. That stick he sometimes holds between his crossed arms would have been so much better. It at any rate could not have been expected to weigh rights and wrongs. It is made of wood.

223

Did I lack sympathy? Did I forget that a letter which would not have hurt me hurt her deeply? No, I think I knew that and knew too that it was her zeal in my service brought that letter upon her. I think it was all just as I have written.

224

August 6 [1910]. As a simplification of *Player Queen*. Yellow Martin should suspect not a follower of Seneca, but some low buffoon, of stirring up the people against them. Some low comedian-poet.[2]

---

[1] '. . . a desolate, windy spot on the coast of Clare': Yeats to John B. Yeats about Burren, 17 July ? 1909, *Letters* (Wade), p. 532. The Gregory house at Burren was 'Mount Vernon', charmingly described by Anne Gregory in ch. VII of her *Me and Nu : Childhood at Coole* (Gerrards Cross, Colin Smythe, 1970).

[2] In an early manuscript version of *The Player Queen* Yellow Martin (Septimus) says to Barrach: 'I can see it all, some rascal, some dunce, that copies Seneca has put you up to this – only writing the play in the market-place.' (National Library of Ireland, MS. 8764 (4).)

225

August 6 [1910]. I have just sent this letter to Gosse: 'My Dear Gosse. Is it ever right to compel a man to choose between two ingratitudes? You showered kindness upon me, and then you insulted my most intimate friend, who had sent you a courteous and fitting answer (for I saw what she wrote) to a letter of yours. You did not get my first letter, because that friend, not wishing me to quarrel, had taken it out of the post-bag. I had just heard this, and a draft of a somewhat milder letter was on my table when your apology came. For so accomplished a writer, you do not write apologies well. I showed yours to Robert Gregory and, on his advice, have not shown it to his mother. However, I thank you for what you have done for me.'

226

August 8 [1910]. Lady Gregory again spoke of the thing today. I said, 'I am amused with Dumas's people. They do good and evil in obedience to a code. They never give a moment's thought to any moral question – all that is settled by their code. They must have been very dull to know. Never for a moment has anybody a modern mind.' She said, 'A code is necessary; there is not time to reason things out.' I knew by her tone of voice that she was thinking again of the Gosse incident, and the next moment she spoke of it. As I look back on the whole thing, I come to see that Lady Gregory and Robert expected me to act at once, on a code. Instead of asking, 'Why has Gosse done this?' instead of being, what is worse really, interested in his character and motives, I should have been in a very simple state of mind. I should have spoken of him with contempt, or written to him with contempt – there was nothing else to do. That whole attitude was so strange to me that, when accused of lacking all right instinct for not thinking in that way, I added to the problem of Gosse the problem of myself and said, 'Do I lack the instinct of honourable conduct?' I see now that for me there was nothing else possible. Since I was fifteen and began to think, I have mocked at that way of looking at the world, as if it was a court of law where all wrong actions were judged according to their legal penalties. All my life I have, like every artist, been proud of belonging to a nobler world, of having chosen the slow, dangerous, laborious path of moral judgment. And yet the moment the code appears before me in the personality of two friends, I am shaken, I doubt myself. I doubted because I talked. In silence I could have thought the whole thing out, kept my vacillation to myself. I could have appealed to what is best in Gosse, perhaps reconciled those who will be enemies, or at any rate I could have recalled him to his better self. My father would have done this because he would have been himself. I neither dealt with the matter like an artist, nor as a man of the world. I allowed myself to accept the code of Punchinello without obeying it. Nothing in which strong passions are involved should, if one can help, be dealt with on general principles as if it were a question of manners. Both Lady Gregory and Robert are Jupitereans. All such create codes or are born into them. Yet does one ever do folly without knowing the right course? I can remember just after seeing Gosse's letter – I was walking up to the house from the sea[1] – it was just as if a voice said to me, 'Speak to no one about it. Go straight in; write at once to Gosse. Remonstrate, but as a man should write to an old friend who has done wrong. But, above all, speak to no one about it.' As I heard this, I knew I should not do it, that I was too timid, too distrustful of myself. So, far from the moral nature having anything to do with the code, it begins with the rejection of it, and attains to power by listening to minute, almost secret, ungeneralized thought. But of all forms of courage this is the most difficult, for this ungeneralized thought has never any support but in itself.

All the time I spoke of the thing with Lady Gregory or Robert, I knew that they thought that I hesitated not because I wished to do right, but because I thought Gosse might be useful to me. If I had kept silent I would have escaped from that.

This has been a painful thing. It has been the one serious quarrel I have ever had with Lady Gregory, because the first that has arisen from unreconcilable attitudes towards life. Being a writer of comedy, her life as an artist has not shaken in her, as tragic art would have done, the conventional standards. Besides, she has never been a part

[1] At Burren.

of the artist's world, she has belonged to a political world, or to one that is merely social.

Why do I write all this? I suppose that I may learn at last to keep to my own in every situation in life; to discover and create in myself as I grow old that thing which is to life what style is to letters: moral radiance, a personal quality of universal meaning in action and in thought.

I can see now how I lost myself. 'I have been trying to re-create in myself the passions,' I wrote, or some such words. Yes, but for me they must flow from reason itself. My talent would fade if I trafficked in general standards, and yet Punchinello too is ancient; they dug up a statue of him among the ruins of Rome.

Is not all life the struggle of experience, naked, unarmed, timid but immortal, against generalized thought; only that personal history in this is the reverse of the world's history? We see all arts and societies passing from experience to generalization, whereas the young begin with generalization and end with experience, that is to say not what we call its 'results', which are generalized, but with its presence, its energy. All good art is experience; all popular bad art generalization.

227

'Put off the mask of burning gold
    With emerald eyes.'
× 'But O my dear you ~~make thus bold~~/are made so bold
'O no my dear you make so bold
    To find if ~~I be dull or wise~~/hearts be wild and wise
    ~~Kind or~~/And yet not cold.'

'I would but find ~~whether~~/what's there to find
    Love or deceit.'
'But 'twas the mask engaged your mind
    And after set your heart to beat
    Not what's behind.'

'For it may be you're my enemy
    I must inquire.'

'O no my dear let the mask be
~~So that~~/What matter ~~if~~/so there but burn fire
In thee and me.'[1]

~~How if you were my~~/But lest you ~~be~~/are my enemy
I must inquire.'
'O no my dear let ~~the mask~~/all that be
What matter so there burn but fire
In thee and me.'[2]

228

~~Every~~/But every powerful life goes on its way
× As if with blind eyes and wild groping hands.
× Too deafened by the cries within the mind
To
Too blinded by the sight of the mind's eye
Too deafened by the cries out of the heart
Not to have staggering feet and groping hands.[3]

229

These are the clouds about the ~~setting~~/fallen sun
The majesty that shùts his burning eye,
The weak lays hand on what the strong has done
Till all be ~~trampled~~/tumbled that was ~~lift~~/~~lifted~~/
~~builded~~/lifted high
And discord follows/followed (or follows) upon unison
And all things at a common level lie
And therefore friend, if your great race were run
And these things came so much the more thereby

---

[1] This stanza is entirely cancelled.
[2] 'The Mask' first appeared as 'A Lyric from an Unpublished Play', the play being *The Player Queen*, in *The Green Helmet and Other Poems* (Cuala Press, 1910), *Collected Poems*, p. 106. 'Among subjective men (in all those, that is, who must spin a web out of their own bowels) the victory is an intellectual daily re-creation of all that exterior fate snatches away, and so that fate's antithesis; while what I have called "the Mask" is an emotional antithesis to all that comes out of their internal nature. We begin to live when we have conceived life as tragedy', *Autobiographies*, p. 189.
[3] Another version of 'Reconciliation'. Cf. entry 72, p. 172.

Have you made greatness your companion.
Although/~~And though~~ it be for children that you sigh.
These are the clouds about the ~~setting~~/fallen sun
The majesty that shuts his burning eye[1]

230

Wine comes in at the mouth
Love comes in at the eye
That's all we shall know for truth
Before we grow old and die
I lift the glass to my mouth
I look at you – and I sigh.[2]

231

May 25, 1911. At Stratford, *Playboy* shocked a good many people, because the Stratford is a self-improving, self-educating audience and that means a perverted and commonplace one.[3] If you set out to educate yourself you are compelled to have an ideal, and if you are not a man of genius your ideal will [be] a commonplace and prevent the natural impulses of the mind, its natural reverence, desire, hope, admiration, always half unconscious, almost bodily. That is why a simple round of religious duties, things that escape the intellect, is often so much better than its substitute, self-improvement.

[1] 'These Are the Clouds', *Collected Poems*, pp. 107–8. The friend is Lady Gregory.
[2] 'A Drinking Song', *Collected Poems*, pp. 104–5. The song was written for *Mirandolina*, Lady Gregory's adaptation from Goldoni's *La Locandiera*: it was first performed at the Abbey on 24 February 1910.
[3] The Abbey players began a two months' tour of England with a performance of the *Playboy*, *Cathleen Ni Houlihan*, and *The Rising of the Moon* at the Memorial Theatre, Stratford-on-Avon, on 1 May 1911. Máire Nic Shiubhlaigh has written of that evening: 'Synge's play, produced now as a rapid comedy, went well with a distinguished audience.' *The Splendid Years* (Dublin, Duffy, 1955), p. 106.

232

August 17 [1911]. Poem written in Paris in May.

Imitated from Ronsard[1]
Good Craoibhin Aoibhin[2] (Douglas Hyde) look into our case
When we are high and airy hundreds say
That if we hold that flight they'll leave the place
While those same hundreds mock another day
Because we have made our art of common things
So bitterly you'd dream they'd longed to look
All their lives through into some drift of wings.
You've dandled them, and fed them from the book
And know them to the bone. Impart to us –
We'll keep the secret – a new trick to please
Is there a bridle for this ~~Pegasus~~/Proteus
That turns and changes like his draughty seas
Or is there none, most popular of men
But when they mock us that we mock again.

233

S.S. *Zeeland*.[3] September 18 [1911]. I noticed in the train, as I came to Queenstown, a silent, fairly well-dressed man, who struck me as vulgar. It was not his face, which was quite normal. I found it was his movements. He moved from his head only. His arm and hand, let us say, moved in direct obedience to the head, had not the instinctive motion that comes from a feeling of weight, of the shape of [an] object to be touched and grasped. There were too many straight lines in gesture of pose. The result was an impression of vulgar smartness, a defiance of what is profound and old and simple by the obvious and trivial.

[1] 'At the Abbey Theatre', *Collected Poems*, p. 107. The Ronsard sonnet is 'Tyard, on me blasmoit, à mon commencement'.

[2] Hyde's pen-name, Irish for 'lovely little branch'.

[3] On 12 September 1911, Yeats sailed with the Abbey players from Queenstown (now Cobh) to Boston, where they were to begin their stormiest tour. He accompanied the players only for a short time, and returned to Ireland when Lady Gregory, delayed for some days in Dublin, joined the company in the United States. The tour is well described in *The Splendid Years*, pp. 108–39.

I have noticed that beginners sometimes move this way on the stage. They are told to pick up something and show in their way of doing so that the idea of doing it is more vivid to them than doing it. This is especially true of actors with a critical faculty. One gets an impression of thinness of nature. I am watching Miss Nic Shiubh-laigh[1] to find out if her stiffness on the stage comes from this or if she is stiff in life. I watched her sitting in a chair the other day to see if her body, as it were, felt its size and place before she reached it. If her body is not stocked with these impressions in great abundance, she will never be able to act, just as she will never have grace of movement in life. But she may have them and stop them artificially. As I write I see through the cabin door a woman feeding a child with a spoon. She thinks of nothing but the child, and every movement is full of expression. It would be beautiful acting. On the other hand her talk – she is talking to someone next her – in which she is not interested, is monotonous and thin in cadence. It is a mere purpose in the brain, made necessary by politeness.

234

January 4 [1912]. The night before last went to see George Moore, urged on by W. F. Bailey, and came back in a fury. Walked most of the way back to get my mind quiet enough for sleep, and even then felt that it was no use going to bed, so sat up till three. Moore had some friends; the Englishmen left early and no one was left but G. Moore, Colonel Moore,[2] and George Russell. I stayed, for there was a matter I wanted to see Moore about. Moore spoke with pride of a letter he had written to Beecham because of some trumpery dispute about an essay Beecham had accepted and then would not publish and pay for because he had given up his idea of editing a review – had lost money. Moore wrote that he was fit for nothing but conducting his father's opera, 'which made the entrails of servant girls sing'.[3] He repeated this twice, so proud he was of its wit. Then he and

---

[1] Miss Nic Shiubhlaigh had returned to the Abbey Company in November 1910 at the request of Lady Gregory. She replaced Máire O'Neill, who was ill, on the American tour.

[2] Colonel Maurice Moore, George Moore's brother.

[3] Sir Thomas Beecham (1879–1961) was associated with Cecil Chesterton (1879–

Russell began urging me to make peace with George Roberts. I told the story of his agreement with Edward Synge and his treatment of myself and said that it amounted to fraud. George Moore said, 'Oh nonsense, Yeats, anybody might do a thing like that,' and Colonel Moore said, 'No, not fraud, merely sharp practice.' I accepted the correction, and then Russell began to defend Roberts – it was mere muddleheadedness, and so on. He was vehement, as I have heard him so often in the defence of the mischief-makers or the incompetent. I got angry and described the dishonesty of the muddle-headed whose darkness has always one light, that of self-interest; there, though there alone, attention does not wander. I was all the angrier because I knew I was making a bad impression, appearing to denounce Roberts from mere personal resentment, and knowing that some impish instinct made it impossible to tell the truth, which is that I was angry because Roberts's trickery left Synge's image in the world's memory less perfect than it should have been.[1] Why do I constantly represent my motives as worse than they are? The casual stranger is always Russell's friend, because Russell has never represented his motives as anything but high. What is this instinct or perversity? I find myself again and again representing my actions as based on some merely clever motive when the real one was high enough. Is it dislike of facile fervour, or is it that the constant strain of writing where style, emotional nobility, is the end requires relaxation? I often feel while putting something in a bad light, when giving way to momentary irritation with all the exaggeration that follows, that I am doing it from a kind of conscious self-indulgence, or as if a bond of control broke. Then again the instinct seems deeper than reason, as if there is always a secret in the moral nature that must be kept, a sort of savage *geasa*.[2] In public speech, or any expression which is formal, I escape, recovering style.

1918) in founding *The New Witness* in 1912. Chesterton edited the magazine from 1912 to 1916. The reference to 'his father's opera' is evidently a gibe occasioned by Sir Joseph Beecham's financial contributions to the cause of opera in England; many of his operatic productions featured Sir Thomas as conductor. The reference to servant girls recalls the advertising motto, 'worth a guinea a box', devised for the sale of Beecham's Pills, a medicament patented by the conductor's grandfather, Thomas Beecham (1820–1907), in 1847.

[1] Entry 215, p. 247.

[2] *geas*, plural *geasa*, Irish for 'magical injunction laid upon someone'.

235

April 3, 1912.

On hearing that the students of the new National University, having joined the Ancient Order of Hibernians, are taking part in its campaign against immoral literature:

> Where, where but here have Pride and Truth,
> That long to give themselves for wage,
> To stand and laugh at timid youth
> Restraining reckless middle age.[1]

236

April 10 [1912]. Went last night to Cambridge House, Wimbledon, to attend séance by Mrs Wriedt. Eight people including myself, and in addition Mrs Harper and Miss Harper.[2] We sat round room not holding hands or touching, but were told to put our feet flat on the floor. There was the usual trumpet and Mrs [Wriedt] was two off to my right. It was perfectly dark. We were seated a very few minutes when we were sprinkled with some liquid – I felt it on my head and hands, a few drops. Medium said it was a baptism. Then there came a very loud voice through the trumpet. It had come for 'Mr Gates.'[3] Or so the medium heard the voice. I said that was me. Then the voice said, 'I have been with you from childhood. We want to use your hand and brain.' 'You possess key,' or, 'you are a key mind', I forget which. 'I am Leo the writer – writer and explorer.'[4] I tried by questions to get more. 'When did he live; in eighteenth century?' He then said, 'Why man,' or such expression implying impatience, 'I am Leo, the writer. You know, Leo the writer.' When I said I did not, I thought he added, 'You will hear of me at Rome.' He then went. After him came a feeble voice of which we could get

---

[1] 'On Hearing that the Students of our new University have joined the Agitation against Immoral Literature', *Collected Poems*, p. 105.

[2] The correct date of this séance is 9 May 1912. Mrs Etta Wriedt, a Detroit medium, was then living in Hampstead. The participants included Mrs S. A. Adela Harper and Miss Edith K. Harper, secretary to W. T. Stead.

[3] 'Gates' is the name by which Yeats is referred to in Aleister Crowley's novel *Moonchild*.

[4] Leo Africanus, Italian geographer, who became Yeats's attendant spirit.

little that was clear. This voice was suddenly interrupted by the very loud voice again, telling me 'to sit up straight in my chair'. I was leaning forward. At this point the influence was broken. One terrified lady had already left, and now two left. We got nothing more except that after about half-an-hour I was twice touched on the hand, somebody else to my left once, and that I saw a vague but unmistakable light before me, about as large and the same shape as a sixpenny loaf. After the two ladies left, the medium had seated herself next me. She was not next me, however, at the time when the voice told me to sit up in my chair, and it was too dark for her to see me.

237

May 18 [1912]. When any part of human life has been left unexpressed, there is a hunger for its expression in large numbers of men, and if this expression is prevented artificially, the hunger becomes morbid, and if the educated do not become its voice, the ignorant will. From this cause have come the Victorian charlatanic mystics and the obscene sentences written upon the walls of jakes.

238

May 24 [1912].

> To toil and grow rich
> Is all night to lie
> With a foul witch
> And after be brought
> Weary and drained dry
> To a lady fair
> Long loved and sought
> With despair.

> Toil and grow rich
> What's that but to lie
> With a foul witch
> And then when drained dry
> To be brought
> To a lady fair

Long loved and long sought
With despair.[1]

239

Transcribe *Proceedings* of A.S. for P.R. 1912, page 629.[2] Control reporting pictures in mind of Robert Hyslop, of a crowd, says, 'Then I walk on with the crowd,' showing that it shared in the vision in some way, became his past.

240

October 1912. I notice that in dreams our apparent subjective moods are almost limited to very elementary fear, grief and desire. We are without complexity or any general consciousness of our state. If we are ill, our discomfort is transferred apparently from ourselves to the dream image. An image created by sexual desire, when our health is bad, may for instance be a woman with a swollen face or some disagreeable behaviour. Indeed, when we are ill we often see deformed images. I suggest analogy between the form of mind of the control, also superficial, and our apparent mind in dreams. The sense of identity is attenuated in both at the same points.

241

July 1913. Having now proved spirit identity – for the ER case[3] is final – I set myself this problem. Why has no sentence of literary or speculative profundity come through any medium in the last fifty years, or perhaps ever, for Plutarch talks of the imperfect expression of the Greek oracles in which he believes? By medium I mean spirit impulse which is independent of, or has submerged, the medium's conscious will. I re-state it thus: All messages that come through the senses as distinguished [from] those that come from the

---

[1] 'The Witch', *Collected Poems*, p. 135.
[2] American Society for Psychical Research. See Appendix F, pp. 292–302 especially p. 295.
[3] ER, a young woman gifted in automatic writing, is described in Yeats's 1912 notes book, a present from Maud Gonne at Christmas 1912. One part of the description is entitled 'Spirit Identity': it offers evidence that spirits maintain their identities after death: the spirits, in ER's case, included Thomas Creech, John Mirehouse, Henry Larkin, and Thomas Emmerson. Yeats met ER in the spring of 1912.

apparently free action of the mind – for surely there is poetic inspiration – are imperfect; that is to say, all objective messages, all that come through hearing or sight – automatic script, for instance – are without speculative power, or at any rate not equal to the mind's action at its best. All that is objective – and this is more true of all where there is the greatest degree of objective materialization – suggests a mirror life or at times a fragmentary consciousness as if cast from a distance, or from a sphere which has no real likeness to this sphere. The power of thought and expression is, however, sufficient for the practical, in which the spirits excel us often as they always do in knowledge of fact. It is only in speculation, wit, the highest choice of the mind, that they fail. Upon the other hand, the mind when it seems in contact with their life directly, that is to say without any understanding through the senses, does not receive messages as to matters of fact.

242

If you that have grown old were the first dead
Neither catalpa tree nor scented lime
Should hear my living feet nor ~~should~~/would I tread
Where we wrought that shall break the teeth of time
Let the new faces play what tricks they will
In the old rooms. For all they do or say
Our shades will rove the garden gravel still
The living seem more shadowy than they.

December 1912
For all they'll do or say
Our shadows rove the garden gravel still
The living seem more shadowy than they.[1]

243

I am troubled over Lady Gregory's journey to America,[2] I have a

[1] 'The New Faces', *Collected Poems*, p. 238. The poem is addressed to Lady Gregory, the catalpas and limes are at Coole Park. Lady Gregory's *Coole* has a fine description of the Park's catalpas.

[2] To take charge of the Abbey's second American tour, and to collect money for Sir Hugh Lane's projected gallery.

sense of ill luck about it. I wish I had her stars. (She was ill a good deal of the time, and hurt her hand badly on the way home. July 1913.)

Dr Maitra[1] came to see me today. I told him how Sarojini's[2] brother had said to Maud Gonne, 'What can we do? A man who is the spiritual leader of our race has written a poem welcoming the King.' Maitra's face was full of amusement. He said, 'I think I know what he was speaking of. The National Congress asked Tagore to write them a poem about the King. He tried that night and could not do it. He got up very early next morning and wrote a poem, a beautiful poem though not one of his best. He gave it to one of us and said, "There is a poem which I have written. It is addressed to God, but you can give it to the National Congress. They will be pleased. They will think it is addressed to the King." December 28 [1912].

244

July 1913. I told the control that I had evoked in a girl's mind a Diana in a cave by imagining geometric symbols and a moon, which she did not see, for her eyes were shut. I had not foreseen the Diana. Her trance grew too deep, and I tried to lighten it by making an exorcism very faintly – a stupid action – with the result that the girl started and said, 'Diana is angry, you are driving her away too quickly.' She had not seen my gesture and would not have understood if she had. I asked [if] Diana was a symbol, and yet she acted as if she lived: are then symbols living things? He said, 'She completed your thought as you would if you had followed your clue.'

If symbolic vision is then but thought completing itself, and if, as we must now think, its seat is but the physical nature, and if thought has indeed been photographed, is symbolic thought, as all

---

[1] Dr D. N. Maitra (1878–1950), Resident Surgeon of the Mayo Hospital in Calcutta from 1901. In 1912 he took a postgraduate course in surgery at the Royal Infirmary and University of Edinburgh, also at the West London Hospital. In 1925 he founded the Bengal Social Service League, with Tagore as its President from 1925 to 1930. He is the 'distinguished Bengali doctor of medicine' with whom Yeats discussed Tagore's poems in the summer of 1912 (*Essays and Introductions*, p. 387). The anecdote about Tagore's royal poem is repeated in Ezra Pound's letter to his father, January 1913, where the doctor is described, inaccurately, as 'one of Rabindranath's students' (*The Letters of Ezra Pound*, ed. D. D. Paige, London, Faber & Faber, 1951, p. 49).

[2] Sarojini Naidu, poetess: her books include *The Bird of Time*, *The Golden Threshold*, and *The Broken Wing*. Her brother was Harindranath Chattopadhyay (Chatterji).

thought, a reality in itself going its appointed course when impulses are given in heaven or earth, moving when we do not see it as when we do, a mid-world between the two realities, a region of correspondences, the activities of the daimons?[1]

245

George Moore in an outrageous article in *English Review*[2] attacks Lady Gregory and myself. Lady Gregory has threatened a libel action and Moore has apologized and withdrawn a statement about her proselytizing in early life.[3] The statements about me are too indefinite for any action, though equally untrue. Some years ago I made a speech at a lecture of Moore's for which Lane thanked me at the time, saying it was the one speech that might have some good effect. It was an appeal to the Irish aristocracy to support Lane's gallery, and I heard afterwards that it offended Lady Ardilaun.[4] Moore has turned this into an attack on the middle classes, confusing it with a speech, probably, which he did not hear but would have heard of, delivered at the National Literary Society (which speech is reported, verbatim I think, in the *Irish Times*). Much of his report is, however, mere novel writing.[5] He takes up the common defence

[1] 'the sensible world that surrounds all spirits.' deleted.

[2] 'Yeats, Lady Gregory, and Synge', *English Review*, vol. XVI, pp. 167–80 and 350–64, January and February 1914. The reference to Lady Gregory's alleged proselytizing is as follows: 'A staunch Protestant family, if nothing else, the Roxborough Persses certainly are. Mrs Shaw Taylor is Lady Gregory's sister, and both were ardent soul-gatherers in the days gone by; but Augusta abandoned missionary work when she married, and we like to think of Sir William saying to his bride, as he brought her home in the carriage to Coole, "Augusta, if you have made no converts, you have at least shaken the faith of thousands. The ground at Roxborough has been cleared for the sowing, but Kiltartin can wait."' (p. 175.)

[3] Lady Gregory wrote to Moore on 17 January 1914: 'The suspicion of me began when I had to take the part of an ill-treated woman against both churches, but that is a long story.' (Berg Collection, New York Public Library.)

[4] Olive, wife of Sir Arthur Edward Guinness (1840–1915), Baron Ardilaun of Ashford. Yeats, sending to Hugh Lane a copy of the poem 'To a Wealthy Man who Promised a second Subscription to the Dublin Municipal Gallery if it were Proved the People Wanted Pictures', said: 'I have tried to meet the argument in Lady Ardilaun's letter to somebody, her objection to giving because of Home Rule and Lloyd George, and still more to meet the general argument of people like Ardilaun, that they should not give unless there is a public demand.' *Letters* (Wade), 1 January 1913, p. 573.

[5] Moore wrote to Rev. James O. Hannay ('George A. Birmingham') on 27 October 1911 about *Ave*: 'The reviewers look upon my book as a book of reminiscences, whereas

of the middle classes, a gibe against the critic because the critic is of them, a pretence that only the aristocracy or perhaps the working classes have a right to criticize. The word 'bourgeois' which I had used is not an aristocratic term of reproach, but, like the older 'cit' which one finds in Ben Jonson, a word of artistic usage. 'God created the nobles, God created the clerks, God created the poor, but who the devil created these people?' wrote a fourteenth-century poet.

Moore, however, is the born demagogue and in nothing more than in his love of the wealthy. He has always a passion for some crowd, is always deliberately inciting them against somebody. He shares the mob's materialism and the mob's hatred of any privilege which is an incommunicable gift. He can imagine himself rich, he cannot imagine himself with fine manners, and the mere thought of such manners gives him a longing to insult somebody. He looks at style, or the pursuit of it, in the same way. On the other hand he has the demagogic virtues which are all bound up with logic. When logic is master and his personality is for the moment quiet, he has intellectual honesty and courage. These impersonal moods alternate with orgies of personal vanity during which he sees all the closed doors of the world and bangs them with his fist and shrieks at the windows. If his vanity had not made self-possession impossible, substituting a desire to startle and to shock for the solitude [which is] the first laborious creation of genius, he might have been a great writer, or at any rate as great a writer as a man of wholly external vision can be. That antithesis which I see in all artists between the artistic and the daily self was in his case too crude and simple, and the daily part too powerful, and his ignorance – and ignorance often helps external vision – deprived him of all discipline.

I have been told that the crudity common to all the Moores came from the mother's family, Mayo squireens, probably half-peasants in education and occupation, for his father was a man of education

---

I took so much material and moulded it just as if I were writing a novel, and the people in my book are not personalities but human types. Edward Martyn, for instance, is as typical of Ireland as anything can well be; he seems to me to reflect the Irish landscape, the Catholic landscape, and as a type of the literary fop one could not find a more perfect model than Yeats.' (National Library of Ireland, MSS. 8271.)

and power and old descent. His mother's blood seems to have affected him and his brother as the peasant strain has affected Edward Martyn. There has been a union of incompatibles and consequent sterility. In Martyn too one finds an intellect which should have given creative power, but in Martyn the sterility is complete, though unlike Moore he has self-possession[1] and taste. He only fails in words. It is as though he had been put into the wrong body. Both men are examples of the way Irish civilization is held back by the lack of education of Irish Catholic women. An Irish Catholic will not marry a Protestant, and hitherto the women have checked again and again the rise, into some world of refinement, of Catholic households. The whole system of Irish Catholicism pulls down the able and well-born if it pulls up the peasant, as I think it does. A long continuity of culture like that at Coole could not have arisen, and never has arisen, in a single Catholic family in Ireland since the Middle Ages.

Stone Cottage.[2] January 1914.

246

A good writer should be so simple that he has no faults, only sins.

October 1914

247

Last Monday Madame Du Pratz said that she would die – 'disappear' was her word – between Dec. 2 and Dec. 5 next. Pound and Sturge Moore were present.

November 23, 1915

Now Clare Du Pratz is in excellent health.

January 23, 1917

The editor of *Light*[3] brought a clairvoyant on Saturday. She did not know my name (I had even covered the door plate with a patch

---

[1] 'charm' deleted.
[2] Coleman's Hatch, Sussex, where Yeats spent December and January, with Ezra Pound as companion and secretary.
[3] *Light : A Journal of Psychical, Occult, and Mystical Research*, edited by E. Dawson Rogers.

of brown paper pasted on). The moment she came in she seemed upset. I heard her muttering about death, then she told me I would be shipwrecked. (I have been for some time busy with Hugh Lane's affairs and he has come through various mediums. However, clairvoyant did not completely accept this explanation.) Then she told me I would have a son, perhaps not legitimate, and go to a far land. She got correct that I was a poet and writer, but fished a good deal and was full of flatteries, very gross, and even hinted at Royal Blood (in a past life).

January 23, 1917

248

Annunciation[1]

Now can the swooping Godhead have his will
Yet hovers, though her helpless thighs are pressed
By the webbed toes; and that all powerful bill
Has suddenly bowed her face upon his breast.
How can those terrified vague fingers push
The feathered glory from her loosening thighs?
All the stretched body's laid on that white rush
And feels the strange heart beating where it lies
A shudder in the loins engenders there
The broken wall, the burning roof and tower
And Agamemnon dead . . .
                   Being so caught up
Did nothing pass before her in the air?
Did she put on his knowledge with his power
Before the indifferent beak could let her drop.

September 18, 1923

---

[1] 'Leda and the Swan', first published in *The Dial*, June 1924, *Collected Poems*, p. 241.

The ~~trembling~~/swooping godhead is half hovering still,
Yet climbs upon her trembling body pressed
By the webbed toes; and ~~through~~/that all powerful bill
Has suddenly ~~bowed/thrown~~/bowed her face upon his breast
How can those terrified vague fingers push
The feathered glory from her loosening thighs
All the stretched body ~~leans~~/laid on that white rush
                              or
Her body can but lean on the white rush
                              or
His falling body thrown on the white rush
Can feel etc.

But mounts until her trembling thighs are pressed
By the webbed toes; and that all powerful bill
Has suddenly bowed her head on his breast
Now[1] ~~all~~/that her body's laid on that white rush
×   All the stretched body, laid on that white rush
×   Now that whole
Now that her body, on the white rush
Can feel

Final Version[2]

Annunciation

The swooping godhead is half hovering still
But mounts until her trembling thighs are pressed
By the webbed toes; and that all powerful bill
Had suddenly bowed her head/Has hung her helpless body,
                              upon his breast.
How can those terrified vague fingers push
The feathered glory from her loosening thighs?
Now that her body's laid on that white rush
×   All the stretched body, laid on that white rush
×   Now that whole

[1] The lines from this point to 'feel' are deleted.
[2] This entire 'Final Version' is deleted.

Now/how that her body, on the white rush
Can feel the strange heart beating where it lies.
A shudder in the loins engenders there
The broken wall, the burning roof and tower
And Agamemnon dead . . .

×   Being so caught up/Being wrought so
So mastered by the brute blood of the air
×   Being wrought so
× Did nothing pass before her in the air?
Did she put on her knowledge with his power
Before the indifferent beak could let her drop.

                               WBY September 18, 1923

A ~~rush~~/swoop upon great wings and hovering still
× He sinks until
× He has sunk on her down, and her hair
× The great bird sinks, till
The bird descends, and her frail thighs are pressed
By the webbed toes; and that all

249[1]

When the Queen of Sheba's busy
~~Great~~/King Solomon is mute
'Busy woman,' ponders he
'Is a savage brute.'

The Queen of Sheba's busy
King Solomon is mute
Because a busy woman
Is a savage brute.

250

Final Version

Leda and the Swan
× A rush, a sudden   and   A rush, a sudden wheel,
                                   and hovering still

[1] An epigram addressed to Mrs Yeats.

✕   A sweep upon great wings
The bird descends/sinks down, her frail bare/frail thighs are
                                                    pressed
By the webbed toes, and that all powerful bill
Has driven/laid her helpless face upon his breast.
How can those terrified vague fingers push
The feathered glory from her loosening thighs
All the stretched body's laid on that white rush
And feels the strange heart beating where it lies.
A shudder in the loins engenders there
The broken wall, the burning roof and tower
And Agamemnon dead.
                          Being so caught up
So mastered by the brute blood of the air
Did she put on his knowledge with his power
Before the indifferent beak could let her drop.

251

October 30, 1930. Last night I saw the second half of Denis Johnston's production of *King Lear*.[1] A few days earlier when I saw the
first half I thought part of my unfavourable impression might be
fatigue, but last night increased my dislike. Production of imaginative
drama should be regulated by definite principles. First of all, there
must be visibility and audibility, and if these are absent nothing can
be right. Lack of visibility is the curse of all the amateur producers
now. They have learned that they should avoid realistic painted
scenes, and yet insist on realistic light effects which sacrifice their
whole dramatic life to a single pictorial moment of dim or broken
light. Far better the old painted scenes which permitted a blaze of
light. I would like to compel Denis Johnston to produce some
Shakespearean play with all the stage lights in every scene. He could

---

[1] '. . . the state of irritation into which I was thrown by *King Lear*, which I thought but
half visual and badly acted by everybody. I was too tired to stay beyond the middle but
will see the second half to-night.' Yeats to Lady Gregory, 29 October 1930, *Letters*
(Wade), p. 778. Denis Johnston (born 1901), actor, dramatist, author of *The Old Lady
Says 'No'*, *The Moon in the Yellow River* and other plays.

still reject realistic painting, he could get his effects by stylized scenery.

I once saw the George MacDonald[1] family play *Pilgrim's Progress* with scenery worked with wool on bleached canvas, and always in full light, and the result was beautiful and simple, always the right thing, never 'arty'. My own *Hour-Glass*, played in full light except for a slight and perhaps unnecessary dimming where the angel enters, was in its different way simple and beautiful. Craig[2] once wrote that I could make a forest scene by painting patterns of boughs on one-foot screens arranged in a semicircle. The lighting of such a scene might, as did that of the screens in *The Hour-Glass*, prove beautiful. Lighting, which the stage has and the painter has not, has always to be considered. My objection is to naturalistic effects, which every fool can create, effects which impose themselves between the poet and the audience as the old painted scenes never did, and make all or some of the players, at a moment when they need one's whole attention, half invisible.

Some of the inaudibility was mere incapacity to articulate, but much arose out of the stage arrangement which for the sake of a few pictorial effects cut off the inner half of our small stage by a kind of dais. In all principal scenes one actor had to stand on this and face another actor whose back was turned to the audience. The lack of light increased inaudibility, for the ear had no help from gesture and expression and the mind behind the ear was jaded, inattentive through the strain upon the eye. Pictorial effects by which the whole movement of a drama is helped were sacrificed to get a space between curtains at the back for sky effects. There are moments when a play loses vitality if one cannot make the actors silhouette themselves against some one colour – white on black, red on black, or the like. The Abbey black velvet curtains should have been used once at any rate as such a background.

The costumes suffered from the general lack of any idea of the play as a whole on the part of producer and decorator. Probably the

[1] George MacDonald (1824–1905), poet and novelist, author of *At the Back of the North Wind* (1871), *The Princess and the Goblin* (1872) and other stories for children.

[2] Edward Gordon Craig prepared costumes and screens for the Abbey production of *The Hour-Glass*, 12 January 1911.

decorator never knew upon what background anybody could be posed – there was the general impression of the rag bush at a blessed well. Better go back to the old Abbey principle: two colours and a third for accent, each colour in scene and costumes alike becoming in its turn accent, one colour always predominant in the background. This permitted Robert Gregory to build up a most beautiful effect in Lady Gregory's *Kincora*, and all for about twenty pounds. But the essential thing is always full or almost full light, because the actor comes first. Once accept that and 'artiness' is impossible. A production that disturbs and obstructs the actor should be abandoned at once.

Strong naturalistic light effects seem most suitable to prose plays and quickly played brief scenes where words and the effect are not in competition. I used to think it impossible to talk about the martlet's 'procreant cradle'[1] in front of a painted castle, but nothing can be said outlined against a night or sunlit sky that needs more attention than 'who killed Cock Robin?'

Some improper words very audible – this also very 'arty'. Some of the backgrounds were in themselves good, though never good there. Under modern circumstances one is expected to make the scene on the heath dark – probably I should allow it, though the darkness has made every representation of the mad scene I have seen a disappointment. I would prefer such a method of presentation as would leave the words to do all the suggesting. How can an actor compete successfully with a wind machine? Probably Shakespeare used nothing but some claps of thunder, which have come down through the ages and are always effective.

252

October 30, 1930: Corrections for *A Vision*.

Use 'necessity' instead of 'Fate'.

The Celestial Body confers 'necessity' upon truth – 'necessary truths'. The Spirit is truth or unity. 'Spirit is Celestial Body' – truths seen as in an 'Others'. 'Celestial Body and Spirit' necessity

---

[1] *Macbeth*, I i 8.

found in one's consciousness. The first says 'it is true because it is', the second, 'it is because it is true'. Truths are necessary. Passions are predestined.[1]

[1] 'The ideas, which decide what is necessary are in Celestial Body. They are "constituent" or else the ideas are the union of *Spirit* and *Celestial Body*.' deleted.

Appendixes

Appendix A

The following is a transcription of 'Occult Notes and Diary, Etc.', Yeats's copy-book journal dated October 1889, National Library of Ireland MSS. 13570:

Esoteric Section Journal: October 1889.

About Xmas 1888 I joined the Esoteric Section of TS. The pledges gave me no trouble except two – promise to work for theosophy and promise of obedience to HPB in all theosophical matters. Explained my difficulties to HPB. Said that I could only sign on the condition that I myself was to be judge as to what Theosophy is (the term is wide enough) and I consider my work at Blake a wholly adequate keeping of this clause. On the other matter HPB explained that this obedience only referred to things concerning occult practice if such should be called for. Since then a clause has been inserted making each member promise obedience subject to the decision of his own conscience.

Last Sunday (this is Oct. 24, 1889) at a private meeting of members of London Esotericists we passed a resolution that amounts to this, (1) we believe in HPB, (2) we believe in her teachers, (3) we will defend her, subject to our own consciences. I had some doubt as to whether I could sign this second clause. M^d Zambucu who probably thinks much as I do on this matter of Mahatmas left the Section rather than sign: still, I think I was right in signing. I take it in this sense. 'I believe Madame Blavatsky's teachers are wholly righteous, learned teachers and that I have in them all due confidence as from pupil to teacher.' M^d Zambucu and some who signed seem to have considered it as a committal to a particular theory of their nature. I tried to explain my view of this clause but somehow did not succeed. I as yet refuse to decide between the following alternatives, having too few facts to go on, (1) They are probably living occultists, as HPB says, (2) They are possibly unconscious dramatizations of HPB's own trance nature, (3) They are also possibly but not likely, as the mediums assert, spirits, (4) They may be the trance principle of nature expressing itself symbolically. The fraud theory in its most pronounced form I have never held for more than a few minutes as it is wholly unable to cover the facts. The four other hypotheses do cover them.

I came to the conclusion that my view of the clause was right on considering the yankee insubordination that made some such clause needful and the statements in some entry instructions about there being no need for any esotericist to commit himself[1] on the question of the masters, but also came to this conclusion that owing to the extreme vagueness of E.S. resolutions, the way various members have various meanings, to keep a diary of all signings I go through and such like, for my own future use; and always to state my reasons for each most carefully and when in doubt as to the legitimacy of my reasons to submit them to some prominent member in whom I have confidence. As to the personnel of Section (having seen them now together): they seem some intellectual, one or two cultured, the rest the usual amorphous material that gathers round all new things – all, amorphous and clever alike, have much zeal – and here and there a few sparkles of fanaticism are visible. This Section will not in any way (I believe) influence educated thought – for this as yet unattempted propaganda the society has so far neither men nor method. What effects it has produced upon it are wholly owing to the inherent weight of the philosophy – the method of propaganda has repelled many educated people. In India things seem to go better, and Mohini's made, while over here, the one adequate appeal that has been made to educated people, but then he could not write decently.

Dec. 20th. Was at Esoteric Section meeting last Sunday, renewed with others – Mrs Besant, Burrows, etc. – pledge. Mead, whose intellect is that of a good sized whelk, was a little over-righteous as usual; otherwise meeting interesting. A private soldier with intense face last addition. Members taking a town each for propaganda by letter. NB keep out of propaganda, not my work. The whelk may look righteous in vain. I proposed scheme for organization of occult research – matter referred to HPB. HPB will refuse probably on the ground of danger by opening up means of black magic.

Dec. 30: Proposals for experiment accepted, to HPB, last week.

Jan. 19th: Meeting of ES at Duke St. Proposals for experiment accepted by Section, and Research Committee appointed with myself as Sec. New members seem turning up plentifully – some sparks of culture here and there. What now shall Research Committee find to do with itself?

On a Saturday a week or two after last entry we, Research now Recording Committee made experiment in clairvoyance with Monsey as medium – Mrs Besant has the detailed account.

---

[1] 'In Preliminary Memorandum rule 17 page 24.' (Yeats's note on opposite page.)

Appendix B

'A Symbolic Artist and the Coming of Symbolic Art': *The Dome*, new series, vol I, December 1898, pp. 233–7.

The only two powers that trouble the deeps are religion and love, the others make a little trouble upon the surface. When I have written of literature in Ireland, I have had to write again and again about a company of Irish mystics, who have taught for some years a religious philosophy which has changed many ordinary people into ecstatics and visionaries. Young men, who were, I think, apprentices or clerks, have told me how they lay awake at night hearing miraculous music, or seeing forms that made the most beautiful painted or marble forms seem dead and shadowy. This philosophy has changed its symbolism from time to time, being now a little Christian, now very Indian, now altogether Celtic and mythological; but it has never ceased to take a great part of its colour and character from one lofty imagination. I do not believe I could easily exaggerate the direct and indirect influences which 'A. E.' (Mr George Russell), the most subtle and spiritual poet of his generation, and a visionary who may find room beside Swedenborg and Blake, has had in shaping to a definite conviction the vague spirituality of young Irish men and women of letters. I know that Miss Althea Gyles, in whose work I find so visionary a beauty, does not mind my saying that she lived long with this little company, who had once a kind of conventual house; and that she will not think I am taking from her originality when I say that the beautiful lithe figures of her art, quivering with a life half mortal tragedy, half immortal ecstasy, owe something of their inspiration to this little company. I indeed believe that I see in them a beginning of what may become a new manner in the arts of the modern world; for there are tides in the imagination of the world, and a motion in one or two minds may show a change of tide.

Pattern and rhythm are the road to open symbolism, and the arts have already become full of pattern and rhythm. Subject pictures no longer interest us, while pictures with patterns and rhythms of colour, like Mr Whistler's, and drawings with patterns and rhythms of line, like Mr Beardsley's in his middle period, interest us extremely. Mr Whistler and

Mr Beardsley have sometimes thought so greatly of these patterns and rhythms, that the images of human life have faded almost perfectly; and yet we have not lost our interest. The arts have learned the denials, though they have not learned the fervours of the cloister. Men like Sir Edward Burne-Jones and Mr Ricketts have been too full of the emotion and the pathos of life to let its images fade out of their work, but they have so little interest in the common thoughts and emotions of life that their images of life have delicate and languid limbs that could lift no burdens, and souls vaguer than a sigh; while men like Mr Degas, who are still interested in life, and life at its most vivid and vigorous, picture it with a cynicism that reminds one of what ecclesiastics have written in old Latin about women and about the world.

Once or twice an artist has been touched by a visionary energy amid his weariness and bitterness, but it has passed away. Mr Beardsley created a visionary beauty in *Salome with the Head of John the Baptist*, but because, as he told me, 'beauty is the most difficult of things', he chose in its stead the satirical grotesques of his later period. If one imagine a flame burning in the air, and try to make one's mind dwell on it, that it may continue to burn, one's mind strays immediately to other images; but perhaps, if one believed that it was a divine flame, one's mind would not stray. I think that I would find this visionary beauty also in the work of some of the younger French artists, for I have a dim memory of a little statue in ebony and ivory. Certain recent French writers, like Villiers De L'Isle Adam, have it, and I cannot separate art and literature in this, for they have gone through the same change, though in different forms. I have certainly found it in the poetry of a young Irish Catholic who was meant for the priesthood, but broke down under the strain of what was to him a visionary ecstasy; in some plays by a new Irish writer; in the poetry of 'A. E.'; in some stories of Miss Macleod's; and in the drawings of Miss Gyles; and in almost all these a passion for symbol has taken the place of the old interest in life. These persons are of very different degrees and qualities of power, but their work is always energetic, always the contrary of what is called 'decadent'. One feels that they have not only left the smoke of human hearths and come to The Dry Tree, but that they have drunk from The Well at the World's End.

Miss Gyles' images are so full of abundant and passionate life that they remind one of William Blake's cry, 'Exuberance is Beauty', and Samuel Palmer's command to the artist, 'Always seek to make excess more abundantly excessive.' One finds in them what a friend, whose work has no other passion, calls 'the passion for the impossible beauty'; for the beauty which cannot be seen with the bodily eyes, or pictured otherwise than by symbols. Her own favourite drawing, which unfortunately cannot be printed here, is *The Rose of God*, a personification of this beauty as a naked woman, whose hands are stretched against the clouds, as upon a cross, in the traditional attitude of the Bride, the symbol of the microcosm in the Kabala; while two winds, two destinies, the one full of white and the other full of red rose petals, personifying all purities and all passions, whirl about her and descend upon a fleet of ships and a walled city, personifying the wavering and the fixed powers, the masters of the world in the alchemical symbolism. Some imperfect but beautiful verses accompany the drawing, and describe her as for 'living man's delight and his eternal revering when dead'.

I have described this drawing because one must understand Miss Gyles' central symbol, the Rose, before one can understand her dreamy and intricate *Noah's Raven*. The ark floats upon a grey sea under a grey sky, and the raven flutters above the sea. A sea nymph, whose slender swaying body drifting among the grey waters is a perfect symbol of a soul untouched by God or by passion, coils the fingers of one hand about his feet and offers him a ring, while her other hand holds a shining rose under the sea. Grotesque shapes of little fishes flit about the rose, and grotesque shapes of larger fishes swim hither and thither. Sea nymphs swim through the windows of a sunken town and reach towards the rose hands covered with rings; and a vague twilight hangs over all. The story is woven out of as many old symbols as if it were a mystical story in 'The Prophetic Books'. The raven, who is, as I understand him, the desire and will of man, has come out of the ark, the personality of man, to find if the Rose is anywhere above the flood, which is here, as always, the flesh, 'the flood of the five senses'. He has found it and is returning with it to the ark, that the soul of man may sink into the ideal and pass away; but the sea nymphs, the spirits of the senses, have bribed him with a ring taken from the treasures of the kings of the world, a ring that gives the mastery of the world, and he has given them the Rose. Henceforth man will seek for the ideal in the flesh, and the flesh will be full of illusive beauty, and the spiritual beauty will be far away.

The Knight upon the Grave of his Lady tells much of its meaning to the first glance; but when one has studied for a time, one discovers that there is a heart in the bulb of every hyacinth, to personify the awakening of the soul and of love out of the grave. It is now winter, and beyond the knight, who lies in the abandonment of his sorrow, the trees spread their leafless boughs against a grey winter sky; but spring will come, and the boughs will be covered with leaves, and the hyacinths will cover the ground with their blossoms, for the moral is not the moral of the Persian poet: 'Here is a secret, do not tell it to anybody. The hyacinth that blossomed yesterday is dead.' The very richness of the pattern of the armour, and of the boughs, and of the woven roots, and of the dry bones, seems to announce that beauty gathers the sorrows of man into her breast and gives them eternal peace.

It is some time since I saw the original drawing of *Lilith*, and it has been decided to reproduce it in this number of *The Dome* too late for me to have a proof of the engraving; but I remember that Lilith, the ever-changing phantasy of passion, rooted neither in good nor evil, half crawls upon the ground, like a serpent before the great serpent of the world, her guardian and her shadow; and Miss Gyles reminds me that Adam, and things to come, are reflected on the wings of the serpent; and that beyond, a place shaped like a heart is full of thorns and roses. I remember thinking that the serpent was a little confused, and that the composition was a little lacking in rhythm, and upon the whole caring less for this drawing than for others, but it has an energy and a beauty of its own. I believe that the best of these drawings will live, and that if Miss Gyles were to draw nothing better she would still have won a place among the few artists in black and white whose work is of the highest intensity. I believe, too, that her inspiration is a wave of a hidden tide that is flowing through many minds in many places, creating a new religious art and poetry.

W. B. Yeats

Appendix C

'Althea Gyles': in *A Treasury of Irish Poetry in the English Tongue*, ed. Stopford A. Brooke and T. W. Rolleston (London, Smith, Elder, 1900), p. 475.

Miss Althea Gyles may come to be one of the most important of the little group of Irish poets who seek to express indirectly through myths and symbols, or directly in little lyrics full of prayers and lamentations, the desire of the soul for spiritual beauty and happiness. She has done, besides the lyric I quote,[1] which is charming in form and substance, a small number of poems full of original symbolism and spiritual ardour, though as yet lacking in rhythmical subtlety. Her drawings and book-covers, in which precise symbolism never interferes with beauty of design, are as yet her most satisfactory expression of herself.

W. B. Yeats

[1] 'Sympathy' ('The colour gladdens all your heart').

Appendix D

From Elizabeth A. Sharp, *William Sharp: A Memoir by His Wife* (London, Heinemann, 1910), pp. 421–2:

In a letter to Mr W. B. Yeats signed 'Fiona Macleod', and written in 1899, about herself and her friend (namely himself) William tried 'as far as is practicable in a strange and complex manner to be explicit'. 'She' stated that, 'all the formative and expressional as well as nearly all the visionary power is my friend's. In a sense only his is the passive part, but it is the allegory of the match, the wind, and the torch. Everything is in the torch in readiness, and as you know, there is nothing in the match itself. But there is a mysterious latency of fire between them . . . the little touch of silent igneous potency at the end of the match – and in what these symbolise, one adds spiritual affinity as a factor – and all at once the flame is born. The torch says all is due to the match. The match knows the flame is not hers. But beyond both is the wind, the spiritual air. Out of the unseen world it fans the flame. In that mysterious air both the match and the flame hear strange voices. The air that came at the union of both is sometimes Art, sometimes Genius, sometimes Imagination, sometimes Life, sometimes the Spirit. It is all.

'But before that flame people wonder and admire. Most wonder only at the torch. A few look for the match beyond the torch, and finding her are apt to attribute to her that which is not hers, save as a spiritual dynamic agent. Now and then the match may have *in petto* the qualities of the torch – particularly memory and vision: and so can stimulate and amplify the imaginative life of the torch. But the torch is at once the passive, the formative, the mnemonic, and the artistically and imaginatively creative force. He knows that in one sense he would be flameless or at least without that ideal blend of the white and the red – without the match: and he knows that the flame is the offspring of both, that the wind has many airs in it, and that one of the most potent is that which blows from the life and mind and soul of "the match" – but in his heart he knows that, to all others, he and he alone is the flame, his alone both the visionary, the formative, the expressional.'

Appendix E

GOSSE, LADY GREGORY AND YEATS

The possibility that Yeats would be granted a Civil List pension arose at the end of November or the beginning of December 1909. Yeats wrote to Lady Gregory, 9 December 1909, mentioning Agnes Tobin: 'Miss Tobin told me the other day that Gosse has asked her to sound me as to my getting a government pension. He has said very generously, "We cannot neglect our greatest poet." Miss Tobin told him that she knew I felt it impossible to accept anything from government owing to Irish conditions.' *Letters* (Wade), p. 542. Yeats had a second conversation with Miss Tobin on the matter, 12 December 1909. He told her 'that no Irishman in my position could accept anything from the government which limited his political freedom, no matter how little he wished to use that freedom. Gosse it seems says it would not, but Miss Tobin I think shares my doubts as to its being possible.' *Letters* (Wade), p. 544. On 25 December Yeats saw Gosse, but the matter was postponed, nothing could be done 'during the present political excitement'. (The excitement arose from the rejection of the Finance Bill by the House of Lords on 28 November, the dissolution of Parliament on 3 December, and the General Election campaign between that date and polling day, 14 January 1910. The question of a pension for Yeats could not have been brought to Asquith during those weeks.) On 12 April 1910, Yeats accepted Gosse's invitation to become a member of the proposed English Academy of Letters. *Letters* (Wade), p. 549. At some date shortly thereafter Gosse appears to have consulted Lady Gregory, asking her to prepare material for a petition in Yeats's favour. On 22 July he wrote to thank her and to say that 'the nature and cause of Yeats's poverty ought to be very clearly stated in your letter to Mr Birrell'. (Berg Collection, New York Public Library.) Birrell was then Chief Secretary for Ireland. But at that point a misunderstanding developed between Gosse and Lady Gregory. On receipt of a letter from her which she had already shown to Yeats, Gosse replied on 25 July 1910:

> Dear Madam,
>   I cannot express my surprise at the tone of your letter. If this is your attitude, I wish to have no more to do with the matter, and I am lost in wonder at what can have induced you to interfere in an affair

when your opinion was not asked, and when you seem to intend neither to give any help nor to take any trouble.

I have the honour to be

Yours faithfully
Edmund Gosse
(Berg Collection)

This is the insulting letter. Yeats then wrote the following letter to Gosse, but he did not post it: he showed it to Lady Gregory and asked her to post it. She chose not to send the letter, however. The date is 24 July, but this is evidently a mistake for 27 July. The letter reads:

Dear Mr Gosse,

I was shown last night a letter beyond explanation or apology, written by you to Lady Gregory, who had sent you in my service[1] a fitting and courteous letter, which she had first shown to me. I had not thought it possible that you could write to any woman a letter so insolent – I can use no lesser word – and when I remember that it was sent to my best and oldest friend I am amazed that you should think so little of me and so little of yourself. Apology cannot amend what is done but lacking it even the most formal intercourse between you and me will be impossible. You have tried to be of service to me in the past, and you are a much older man than I am but even these considerations are annulled by insolence to an old and dear friend.

Yours,
W. B. Yeats
(Berg Collection)

On 29 July Gosse wrote to Yeats, telling him that the petition was now with the Prime Minister and to caution Yeats 'to be absolutely passive'. (Berg Collection.) On 29 July also Lady Gregory wrote to Birrell, as follows:

Dear Mr Birrell:

I have had a little check, for I thought as Mr Gosse had first mentioned the Civil List's possibility to Mr Yeats, it was but polite to tell him what was happening, and I sent him at the same time a draft Memo or Petition, much like that which I enclose. He enlarged it, especially the allusion to the new Academic Committee, which he takes credit for having put Yeats in, and wrote a letter which I enclose – I answered, as I thought in the true friendly manner, and asked him to get the signatures mentioned. I wrote myself to Sir Ian Hamilton – What there was in the letter (which Mr Yeats

---

[1] 'and after showing it to me' deleted.

saw and approved of) to call forth his extraordinary letter of the 25th I cannot imagine, unless he has gone out of his mind. Anyhow, as we are deprived of his art, I have written out another draft and I must appeal to your kindness to ask you ... to put it in proper form and return, together with the Gosse letters, which are a literary curiosity. I am afraid this is asking you to gather the straw as well as bake the bricks – but I can't help it. ...

(Berg Collection)

On 2 August Yeats drafted a letter of explanation to Robert Gregory, committing the draft to his Journal. Between 2 and 6 August an apologetic letter arrived from Gosse, but Yeats and Robert Gregory decided not to show it to Lady Gregory, on the grounds that it was such an inadequate apology. On 6 August Yeats wrote entry 225, but it appears probable that no such letter was in fact posted to Gosse. On 10 August Yeats heard from the Prime Minister that he had been granted a Civil List pension of £150 a year. He immediately wrote to Gosse, *Letters* (Wade), p. 550, to thank him for his efforts: the letter shows no sign of ill-feeling. On 13 August Gosse replied with warm congratulations (Berg Collection). It seems evident that none of Yeats's stern letters was posted to Gosse.

Appendix F

PROCEEDINGS OF THE AMERICAN SOCIETY
FOR PSYCHICAL RESEARCH

Mrs C. J. H. H. April 29th, 1911. 10 A. M.
[Normal.]

I hear a name like Rue, Reuben or Ruth. I don't see any person. I think it is Reuben. [Pause.] [Note 553.]

I have a funny little experience when I get into the trance lately and the same occurs when I go to sleep or close my eyes. I seem to look into liquid blackness, as if looking into an open cave. The blackness looks very palpable and like deep space. Then it suddenly changes and is light again. All I can say is that it is like looking into a void and is as if I started into a black abyss, tho I don't move. But I see it as tho the atmosphere was taken away and the clouds so that nothing is left. Then the clouds come back. But I never see anything beyond that black. [Pause.]

Somebody has a hand on my head, like a finger on top of my head, and I begin to see things. I am still conscious. [Pause.]

[Hand clinched slightly and a slight groan. Pause and the Indian or French gibberish and a pause again.]

[Automatic Writing.]

[The automatic writing began and continued very slowly throughout the period of the first communicator and from the way that the pronoun 'I' was made twice I supposed that Mr Myers was present and controlling the writing, but the manner of making the letter 't' at the end of a word soon betrayed the presence of 'The Teacher', and I remained quiet till the end when it was explained in a manner which the reader may see for himself.]

* * I am with you.

(Greetings this morning.)

even unto the ends of the earth. [Pause.] [Probably due to my moving the pad down to prevent superposing which began.] I am here to give you peace and the peace of the spirit passes the understanding of men.

553. The name Reuben or Ruth has no recognizable significance.

The day of materiality is doomed and will pass away and the life and light of the spirit will supersede the merely intellectual authority of the men who strive to lead the world today but the expressions and exhibitions of spiritual power will be intellectually perceived and comprehended and become the light of the world. The intellectual is but the channel which leads to the open sea of [French sounds whispered.] spiritual Truth. How then is the mind of man the servant of God and the more illumined the mind the brighter the glory which encircles the universe. So does intellect wait upon knowledge and knowledge serve Truth and Truth reveal [read 'served' and hand pointed till read 'reveal'.] God. Teacher.

(Thank you. Did any one help you in the writing? I recognized you by your sign and there were indications . . .)

Yes your other friend F. Myers. [Very slowly written.]

(Thank you. I thought so.) [Note 554.]

[Change of Control.]

[Two pencils rejected and I first rubbed the third before giving, and it was retained.]

Good morning Hyslop. I guess they thought they would not let any tramps [not read tho clear enough.] tramps [not read.] in . . . spirit tramps yes [to reading.] hoboes as you remember yesterday.

(Perfectly.)

Myers said he did not think that ought to be done even for experiment, so he brought his friend and they opened the circle in a fitting manner.

(No epithets.)

No epithets no prayers to the Unknown. It was the Unknown to that man I think but perhaps they are right. Anyway what Myers says has to be done in this particular case for he has an agreement with Madam to let no harm come to the light while under our experiments. Ys [yes.] [To correct reading of 'under' which was delayed in reading.]

We all are under orders to do our missionary work in heaven so you may never be favored with a like experience, but I think you will not care. Who cares for Society any way. It is not much of an honor to be a member of Society proper is it. There is so little to take away and so much to give.

Seriously when I look on life and see its drawbacks I am glad I did not have to stay and make my way as some have done. There are compensations even for early death. Mine was not too early nor yet too late.

554. This passage again from the Teacher contains an interesting example of the interfusion of personality even in the writing. As remarked above Mr Myers distinguishes his personality and presence by the manner in which he makes a capital 'I'. The Teacher distinguishes his by the manner of making a final 't'. At the beginning the indication was for Mr Myers but the final 't' soon told who was really present, tho I saw from the contents that it was not like Mr Myers usually. My conjecture, the reader will see, was confirmed by the answer to my last question.

Now about our specific work yesterday. How did it turn out.

(It was fine, tho I wish some facts had been clearer and fuller, but that may have been impossible.)

I believe that the first communicator jarred the conditions a little.

(Likely.)

but all that is essential to evidence too.

(Yes.)

We would like to go on in the same way if you desire. What we want and like to do is to get hold of a person and keep that person at the point until we have a good set of circumstances. Some spirits lend themselves more readily to this work than others and so when we find one who does not prove good as a communicator we drop the matter and take another.

Do you know anything about a well with a long pole [read 'pile'] pole on which is put a pail [read 'part', tho clear enough, and hand pointed till correctly read.] yes. I hear a sound like tin or something light [read 'bright'] light against stones and I look and see a well with a low wooden frame around it and there I see a long pole and a hand pulling [read 'putting' and hand pointed till read correctly.] a pail by some method of clasp and then it is lowered and up comes water which is taken into a house for use. Do you know about one.

(No, I do not unless you tell where.)

It seems to be in those conditions where we were yesterday.

(I do not recall it, but it may have been before my time.)

It is not on a chain or a crank but is a pole lowered like a dip.

(I have seen such poles and wells in my life, but do not recall any about my old home.)

Do you know any one by the name of Solomon. This seems to be connected with the well and is some time ago but your father knows it and speaks of it and the name [pause.] [Note 555.]

I want to tell you something else I see and we will see if we are on the right line again.

Do you know anything about a trip away when you and your father and another boy went when you were a young lad. It is to a small town where there are stores and business and some special activities on the day you go. It looks like town meeting day. Do you know anything about town meeting day.

(No, it must have been too early for my memory.)

Do you not know of some special day like voting day. (Yes.) When [read 'what' hastily and without excuse for it.] you ... when ... and your

---

555. This incident of the 'well with a long pole' was mentioned in another connection in the New York experiments a few years ago, and was not then verifiable. My Aunt who is the only living person who might be expected to verify it cannot identify the place or person, tho recalling that some one in the neighborhood had a well sweep. Whom she does not remember.

father and another boy went to a small town. It is like taking the boys along for some other purpose but it is on a special day as I wrote. Do you know about that.

(I remember a special day when we were taken. Tell all about it.)

I see people and some excitement unusual not wild but a little commotion [read 'connection' tho clear enough.] commotion [read 'commemoration' tho clear enough.] commot . . . [read.] yes [to correct reading.] it is not Sunday but I hear the church bells ring and see people glad and happy. Do you know about this.

(Yes, go ahead.)

Your father thought you would remember it because he was so happy over it himself.

(But he must tell me something more specific to make the evidence conclusive.)

Of course he intends to but this is a beginning. Just a moment till I get started. [Moment's pause.]

Were there flags flying. I see something like flags and hear a sound of joy almost as if good news had come from another [read 'mother' and these are undoubtedly the letters, but the hand pointed till read 'another'.] center. It is not a town affair but one of greater importance and I se [see] it is all bright and sunny and rather warm but not extremely so. There I see your father a center of a group of men and he is talking emphatically and energetically while you look on in wonder and are taking in the situation [not read.] situation. Then I walk along with the crowd to a place out of doors where there is something going on. This is a celebration of an event. Do you remember.

(Yes.)

Was there a bridge and some water in that town like a small river.

(Yes.)

I se [see] it at one end of the town but I think you go over it in a carriage for I hear the sound of hoofs and then I come to a road again and dust and less noise of hoofs. Do you know.

(Yes, go ahead.)

Then I see a strange little shop or place where is a large wheel outside. It looks like a blacksmith shop not far from that bridge but all this is before I get to the real scene of the day.

Was there a red brick building of some pretension near the center of the town. I see a red building and it looks like stores [read 'stones' and hand pointed till read correctly.] or some business buildings and I see a long very pretty street with trees and houses on each side. I see it for a long distance and a curve toward the right as I look at it coming into the town after I have passed through some of the crowd and there I stop at a house and see some one. It seems like a friend's house but there is no long stay at any house for the day is one of general activity.

(What else on that long street besides trees?)

[I had in mind another street than the communicator. See later.]

You mean besides houses also (Yes.) I suppose. I do not know as I can see what you have in mind but I will try. I see a tall [pause.] something [pause.] I don't know whether it is a pole or what but it is tall and straight. Do . . .

(Yes, there was a pole.)

you know what a liberty pole is (Yes.) Was not that what it was.

(That was on the street crossing the one in my mind.)

Do you know about a watering trough which was somewhere in the center of the place. (Yes.) I see you drive up there and let [not read.] let the horse drink. [Note 556.]

I se [see] another thing. It is an open space and then a sort of hill and some monuments [not read.] monuments up there. Not very high and then I se [see] a big building like a church or public building but it is white. Do you know that.

(I don't recognize that as described, but tell more about the place of the monuments.)

Let me see. the monuments are not by the church at all but I see them and then I turn back and find my church. you know what I mean I think.

(Yes.)

Now I see some people at the place where the monuments are and they seem to be there for a special purpose but it does not seem like a funeral. It is more joyous than a funeral. It might be a dedication or something of that sort but I cannot tell precisely what it is. [Note 557.]

556. This long passage is a good account of the national celebration of the 4th of July in 1876, in which my father had an important part from his township. We stopped our harvesting to take part and we boys were taken to see it. There were important speeches made and all that I remember of the details is the place of the speaking and the name of the chief speaker from that place. The church bells were probably rung on the occasion. It was not a town but a national affair.

There was a small stream at the west end of town and across it a bridge with a road to the cemetery. Just after you crossed this bridge, at the cross-roads, there was a blacksmith shop. There were always wheels lying about such blacksmith shops.

The red brick building 'of some pretension' was the Court House, made of brick, and in front of it were the stores and the long street mentioned and leading to the bridge referred to above. There were trees on its sides. It was not the flag or liberty pole that I had in mind in my question, but a railway which passed through the heart of the town on one of its principal streets. The flag pole was a tall one in front of this Court House. There was also there a watering trough.

557. The reference to 'the monuments' seems to be to the cemetery in the place which is very near the town and situated on a hill. Inquiry shows that no mention is made in the town papers of any exercises in the cemetery tho they give full accounts of the other things. It is therefore practically certain that none were there. I do not know why a church is referred to in this connection, especially in speaking of it as white. While there were one or two white churches in the place it is not probable that they figured in this occasion. But it is possible that the confusion here is due to an incident which the

(Was there any speaking that day?)

Yes out of doors and some in another place.

(Who spoke out of doors?)

I don't know whether your father did or not but I see him with his hat off and I see a lot of people looking up at him and listening to what he says. Did he make [not read.] an address ... make.

(I do not know, but can inquire. A man whom he knew well and prominent in the town did speak.)

Yes I knew there was speaking but also see your father speaking and being listened to as if he had some word to say. It was all red white and blue day any way [not read.] any way. It was a national day as well as town day. You will know that I think.

(Yes.)

Was there anything about Lincoln in that.

(Very probably. I was too young to remember.)

Strangely enough [superposed and read 'though'] enough I see constantly a picture of Lincoln and I think the thought of him [not read.] of him was in the minds of all. You know what the name of the principle [principal] speaker was.

(Yes I do. Tell it.)

I will if I can. I thought I was going to ge [get] it at once. [pause.] [Just at this moment I could not recall it myself, tho having it previously clear in my mind. It had suddenly slipped from me, the first experience of the kind in this connection.]

Was it R. or B.

(No.)

It looks like that letter to me.

(No neither letter.) [I recalled the name in time for this answer.]

[If the letter K could be mistaken for 'R' in G. P's or Jennie P's mind, it would have been on the right track.]

I had b ... [superposing.] I had better let it wait and if he can give it we will drop it in. I see such a look of satisfaction on your father's face

---

cemetery and the mention of the way to it would inevitably call to my father's mind. This is suggested to me by the statement that 'the monuments are not by the church at all'. Early in the history of the town there was a cemetery of some size in it and connected with a church. The town had grown around it. This cemetery had to be moved and an incident was connected with it of much interest to my father and his sisters. All the bodies were removed to the present cemetery, or the remains of them. I happened to have the incident told me or in my presence many years ago by my Aunt. The event had no relation to the day which my father is describing, but it might easily enough in this picture panorama have passed before his mind and have been caught by Jennie P.

The speaking was in the open air in a forest, and it was a bright clear day, probably warm, tho often after a rain in this locality, the day was not so warm as July days usually are.

all that day. He just beamed when he was in such an atmosphere, for he was patriotic to the last degree.

(Yes.) [Note 558.]

Do you know Henry some one whom he knew in those days.

(Yes, tell about him.)

He speaks of him as a friend and some one who was more than ordinarily near to him. Immediately after I speak of Henry I see a very large house in the same place I think where I have been. It is a house with a door yard yes [to correct reading of the two last words.] and it [read 'a'] large . . . it is large, the house I mean, and has trees all around it and some out buildings . . . out [read 'one' the first time.] like a barn or shed and has a look of thrift and well [read 'will'] to do . . . well [read 'will'] well . . . conditions about the place. Was that where [letters spell 'when'] Henry lived.

(Make it clearer.)

all right. I go into the house and I can go two ways. a front door and a side door which was the one used most. The side door is into a smal [small] entry or hall which leads [read 'lends'] more * * [possibly for 'directly'] leads . . . into a room where everything is going on like a living room.

(What kind of trees behind the house.)

[I had in mind 'behind' the front entrance. The answer shows that the communicator had in mind 'behind' the side entrance.]

[Pause.] Dark dark trees. I se [see] quite a cluster of them but the trees in front are different more leaves and lighter green. Do you know about that.

(Go on, not clear.)

Am I making a bungling mess of it today. Do you know hemlocks and . . . hemlocks [not read first time.] . . . and pines and such trees back of the house.

(No, but I think there was an evergreen or two at the side in the yard, but I am not certain. Behind the house were trees of which I am certain.)

and you want those. I must pass through this bit of evergreen and come to some large leafy ones. Say Hyslop I don't know whether this is an orchard or not but I seem to be hunting under the trees for something like fruit.

(Yes, go on.)

558. My father did no speaking on that occasion and I doubt if he ever spoke to any considerable assembly of men outside his church. I wanted to see if he would mention a certain man whose ability he had always to recognize but whom he always criticized for his religious unbelief. It is possible that this man's personality in connection with this occasion did not impress his memory as it did mine. It is more than probable that Lincoln would have a prominent place in the speeches of the occasion and for evidence it is not worth inquiring whether he did or not. The speaker's initials were not R. B., and who could have been meant by them here I do not know.

and as I walk along I pick up something red and bite into it and it is juicy. It is not pear but seems like a firm [not read.] firm fruit more like apples but it may be peaches.

(Yes, there were both apples and peaches there.) [Note 559.]

Good. I couldn't tell which but do you know anything about a very small red fruit. It seems as if there were only one or possibly two trees of it. It looks like a red plum red on the outside and a yellow meat. I think it is not a peach for it is too small. Do you know anything about a plum tree.

(Yes, but not at that place, tho there may have been one there and another person will know.)

I am still here and find it so I think you find it true. I find a low bush of berries at the same place. They are more like currants.

(Probably.)

and are near a wall or fence made of wood but not nailed [read 'mailed' questioningly, tho it is clearly 'nailed'] like . . . mailed [read so and when hand paused read 'nailed'.] . . . slats but laid up on some wall or stones for a beginning and then cross crossed and recrossed in a peculiar way. (Yes.) It is unpainted and is not for show but for protection. To keep the cattle out I think.

(Yes, can he describe some of the apples near that fence.)

Yes I see a large yellow apple. It looks like an early Summer or Fall apple. It has no lasting quality like some of the others but is fairly good to eat right there. you must know that one.

(Yes, go ahead.)

Now do you know a little rough red one. It seems unshapely but a good apple good flavor. It is rather peculiar in shape but red in color [French or Indian.] and now I come to a good apple. It is hard as a rock in Summer but it grows good later. It really looks green. I don't know whether that is is [for 'its' probably] name but it looks like a Greening.

(Yes.) [Note 560.]

559. The name Henry at once suggested the man who lived on the place and worked for us. The house, so far as the description went, was correctly described. It was a very large house for a hired tenant to occupy, having been the old dwelling house on the farm which we bought. There were trees and outbuildings of several kinds about it, and the side door was the one almost wholly used by the tenant, the front door rarely, and most of the life of the family was spent in the rear room. There were a few evergreen trees in the yard, cedar I think, certainly not hemlocks, and I do not know whether there were any pines. It was a correct answer to my question to say the orchard, and also to specify peaches; for I wanted to see if peaches as well as apples would be mentioned, there being a large peach orchard there, the peaches all being red by the way, and only a few apples that were red.

560. There were a few old plum trees on the place, but none of us recall the red plum with yellow meat. There was such a plum on the home place. The plums on the place under review, as we remember them, were blue damson. There were plenty of currants there, but probably so on every farm. The most striking incident, however, in this

Do you know any apple named Duchess [pause.] de [pause.]
(Go ahead.)
I fear I can't get it. [Pause.] Was it O——
(No.) It was not Pomar was it. Yes [to reading of 'Pomar'] (No.)
I can't get it but he makes a mighty effort. [Pause.]
(That fruit was not an apple was it?)
Is it Quince. (No.) Youve got me Hyslop. Wait and let me see. It is
not peach [read 'peace'] but . . . peach . . . not peach but more like pear.
Yes [to correct reading.] but I don't know it and he doesn't seem able to
show me so that I can tell.
   (Let me tell. Duchess d' Angoulême.) [Repeated.]
Pretty good. He got the first part all right did he not.
(Yes.) [Note 561.]
Do you know anything about crabs.
(Go ahead.) [Thinking of crayfish in that region.]
He speaks of a special crab apple. Do you know if he raised them.
(Yes.)
They are his delight. He is fond of them for some reason. Do you know
that. This one I se [see] is a dark red and smooth as the best of fruit and
excellent for some purpose in the house.
   (Go ahead.) [Note 562.]
Do you know about grafts from that tree and did he make money from
his orchard.
   (Somewhat.)

---

account is the reference to the fence. It was not a nailed fence of slats, but made of rails
'crossed' as loosely as indicated and for protection against the stock to keep them out of
the orchard.
   Most of the apples in the orchard were yellow, and the absence of 'lasting quality' was
their characteristic. They were 'good to eat right there' and also to cook, but they would
not keep. We often made cider of them. The little *rough* red one I do not recall, but there
was a *small* red apple, the Snow apple I think, but not rough. There was a large *rough* red
apple that was a good eating apple, but farther off. Near this fence was a good apple that
was very green and hard in the summer, but was a good eating apple in the winter, and
resembled the Greening in color, tho larger in size, the Tolpahockan, if I spell it correctly.
   561. The reference to the Duchess d' Angoulême pear is remarkably interesting. It
was not connected with this tenant's place. It was on the home farm and also behind the
house and garden. It stood second in the row of trees and was one of father's favorite
pears, of which fruit he was very fond. The tree died and disappeared fully thirty or more
years ago. There was another one, however, in the yard that lived much longer than this.
It was natural to the subconscious to slip on its being an apple in connection with apples
generally.
   562. My father was very fond of crab apple jelly. He had a tree of crab apples which
stood right next to this Duchess d' Angoulême pear in the yard. The fruit was a dark red.
It was also a special kind, named the Hyslop crab apple, and it is interesting to see that
this name does not come through which it would have been most natural under the
circumstances for it to have done, but it is evidently an illustration of the difficulty with
proper names.

The grafts from his tree were taken to another place and used with success. Your fth . . . Your father says most grafts are successful but this is not political graft just legitimate fruit growing.

There are two kinds of crabs one yellow one red and the graft made stripes. what do you know of that. Do you know anything about it. (No.) [Note 563.]

[Pause.] Now I feel I am losing power. Is it late.

(Yes it is.) [Looked at my watch and found it later than I supposed.] Just a moment if I may stay. Have I not seen this Henry before.

(He has been mentioned and if you could give the first name of his daughter which I think has been mentioned before I would be sure.)

I will try and bring it tomorrow and will get more if I can. Do you know anything about a little corner [not read.] brackett [bracket] . . . corner [read 'comer' tho I should have known better.] corner brackett [bracket] in his house.

(Whose house?)

Henry's. (No.) I se [see] a bracket made of plain wood and stained dark. it is in the living room and on it are spectacles and a few little things used often. Did he smoke.

(I do not remember.)

It looks like a pipe there with the spectacles. I must go but do you know L——

(Go ahead.)

[Pause.] L [Pause.] Lizzie I think but I am not sure. Do you know Lizzie in connection with him.

(No.)

It is Laura.

(No.)

I am too far gone. G. P. [Note 564.]

[*Subliminal.*]

[Pause.] Goodbye. You get anything good?

563. My father did a great deal of grafting with fruit trees, but no one remembers grafting the Hyslop crab apple. It is quite certain that no such effects as is described would take place if he had grafted it. The allusion to political graft is evidently a sub-conscious diversion, or some of the control's attempt at wit.

564. No one can recall this incident of the bracket and it would astonish me to know that my father would remember such an article, as he rarely ever went to the house of this tenant. Besides it is the firm belief of my stepmother and myself that this Henry did not smoke or wear spectacles. He may have chewed tobacco and my stepmother thinks he did. But there was another old negro who had also been a tenant there who did smoke and wear spectacles. No one could verify the bracket incident in connection with him.

The name Lizzie would not identify any one in connection with this Henry or the other negro. Neither would the name Laura, but the name Lucy would, as it was the name of Henry's daughter and she worked for us often.

(Yes.)

[Opened her eyes and I thought her awake.]

(There we are.)

No, who said so. [Pause, and looking about.] I see nothing but chickens everywhere.

(Whose?)

Goodness knows, not mine. I don't see how they can be yours. They belong to the farm.

(Who are you?)

[Awakened as I asked this question.]

Appendix G

Key to Passages from the Journal published in *Estrangement*
(1926) and *The Death of Synge* (1928)

Journal	Estrangement	Journal	Estrangement
4	II	50	XXVIII
5	I	51	XXIX
6	III	53	XXIX
9	IV	54	XXIX
11	V	55	XXXV
14	VI	56	XXX
16	VII	58	XXX
18	VIII	59	XXXI
19	IX	60	XXXII
20	X	61	XXXIII
21	X	64	LIV
22	XI	65	XXXVI
24	XII	68	XXXVII
25	XIII	71	XXXVIII
26	XIV	74	XXXIX
27	XV	75	XL
28	XVI	76	XLI
29	XVII	78	XLII
30	XVIII	79	XLIII
31	XIX	80	XLIV
32	XX	81	XLV
33	XXI	82	XLVI
34	XXII	83	XLVII
35	XXIII	84	XLVIII
36	XXIV	85	XLIX
37	XXIV	87	L
38	XXV	88	LI
39	XXV	93	LII
42	XXV	94	LIII
46	XXVI	95	LV
47	XXVII		

Journal	Death of Synge		Journal	Death of Synge
97	I		137	XX
98	II		138	XXI
99	III		140	XXI
100	IV		141	XXII
101	IV		143	XXIII
102	IV		144	XXIII
105	V		145	XXIV
107	VI		147	XXV
108	VII		150	XXVI
109	VIII		152	XXVII
114	IX		153	XXVIII
116	X		154	XXVII
117	XI		156	XXIX
118	XII		173	XXX
119	XIII		178	XXXI
120	XIV		191	XXXII
122	XV		192	XXXIII
123	XVI		194	XXXIV
126	XVI			and XXXV
127	XVI		195	XXXVI
128	XVII		203	XXXVII
129	XVIII		204	XXXVIII
130	XVIII		231	XXXIX
131	XIX		233	XL
134	XX		246	XLI

Index

INDEX

Stenbock, Count Stanislaus Eric (1860–95), 118 and n
Stephens, Annie, 200 n
Stephens, Edward M., 208 n
Stephens, Harry, 200, 203, 207–8, 216–18, 219, 220, 221, 222
Stephens, James (1882–1950), 132, 221 n
Stevenson, R. A. M., 39
Stone Cottage, 271
Stratford-upon-Avon, 214. *See also* theatres
Strickland, W. G., 217 n
Sullivan, Alexander, 109
Swedenborg, Emanuel (1688–1772), 130, 283
Sweete, Leonard, 234
Swift, Jonathan (1667–1745), 68, 84
Swinburne, Algernon Charles (1837–1909), 22, 214, 224; 'Statue of Victor Hugo', 41 n; *Tristram of Lyonesse*, 41 n
Symons, Arthur (1865–1945), 36, 37, 86–7, 89–94, 97–8, 99–102, 104–5, 199, 214, 255; 'Amoris Victima', 98; *Aubrey Beardsley*, 98; 'Literary Causerie', 93
Synge, Annie, *see* Stephens, Annie
Synge, Edward H., 208 n, 263
Synge, John Millington (1871–1909): first meeting with Yeats, 104–5; and Young Ireland Society (Paris), 106–7; illness, 154, 161, 177, 199, 202, 203, 205, 220–1; death, 199, 200, 203, 215, 218; obituaries, 201, 211; character, 203–4, 206, 213; his will, 207–8
    WORKS: *Collected Works*, 177 n; *Deirdre of the Sorrows*, 177, 204, 208, 218, 219, 220, 221, 222, 239–40, 241; 'Epitaph', 208; 'Epitaph after reading Ronsard', 208; 'In Glencullen', 208; 'In May', 208; 'Mouvement Intellectuel Irlandais', 204 n; 'Oaks of Glencree', 208; 'Old and New in Ireland', 178; 'On an Anniversary', 208; *Playboy of the Western World*, 121, 141 n, 154,

200, 203, 204, 218, 223, 241, 260; 'On a Birthday', 208; *Poems and Translations*, 212; 'Prelude', 208; 'To a Sister of an Enemy . . . ', 201–2; 'Queens', 208; 'Question', 200 n, 208, 216, 218; *Riders to the Sea*, 211; *Shadow of the Glen*, 144, 211; *Tinker's Wedding*, 204, 217, 219; 'Winter', 208; 'Wish', 208
Synge, Robert, 208

Tagore, Sir Rabindranath (1861–1941), 268
Tarot, 70, 78–9, 125
Taylor, John Francis (1850–1902), 12, 52, 54, 64–5, 66, 68, 198; *Owen Roe O'Neill*, 195; 'Parliaments of Ireland', 52 n
Taylor, Mrs Shaw, 269 n
Tennyson, Alfred Lord (1809–92), 179, 190
Theatre of Ireland, 192, 193 n, 194, 197
theatres
  Dublin: Abbey, 101 n, 143, 171, 172, 174, 180, 190, 194, 227, 229 n, 234, 237, 241, 247, 267–8, 276–7; Gaiety, 122 n; Theatre Royal, 233 n
  London: Avenue, 74; His Majesty's, 217 n; Savoy, 234 n; Theatre Royal, Haymarket, 234 n
  Stratford: Memorial, 260
Theosophical Society, 23–6, 49
Thornhill, 75
Tipperary, 43, 248
Tír na nOg, 200
Tobin, Agnes (1863–1939), 208, 214, 289
Todhunter, John (1839–1916), 37 n; *Helena in Troas*, 41; *Patrick Sarsfield*, 41 n; *Shelley*, 41 n; *Sicilian Idyll*, 72 n
Tolstoy, Leo (1828–1910), 9
Tone, Wolfe (1763–98), 108, 184
Triangle, 109
Tree, Herbert Beerbohm (1853–1917), 171 n, 217, 219